Maurice Zundel

THE INNER PERSON

Finding God Within

A Retreat preached at the Vatican

Preface by Reverend Father Carré
of the French Academy

MÉDIASPAUL

First published as *Quel homme et quel Dieu*, Éditions Saint-Augustin, Saint-Maurice (Suisse), 1989. Translated from the French by Bianca Zagolin.

Canadian Cataloguing in Publication Data

Zundel, Maurice

    The Inner Person: Finding God Within

    Translation of: Quel homme et quel Dieu
    Includes bibliographical references.

    ISBN 2-89420-349-7

    1. Theology. I. Title.

BR85.Z78313 1996   230   C96-940779-3

Phototypesetting : *Médiaspaul*

Cover : *Summum*

ISBN 2-89420-349-7

Legal Deposit — 3rd Quarter 1996
Bibliothèque nationale du Québec
National Library of Canada

© 1996 Médiaspaul
          250, boul. St-François Nord
          Sherbrooke, QC, J1E 2B9 (Canada)

Contents

Epigraph

Est ibi aliud inflammans
animam ad amandum Deum,
scilicet divina humilitas...
Nam Deus omnipotens singulis
Angelis sanctisque animabus
in tantum se subjicit, quasi
sit servus emptitius singulorum,
quilibet vero ipsorum
sit Deus suus. Ad hoc insinuandum
transiens ministrabit illis
dicens in Ps. LXXXI: Ego dixi,
dii estis... Haec autem humilitas
causatur ex multitudine bonitatis,
et divinae nobilitatis, sicut
arbor ex multitudine fructuum
inclinatur...

Opusc. *de Beatitudine*
(S. Thomae, adscriptum, cap. II)

"There is here something else inflaming the soul to
the love of God, namely divine humility... For Almighty
God subjects Himself [so much] to each single Angel and
every holy soul exactly as if He were the purchased slave
of each, and any one of them *were his own God*. To make

this known, He ministers to them as he goes about, saying in Psalm 81: *I have said, You are gods*.... Now, such humility results from the wealth of divine goodness and nobility, as a tree is bowed down by its plentiful fruit..."[1]

[1] Quoted in Jacques Maritain, *Art and Scholasticism and The Frontiers of Poetry*, translated by Joseph W. Evans, New York, Charles Scribner's Sons, 1962, pp. 157-158, n. 39.

Preface

When Charles Du Bos departed this life, Father Maurice Zundel went to offer his condolences to his widow Juliette. Her account of this visit seems to me to express much more than what might have been expected under these particular circumstances. She said: "In his whole person, there was this gentle dignity, a solemn quality and a silence full of compassion, the only thing I would have been able to bear at the time."

Maurice Zundel, in turn, died on August 10, 1975. I met him for the first time when I was a young priest. I had come to see him, on behalf of Father Bernadot, to ask him to write *Notre Dame de la Sagesse* (Our Lady of Wisdom). Although we only saw each other occasionally, our relationship lasted for forty years. My last memory of him is that of being enfolded in the warmth of his broad smile as he was trying to take a few steps in a hallway of the Bois-Cerf clinic in Lausanne, with the assistance of a nurse and a nun.

With his passing, we lost one of the most powerful Christian figures of our times, a kind of spiritual genius. Not everyone understood Fr. Zundel: his stands were often paradoxical, at times baffling, and his ideas were ahead of those of a good number of people. Supported with sensitivity and intelligence by some of his colleagues, Msgr. Ramuz in particular, to mention only those who have passed away, he also relied, and with what joy, on the trust Msgr. Montini placed in him. Not only did the latter, once he was Pope Paul VI, expressly quote him in his encyclical *Populorum Progressio*, but he invited him to preach at the Vatican's Spiritual Exercises in February 1972.

The time has not come yet for biographies or exhaustive studies on Fr. Zundel. However, his friends could not let his Vatican retreat be published without paying a sincere tribute to him. His sermons, together with their testimonies and the letters they exchanged, certainly provided enough subject matter for an entire book. Some limits had to be set. Nevertheless, I do think that, from these pages, drawn from various sources, a distinct profile of the man is beginning to emerge, whose lines are both clearly defined and finely shaded. Fr. Zundel is right before our eyes, literally photographed at times, or rather lovingly filmed. And so it is that simple gestures and remarks on everyday life provide an explanation, shed a new light on his life's work. The essential thing for him, as will be shown here, was "poverty of the spirit totally open as a space which the Infinite alone can fill."

* * *

First, a brief account of his journey on earth, given to us by the nuns of a Benedictine monastery:

Fr. Zundel was born of Swiss parents on January 21st, 1897, in Neuchâtel. He studied in this same city, at the abbey of Einsiedeln, to which he remained attached as an Oblate under the name of Brother Benedict. He then studied in Fribourg until his ordination to the priesthood on July 20, 1919, at the age of twenty-two. After six years as the parish priest of St. Joseph's in Geneva, the young Zundel left for Rome to work on his doctorate in theology. From 1926 to 1928, he was spiritual director at the Benedictine monastery of Saint-Louis-du-Temple, on the rue Monsieur, in Paris. There he met some outstanding people, like Father Montini who later became Pope Paul VI. Montini translated Zundel's *Poème de la Sainte Liturgie* (Poem of the Sacred Liturgy) into Italian, which translation was published a few years later, in 1934. In 1937-1938, Fr. Zundel studied at the School of Biblical Studies in Jerusalem and then spent the war years in Cairo and Beirut. Later, while he was assistant to the priest in the parish of the Sacred Heart at Ouchy-Lausanne, he often returned to Egypt and Lebanon as well as to Paris. He willingly complied with requests made to him to write articles, give lectures and preach retreats. His various books were published throughout the years of his priesthood.

It must be strongly emphasized that this shows how Fr. Zundel devoted all his life to intense intellectual work which was matched by the intensity of his prayer. Even before it resulted in creating a specific work, this intellectual activity aimed first and foremost at studying and in-depth understanding. The author of so many books was not a man to be satisfied with acquired knowledge from which he could easily draw. Even after years of studies in philosophy, theology and Scripture, he constantly pursued his research, always keeping up to date in these fields, striving to discover the latest works and thus providing a solid basis for his inspiration as a poet and mystic.

At the end of two retreats at the Benedictine monastery, Fr. Zundel apologized for his long talks which, he said, "were endless." That was because, he would add, "I am constantly searching: everything is always new to me and I never cease to wonder; for me, every morning, God is new."

* * *

The physician from Lausanne who took care of him for many years gives us a description of Fr. Zundel that should help those who did not know him very well—or knew him only through his writings—to grasp his unusual and fascinating personality.

Under the cape of a Benedictine brother, he wore a white or black cassock over an athletic physique with well-developed muscles. His frail appearance concealed a robust nature, able to withstand an ascetic way of life.

Up at five in the morning, he prepared himself for the Mass he was to celebrate at six. Then he often took a walk at a steady pace before having his breakfast: tea and dry bread. His day was unpredictable: work in his office, consultations, receiving all those who came to him to beg, weep or ask a favor. He also frequently went out of Lausanne to visit people he would never have thought of abandoning.

In Paris, in Lebanon and Egypt, he gave lectures and conducted retreats in very mixed circles, where Christians of various rites and denominations mingled with people of every condition.

He liked to visit contemplative communities. When he preached retreats in their midst, he led the same life as the monks or the nuns. His table fare, however, was even more meager than theirs.

After a light meal in the evening, he would begin a period of serious work. He read, wrote, meditated, took notes, prayed, etc. Late into the night, he would doze off in his armchair until, at five in the morning, he would be wakened by the ring of his three to five big alarm clocks, the constant tick-tock of which I personally found unbearable...

He was a very heavy smoker. When I first met him in 1942 for a short retreat, he took out a box of one hundred cigarettes from under his cassock. That was his supply for the day. His room was overheated (he was sensitive to cold) and, most of the time, filled with a haze. "Father, why do you smoke so much?"—"I don't inhale" he would reply. "I need it to think and, I would add, to control myself." On the other hand, he never drank alcohol, ate neither meat nor fatty foods "which make the mind sluggish". This asceticism, however, did tolerate a few exceptions. I found out that he had eaten a whole chocolate cake while visiting someone who had prepared it especially for him. In the same way, he adapted to the household menu of an Egyptian family who had just returned to France.

All of Fr. Zundel's relationships throughout his life were lived through God. Intelligence was the human quality he revered the most. If he held someone in esteem, he would first say: "He is intelligent"; then other words of appreciation could come. However, intelligence for him was worth something only if it had discovered the divine dimension. Thus he had reservations about Monod's *Le Hasard et la Nécessité* (Chance and Necessity). This book would have been "intelligent" if the author had gone further. "He is almost there," he told me. He had great admiration for Professor Jean Bernard because he presented man in his total dimension. Intelligence is nothing if it believes it can appropriate the truth found in research; it is everything if it acknowledges the source of that truth. For him, intelligence had to be enlightened from within, even if its mission is to apply itself to objects.

To him, only inner enlightenment seemed to be the true criterion of intelligence; he would then trust it completely. This judgment sometimes misled him. Certain intelligent but neurotic individuals, in search of love or some other anchor, often appeared to him as human beings thirsting for knowledge, who only needed, in order to be healed, to be directed toward the view that "I is Another". Zundel's trust, however, was not superficial; it made certain demands. A few years ago, I wanted to give up a woman patient he had entrusted to me. "You cannot abandon her," he told me, "she will die; she lives because of you." I objected that she had only a few months to live. He glared at me, and I remained her doctor... for another five years. He had told me on another occasion: "The fact that she is still alive is a miracle, and you are responsible for it."

The first thing he would ask of those coming to him for spiritual healing was to attend his Mass at six in the morning. He would sometimes assign exhausting tasks to those who offered him their services. But he would also do his own share, and do so generously. Overwhelmed by work, he would still cross the lake to hear confession from an overly scrupulous woman; he would spend the night with patients racked by anxiety; he brought communion here and there every day.

In times of great turmoil and sorrow, he would remain silent, kneel at the foot of the bed and pray. Sometimes, he would spread the hem of his cape over the bed, and this sign of brotherly compassion would be more soothing than any words. I heard him say to a patient who was as terrified of death as of the emptiness of her life: "Do not cry: you are the mother of Christ." In this case, these were not mere words. They were addressed to a woman who had been brought up in a Jansenist milieu and who, at 65, was on the brink of revolt. She died peacefully, filled with love. Fr. Zundel rushed to answer calls everywhere. When someone suggested that he become the chaplain of a psychiatric hospital, he asked for my opinion. I objected to the idea, pointing out reasons that were anything but flattering: his lack of judgment in morbid situations, the fact that he tended to be easily trapped within closed neurotic circuits which led to his quick neutralization. After thirty seconds of silence, I heard him humbly say at the other end of the line: "Thank you, doctor, I shall not go."

Charity for Fr. Zundel was a vital necessity. I asked him to stop receiving beggars, who had free access to his door, and prisoners coming out of jail. "I can't," he said. "I need to do this to be fulfilled." Of course, his wallet was always empty. It was therefore decided that a colleague of his would take care of his funds and give him a weekly allowance. Finding him out of money, one of the regulars went so far as to beat him up. But when one of the curates of the parish intervened energetically on his behalf, Fr. Zundel was profusely apologetic... to the abusive beggar.

Five months before he died, he had a thrombosis of the left cerebral hemisphere with aphasia resulting in loss of speech. Given his age, recovery was impossible. I prescribed readings, songs and guided conversations. Realizing that these were ineffective, he let me know that we would have to seek the help of specialists. One important element of the treatment was rest, leisurely outings, etc. Fr. Zundel refused. What he wanted was to work relentlessly in his room. He fought to the end his incapacity to express himself: he also suffered from the degeneration of his brain and the decline of his mental powers.

During this period, I brought him the news of Cardinal Journet's death. He grew pale, pushed aside the remainder of his meal, and tried to collect his memories. Maritain, Journet: he could not remember their names. He tried to recall them by using circumlocutions, like "the one who entered into silence." That was not Journet but Maritain who had entered a convent. As for the cardinal, a model priest for him, he would have liked him to have a state funeral.

Whenever he was faced with health problems, he always refused treatment. He imagined there might be a risk, some permanent scarring, concoctions which could alter his personality. He constantly misused his strength. In 1973, over ten consecutive nights, he put the finishing touches to this book, his last one, from tapes which had been recorded at the Vatican. It required an enormous effort on his part. He then left for Paris, completely exhausted. He had hardly begun his lectures and homilies when he collapsed. This was a serious warning. And so, throughout 1974, he followed his treatment and rested.

Just before March 1975, having resumed work on his book, he had a relapse. This time it was a coronary with cerebral complications. I have already alluded to these final months. While he continued to make unreasonable demands on himself, he was appreciative of the least attention given him. He would express his thanks, surprised that people should spoil him so. Once, he asked me who was paying his bills at the clinic. I mounted guard at his door and did my best to screen his visitors. He was always thinking, praying, and he was finally able to sleep thanks to some medication. He died suddenly from the migration of a new blood clot that caused an embolism. He had often experienced and shared the anguish of the dying. He was spared that pain.

* * *

An exceptional woman, spiritually and professionally speaking, will now speak on behalf of all those men and women who asked Fr. Zundel "to take them on". Listening to her, we ourselves feel as if we belonged to the huge flock of which he was the Good Shepherd.

Whenever I could and wanted to see him, I would telephone him, sometimes saying just one word. He was always available. He would set up an appointment to fit in with my work, on a day and at a time which suited me. In 1974, the usual two-hour meetings often lasted an hour and a half, rarely less.

It was the same when I needed some advice, and needed it urgently. He would answer kindly and firmly, in a clear and concise manner after a simple "Good day!" in a tone of voice that was filled with meaning: his greeting was for you and nobody else. That was typical of him.

Whenever possible, I would make a detour through Lausanne to go to confession on Saturday, which was his day. Even if he had not previously been informed of my coming, he always recognized me. These confessions were always extraordinary moments, as much for what went on inside the penitents as for the words he addressed to them. How often a friend of mine and myself wished we could have recorded what he said! We never dared. What went on was truly sacred.

It is difficult to speak of this priest without explaining in detail all the facts in which were rooted our respect for him and the absolute conviction of the Truth of what he represented.

In church, he spoke with his eyes closed and without using notes. The way he waited for someone to hand him a ciborium before communion, his genuflexion in front of the Tabernacle spoke louder than words of the real Presence. We felt this was not a matter of knowledge but of personal experience.

In short, in spite of his fundamental humility, he did not go unnoticed. Besides, he never missed a thing. If, after the sermon, he recognized at the back of the church my friend who had just arrived on the six o'clock evening train (and who was therefore late), he would smile and go straight to the confessional.

His welcome? Unforgettable, unique, with that special smile and that look that saw right through you. His extreme gentleness, his care to avoid hurting in the slightest the soul that was opening up to him. Perhaps his silence grew out of this total respect for others. A silence in which a gesture, a sign—a nod, a smile—often took the place of words. Prolonged silence could prompt one to search more deeply inside and discover what was important.

The way he joined his hands or closed his eyes. I should say his ways of doing these things: for he had many ways of closing his eyes. It could indicate listening, concentrating, praying. Sometimes, when the subject of the mystical graces was brought up, whether they be particular graces or particular insights, a certain expression would come over his face, as if he were in the presence of the Adorable One. He would close his eyes, and it seemed as though he was going down to his secret chamber, shedding his own self completely so as to be only an empty space (as he put it) where he merged with God in mutual giving.

He never had an impatient word or gesture, but his piercing gaze revealed to the most unsuspecting observer his incisive lucidity and clear-sightedness. He could read in someone's heart and detect the slightest alteration of the truth. It was enough to make you wish the ground would open up and swallow you, even if the truth had not exactly been altered.

He also knew how to put on an impassive face when he though he should not answer, as for example, with those who were merely curious about spiritual matters.

He was compassionate, his words had a way of surprising you, and his voice...

His comments or questions were brief, concise and to the point.

What a contrast between his unflagging patience and the passion he displayed when speaking of God, of Christ, or when he dissected atheism, etc.

One could confide everything to him. Everything. In certain cases, it caused him pain. In others, he was visibly filled with wonder before the mysterious ways of the Lord. He never judged; he could understand everything and look at the positive side.

His major advice was not to be a screen between God and others, not to hurt others, for in doing so, it was as if we were destroying God's image in them: such a fragile God, handed over to us and made vulnerable through us, a God who surrenders himself to man: "We are responsible for God."

The sight of him, indeed, led us to God. He wrote that what matters is what we are, rather than what we do. He would say this because what is ultimately important "is what is happening on the level of the inner Person". "The Kingdom of God is within us." "It is no longer I who live..." "The Incarnation becomes Life only if we understand that it is God's Life that is unfolding through us. We all possess the Kingdom of God within ourselves, thanks to Christ. It is up to *each one* of us to realize the 'Thy kingdom come'. We utter these words too quickly, without analyzing their wonderful content, a content that commits those saying them in the very depths of their being. We are all concerned: co-crucified and co-sufferers with Christ (Jn 17), but also co-glorified and co-redeemers."

Therefore, it is not God, as it were, who makes the Kingdom emerge from us, but Humanity, which must take upon itself the Assumption of humankind in God, in Love received and shared. Thus bound together, the destiny of humanity and the Kingdom of God will ultimately unfold in our innermost selves.

He used to say: "Life is Someone", "God is an experience", "We know ourselves only when we know ourselves in Him", "God dies rather than compelling us", "To be freedom: to be for others the reflection of this freedom which is an offering."

I shall not say any more about him; others will; they will speak of many things, including his phenomenal culture. When he celebrated the Eucharist, you could feel, as it were, a palpable Presence...

He said "Good-bye" as intensely as he said "Hello". He always added "Thank you." He would stand at the door until you had crossed the threshold and stepped out.

I respected him, I admired him. For me, he really represented God.

* * *

"A mystic of our times": that is how Fr. Zundel was described by a physician whom he had guided and whose thinking has obviously been shaped by Zundel's work.

The last wave of midsummer heat, fearsome for the elderly, carried him off on August 10, 1975, in his seventy-eighth year. He was doubtlessly the most hidden and most dazzling figure of our times.

Fr. Zundel did not let the grime of the world nor the erosion of time affect him. He could say without exaggeration: "Youth is yet to come", for up to his last moment, he believed in man and communicated his faith to him.

"Death," he wrote, "surely holds sway over us as long as we have not transplanted our roots to that immaterial world where our personality asserts itself as source and origin... On the other hand, if this transplanting is carried out to perfection, death will be overcome before it can touch us." Fr. Zundel personified this victory over death and his fervent love changed the course of our lives.

A modest and unobtrusive man, whose frail build showed through the habit, he exerted on many key figures of his time an influence greater than anyone could have imagined. He was not only past master in interpersonal relationships, but also a man of passion and silence. His capacity for undivided attention would soon cause a secret spring to well up in the persons engaged in conversation with him, opening up a boundless space of potentialities in them. If you had the chance of approaching him, his radiant and enigmatic smile, his unfathomable gaze would unexpectedly take you on a great journey within yourself, which you would forever remember longingly.

To let go of oneself, to be *transparent* to divine Reality, inseparable from the one communicating it: Zundel could be the bearer of such a message since he excelled in embodying it. He told it in all his works, the titles of which alone draw our attention to "the only Presence" and to our capacity for being open to the world, until we live Rimbaud's paradox: "I is Another."

His whole life was absorbed in the *joy of others*, in keeping with his definition of holiness which, coming from him, in no way suggested vebal inflation. You could not keep track of his generous deeds, so numerous were they, for which he was only the medium, having nothing of his own. It was his generosity that drove him to get deeply involved in the most difficult and darkest situations. Nowadays, when individual life is languishing in a climate of indifference, he often reminded us that "the greatest sorrow for the poor is that no one needs their friendship."

When he expressed his realistic view of the human organism, imprisoned within the laws or the illusions of biology, he did not mince his words. As he considered "this animal-like teeming mass of human beings scattered over five continents and increasingly bound by their rivalries," he lashed out, along with Jean Rostand, against "the conformism of ignorance in our makers of fashionable rubbish." "Will man ever cease to put up with himself, to be the product of his own biology, the reflection of his moods, the puppet of his glands, the cry of his race or social class... or will he emerge as a creator, bearing within himself the space where each one can suddenly feel liberated, promoted to his own self, accepted in the living silence of a presence, both fulfilling and self-effacing, that opens inside us a field of discovery eternally new?" "Thus there are moments when human beings, perpetually hunting each other down and carrying their genius for massacre to phenomenal heights..., awake from their tragic lack of awareness and suddenly discover in one endangered life the infinite value of all life."

The author then calls on our innate "vocation for freedom, which expresses itself in our refusal to ever be treated as a thing". At the same time, he agrees with Coventry Patmore when he maintains that "virtues are only disciplined passions". And so he would wish that the usual morality, which fits a static view of man in order to "rein in his lusts", be replaced by a (dynamic) morality that will "transform desires into levers for man's fulfillment". Of course, help from heaven is needed, "but since there are no celestial telephone lines to transmit divine information directly to us, all we know about God comes through the human psyche". It reaches its noblest form in Jesus Christ who can lead us away from our visceral self to this unknown self beyond us, buried in trinitarian love. "God's goodness cannot be less than that of the best of men." Zundel passionately sought the true face of the Savior who, unlike the inaccessible monarch frozen in conventional images, reveals himself at the Washing of the feet.

Shaking up our fantasies of a tyrannical monarch, Fr. Zundel invites us to "decrucify" this God so fragile, so easy to kill, whom, as Graham Greene says, we must be willing to protect against ourselves. He once illustrated this with the fresco of the Last Judgment on the façade in Vézelay where, in contrast to Michelangelo's vengeful Christ, Jesus merely shows his wounds to those assembled before him whose eyes have seen the light. One can understand that, when he said mass, Zundel would invite the entire universe to join in the offertory. "God", he wrote, "never plans our lives without our consent, but he sets us before him in the role of creators, making our collaboration essential to the realization of a universe of which Love is the source and the end."

So Maurice Zundel never lost himself in an ethereal or sophisticated theology. For him, the knowledge and communication of God are linked to the transformation of humankind. Who could claim to transform others in the name of a God who would not transform him? This is somewhat like the metamorphosis that Jung called for in the physician in order to make possible the metamorphosis in the patient.

Most probably anticipating his tragic end, Zundel recalled, in one of his last books, these words that Thomas More said to the officer who was taking him to the scaffold: "I pray you, Master Lieutenant, see me safe up, and for my coming down, let me shift for myself."[1] Since the door of "the silent chamber" (as he called death) has closed upon him beyond this visible world, he is beckoning us more than ever to the infinite respect without which "there is no longer anything to communicate or to defend, for there is no longer anyone."

For him, the future of humanity will be a mystical one or there will be no future at all. Never again will we feel the warm clasp of his hands nor see them raised in the act of blessing, but these words from John of the Cross could well be applied to him:

> *He passed through these groves in haste,*
> *And, looking upon them as he went,*
> *Left them, by his glance alone,*
> *clothed with beauty.*[2]

* * *

Finally, a priest, both his friend and confessor, was kind enough—of his own accord—to share a few thoughts with us. They are a valuable complement to what we have just read.

I believe that Fr. Zundel's theology, traditional in pure faith, but thought out, felt and delivered in an existentialist and contemplative mode, through an experience and a testimony in which he totally revealed what he was without

---

[1] Richard Marius, *Thomas More: A biography*, Alfred A. Knopf, New York, 1984, p. 513.

[2] The Complete Works of St John of the Cross, translated and edited by E. Allison Peers, revised ed., 3 vol. Newman Press, 1953, Spiritual Canticle, Vol. 2, Stanza 5, p. 47.

ever speaking of himself, is destined to shed light on the future paths of Christian spirituality. Nevertheless, like every vocation, Fr. Zundel's vocation must be viewed in an overall perspective.

Fr. Zundel's theology was at one with himself. If indeed it came from his deep faith, it came just as much from his painful experience. That is why his theology, a reflection of his inner life, spontaneously took the form of an unsettling pastoral teaching. No! God does not tyrannize man. On the contrary, a defenseless God surrenders to him so that, in turn, man may somehow save God from the blows of the world. This mutual gift of one's whole being forms the basis, in an analogical mode of equality, for this admirable friendship between mankind and its God. Far from reducing man's freedom to nothing, God's sovereign and transcendent freedom exalts it; it allows the human personality to come into being and to meet, in an ineffable manner, the three divine Persons and in them, all created persons.

These are well-known aspects of Fr. Zundel. In order to understand his vocation in relation to itself, one would have to see it hollowed out, as it were. I am speaking of the tormented soul that he always was. I am thinking of some features of his inner face, with all its shades and variations...

However, I would prefer to draw attention to another point, to what appears to me as the very nature and scope of Fr. Zundel's apostolate. I shall mention some limitations, for it is the only way to define someone.

Most of the time, he delivered a fiery message. In its light, each one could or was meant to find his own way and discover his personality. Fr. Zundel did not analyze a situation; he shed light upon it from high above. Perhaps he thought that people only needed a strong light shining in their eyes, and not the modest glow of a flashlight to guide their steps. I recently shared this thought with several people: a priest who was well acquainted with our friend, an elderly working woman who was trained by Fr. Zundel at a time when both were young in St. Joseph's parish in Geneva, and finally, a philosopher physician who had read some of Fr. Zundel's lectures, but who did not know him personally. There are converging elements in their accounts.

The priest thinks, as I do, that, apart from some exceptional cases, a normal spiritual training, individual or collective, requires a clear-sighted, constant "step-by-step" approach in the practice of everyday life. The working woman is aware that she owes much to Fr. Zundel (with whom she remained in contact throughout her life), but that she would never have assimilated his testimony if she had not known the A.C.O. (Action catholique ouvrière or the Catholic Workers Movement). The physician, a former rationalist raised as a Protestant, told me approximately the same thing.

Are these remarks warning us that if Fr. Zundel's ministry is authentic and worthy of admiration, it needs to be completed, at the other end of life, with a totally different ministry? There may be a lighthouse on the shore, but you still need boatmen to ply the oars...

* * *

Indeed, there are many types of vocations. No single "charisma" is enough. That is why St. Paul praised the originality and the value of each different way of serving in the Church, as well as the necessary cohesion of all members to build the Christian Body.

One thing is certain: many boatmen seeking the shore where Christ awaits them will choose, among many others, the light cast by Maurice Zundel's work. One of his key words, *interiority*, is and will increasingly be the answer to the needs of today's world. The timeliness of his message is only beginning.

Those who have spoken about him in this Preface are a living proof of it, and their vision is both lucid and loving. They betray neither the thinking nor the heart of the priest who begot them in the Spirit. And how could they not wish this new birth for everyone? "The flames of love radiate light", a Cistercian monk wrote to me, "and I saw, for one short moment, one of these flames reflected in the eye of the man possessed by God that was Maurice Zundel. Our meeting was coming to an end and, just as I was taking my leave, I begged him to teach me a prayer so that 'I could remain humble'. He stood before me, his eyes all lit up, his face streaming with kindness, and he spoke these words in a loud voice: 'Live in joy, and you will stop looking at yourself'."

This man, so imbued with humility, had just revealed to me the secret of joy, his own joy:

To the man dispossessed of everything, God offers his joy,

the joy of the Poor made transparent by the consuming inner Sun,

the joy of the Risen on Easter Morn!

A.- M. Carré, O.P.
of the French Academy

Introduction

On January 12, 1972, His Excellency the Papal Nuncio to Switzerland summoned me to Berne to hand me the Holy Father's invitation to preach the annual retreat at the Vatican at the beginning of Lent.

Nothing could have been more unexpected. Since an immediate reply was requested, I agreed without carefully weighing the implications of my commitment. The retreat was to begin on February 13, but it was postponed by a few days to February 20.

At that time, I was in charge of some ministries and I could not shirk my duties. It was therefore impossible for me to write out the twenty-two sermons traditionally listed on the program of that week-long retreat. I had to rely on my ability to improvise before the most eminent audience in the world. That prevented me, even if I had wished to do so, from presenting topics other than those that habitually sustained my reflection and had been expressed in my most recent work *Je est un Autre* (I is Another).

As a result, these pages, written from a tape recording that Msgr. Macchi kindly transcribed, will often be reminiscent of that book. Uppermost in my mind was the *crisis* perturbing the Church. Many of its members were caught up in the wave of universal protest that had been sweeping through Western society since May 68. That had to be addressed by pointing out the positive elements of a more or less radical calling into question of the faith, the values and the institutions with which Catholic Christianity had unanimously and officially identified until then.

It seems to me that the most enlightening interpretation of this phenomenon is to see it as the explosive realization of one's autonomy, as it rejects all constraints in its absolute claim to freedom. Such an interpretation finds the roots of protest in an affirmation of the *spirit* that perceives itself as an inviolable interiority. The question the spirit asks and the answer it anticipates lie in those depths.

That does not mean that we ought to close our eyes to the ambiguity of this vast movement of opposition. The freedom demanded by many protesters is one that rebels against established rules but is not likely to provide some of its own. It lacks a precise content and a firm structure. Such a freedom often fails to recognize the inner *necessity* which alone can justify the supreme attachement we claim to vow to it. Also, the rejection of an external norm is meaningful only if it results in creating an inner one, which is both the individual and the common good.

But, indeed, what can this good be, which develops in each person's most intimate *solitude* and tolerates no intrusion, although it constitutes the only specifically human value, the only truly universal good?

We can see the paradox emerging: what is most rigorously personal must also be what is most completely communicable.

But at the cost of what transformation?

Our lusts and our aggressiveness, revolving around a narcissistic prefabricated ego, make our claim to freedom meaningless. For there is no worse enslavement than to be subjected to inner determinisms, whereby we identify with options that in fact emanate from our passions. Literature if full of examples of how fatal these can be.

From this, we begin to understand that freedom implies an inner *liberation*, one that will radically transform us by opening up within ourselves an unlimited space; in it, our instinctual ego, that we have not chosen and that traps us in the false absolute of its biased options, will no longer limit our horizon.

This liberation can only be the work of boundless love, the result of discovering, in the depths of our being, a Presence that will elicit our offering by offering Itself to us. It is precisely because this is a work of love that all outside intervention is inadmissible, and every conscience must be considered inviolable. And it is because this Presence is infinite that the love it awakens embraces the whole universe.

God is at the heart of our freedom, as its *sine qua non* condition: that is what I have tried to say in all I have written.

Man is born from this silent dialogue with the mysterious Host who sets him free from his own self, by making him go from the *given* that subjects him to the *giving* that fulfills him.

What else could I say in Rome where I was invited to speak?

Naturally, I tried to take into account the devotional nature of the talks that constitute the substance of a retreat. Their unity must be derived from the common light they shed rather than from a systematic sequence of ideas. Of course, I could not fail to acknowledge the flaws inherent to improvisation, for which I ask to be forgiven by both my listeners and my readers.

That being said, how can I resist, by way of introduction, recalling briefly all I got out of this unforgettable week? The Vatican was like a monastery, in the contemplative quiet of the liturgical prayer before or after my sermons, as well as in the perfect simplicity of my eminent audience.

The Holy Father's presence was invaluably precious to me and I felt carried along by its radiant effect. I was overwhelmed by his kindness. I can only offer him the most respectful and filial homage of my boundless gratitude.

1

And Little Henry Ceased to Pray...

On February 17, 1967, in the wake of an article of mine, "Man's quest: experiencing God", published in *Choisir*, the Holy Father was good enough to send word to me, urging me to study "the problems of our times" and eventually put in writing whatever sense I could make of them. Nothing could suit my personal inclinations better, since I have spent the better part of my life learning about the ideas and discoveries of thinkers and scientists whose contemporary I was privileged to be. I have endeavored to understand and assimilate their ideas as much as I could.

But I must admit that, at the time I received the letter from the office of the Secretary of State, it was almost impossible to cover all the problems that were being raised, in all areas at the same time, and which were drastically changing traditional ways of thinking.

Nevertheless, an attempt to face them had to be made, since the evangelical message must be presented to the people of our times and in their own language.

In those days, *atheistic existentialism* was continuing to spread, rejecting any preestablished order since, according to Sartre, "every man must create his own path." Marxist atheism, integrated into two great empires and with immense powers at its disposal, thus found, at no cost to itself, an ally of the highest order in the West to promote the disintegration of a part of the world not yet subjected to the political sovereignty of communism. *Freudianism*, for its part, had been so widely popularized that many of its ideas had found their way into everyday language, and were giving rise to widespread mistrust of the old morality, supposedly associated with repression.

A new discipline, the linguistic *structuralism* of Claude Lévi-Strauss and Michel Foucault, was attempting to exclude the *human subject* from objective language, which exists on its own and speaks through us, in particular in the recurring patterns of myths found everywhere and which, through certain structural analogies, can be identified in spite of the variety of their content.[1] Thus, by denying human beings any interiority, *the death of man* was decreed, after the death of God whose nonexistence, according to Marx, was to be the foundation of man's rule.

This negation of man appealed to some *cyberneticians*, like Louis Couffignal, who attribute superhuman faculties to computers, supposing them capable of developing theories beyond any man's comprehension. It was to find a categorical expression among the pioneers of *molecular biology*, like Jacques Monod. According to them, life started by chance, diversified through billions of other chances, stabilizing as many times in a rigorous

---

[1] Cf. Jean Lacroix, "Atheism and contemporary thought", lecture delivered at the Cenacle in Beirut, 9 February 1967.

constant—until a new chance event occurred. Life could in no way be considered as having been intended nor as having, on its own, any meaning.

In a totally different area, the *theologians of the death of God* were shaking up the faithful with some rather adventurous views, the valid elements of which were very difficult to detect.

Everyone listened to the radio, and television was coming into most households; anyone could keep up to date, if not with the questions raised by philosophers and scientists, at least with the conclusions they reached. These often ran counter to all accepted ideas. Unable to pass critical judgment on an ever-increasing mass of conflicting information, many listeners and viewers were thus led to a kind of skepticism that tended to relativize every point of view.

That is where things stood when the demonstrations of May 68 broke out. They spread throughout the "free world" with lightning speed and did not spare the Church. It suddenly found itself confronted with challenging questions one would have thought absolutely impossible.

How did the fire start? How did the established order suddenly find itself radically called into question, to the extent that public authorities had to make concessions and come to terms with a revolt which, at any moment, could become a revolution? What caused such turmoil?

Was it the denial of God and man, which, progressing obscurely through the affective field of the unconscious, lead to the rejection of any absolute and, as a consequence, to the conclusion that all is permissible, even the absurd?

Was it the outrage of two world wars that had revealed the fragility of a civilization unable to respect the values it purportedly held, and which, to this day, keeps on killing people under the guise of defending human rights?

Was it the generation gap that took the explosive form of a collective "Oedipus", rising up against "fathers", determined to supplant them by toppling over all the hierarchies which were meant to guarantee their respectability?

Was this a phenomenon of precocious maturity brought about by the mass media that allowed children to have access, at a very early age, to the same world as adults?

All these factors possibly played a role in the sudden mutation which is giving a new face to our universe. But there are doubtlessly deeper motivations.

Before identifying them, let us point out that two consequences seem to be widely accepted as the aftermath of this ground swell. On the one hand, the collapse of traditional morality, especially on sexual matters, where the notion of guilt is now perceived as anachronistic. Indeed, adolescents claim the right to experiment and many parents—even Christian ones—have decided to turn a blind eye to these inevitable "accidents of life". Meanwhile, "theologians" devote themselves to bringing out the historical character of the norms taught—if not practiced—to this day, and conclude that challenging them is legitimate. On the other hand, all authority is rejected. At the very most do young people accept to discuss everything on equal terms, as among adults, even if they are not even fifteen years old, meanwhile reserving the right to go on strike in support of unmet claims.

I have just implied that some Church people are quite prepared to reassert the value of sexuality, openly accepting it in all its forms, which, they say, can gradually lead to full happiness. The "chummy" style, which is becoming customary in some religious communities, is itself evidence of the erosion of authority in the face of demands from the "grass roots" who intend to have their autonomy respected.

At first glance, to be subjected to no constraints, to be bound by no preexisting order, to agree to do only what is in harmony with one's moods is what constitutes the total freedom so passionately proclaimed as the foundation of a new era.

This analysis, however, needs to be qualified. For someone who sincerely believes that life is the result of chance, any meaning we claim to give it will always remain arbitrary and may be constantly modified. On the other hand, the massive rejection of the established order by even the most vehement protesters does not in itself imply an unrestrained appetite for pleasure. They may be more aggressively sensitive to the loss of liberty in others than inclined to enjoy their own. Furthermore, we cannot deny that what is permitted and what is prohibited have not always been understood in the same way. These notions vary, not only throughout the different civilizations of our history but, to some extent, throughout revealed morality itself. Finally, and this is perhaps the most important point, how can one resolve the antinomy between a moral law, whose commandments seem to be imposed from the outside, and the experience of freedom as the power for self-determination?

Conceivably, it is ultimately on this point that converge all the movements which join in the great rejection we are witnessing. Through secret affinities, this rejection rallies a good number of our contemporaries who are rebelling against all forms of *heteronomy*, that is, against all rules of behaviour received from the outside, judged to be absurd and unfounded by some, and prejudicial to their freedom by others.

This, to my mind, is the common element energizing and uniting demands which, on the face of it, seem unrelated.

I will try to define and express all the *positive* aspects of this element, first, in order to understand the crisis confronting us, and then to discover what is required on the part of the Church, at the pastoral level, so that its voice may be heard.

As I have just suggested, the calling into question of traditional positions which is most worthy of our attention is founded, I believe, on a certain sense of human dignity, on an awareness, no doubt confused and emotional, but all the more vigorous, of the *inviolability* of the person.

A Swiss-German writer of the nineteenth century, Gottfried Keller, uses an infinitely minute incident as an example to illustrate convincingly the discovery of this inviolability. In a novel said to be autobiographical, *Henry the Green (Heinrich der Grüne)*, he tells this episode from the hero's childhood. Little Henry was the only child of a widowed mother; she did her best to bring him up and lavished her tender love on him. He was eight or nine years old at the time. He came home from school one late afternoon; his supper was waiting for him and he sat down at the table without, for the first time, saying grace. His mother, taking this to be a moment of absent-mindedness, gently drew his attention to the omission. He pretended not to hear. She insisted. He stiffened in silent resistance. Then, in a commanding tone, his mother said: "You do not want to say your prayer?—No!—Well then, go to bed without your supper!" The child bravely took up the challenge and went to bed without saying a word. Some time later, the mother, racked with remorse, brought him supper in bed. Too late: from that moment on, the little boy ceased to pray.

This minor incident is heavy with meaning. It makes us see a child becoming aware of his inviolability as a person. He discovers within himself a place his mother cannot enter without his consent, his own personal domain of which he alone can dispose. To be sure, he would be at a loss to define it, but he has such a keen perception of it that, henceforth, he will give up praying in order to constantly maintain, against his mother's infringement, its intangible independence.

We find in this example one of the most basic elements of human experience. The revolt of slaves, throughout history, implies that they too discover in themselves an inviolable inner space which makes them refuse to be instruments in the hands of someone else, who claims ownership over them as mere objects. From that moment on, they know that they can only acknowledge as their own an act of which they are truly the source and origin.

It is undoubtedly spurred on by such a conviction that, between 73 and 71 B.C., with his army of slaves of whom he wanted to make free men, Spartacus managed to hold off the Roman legions for two years. He failed. Finally, he perished in the battle and six thousand of his companions were crucified. In spite of this failure, his heroic feat still proves that man almost always becomes most keenly aware of his dignity in the midst of the indignities he is subjected to.

The driving force behind the process of decolonization, which gave rise to so many new nations, was also the will to self-determination: the people no longer could tolerate to bow to a foreign law which was perceived as denying them status as full members of the human race.

People of the white race surely still have a long way to go in order to rid themselves completely of their superiority complex, a complex that made it seem natural for them to claim supremacy over other races on account of technological superiority. Because of the lack of real personal contact with native populations, they doubtless remained closed to the intimate aspects of indigenous life. In general, their reaction was better when faced with the horrors perpetrated in concentration camps—invented by white men—which touched their sensitivities more directly.

In his *Antimémoires*, Malraux speaks for the best of them when he says that the most profound evil is the will, apparently the only law governing these infernal jails, to trample man underfoot, to strip him of all that is human, and finally to reduce him to such a state as to make him feel, out of despair, disgust for himself.

I remember a colleague, a missionary in China, who was subjected to horrendous brainwashing. Hands chained behind his back and feet shackled with balls and chains, he had to eat his meals in this position. He was forced to lap his food like a dog and, spilling half of it most of the time, he had to lick this food, essential to his survival, right off the ground. Moreover, beaten up, insulted and spat at, he lost all semblance of a human face.

It is impossible for us to imagine such a situation without recognizing, through the indignation and compassion we feel, the interiority and inviolability that make us human, the right and the duty for a person to be the source and origin of his actions. And also, the crime of reducing a human being to this tragic puppet, forced to collaborate by degrading gestures to the disgrace inflicted upon him.

An opinion poll on the subject of such indignities would undoubtedly reveal an almost universal disapproval. When man becomes a mere object in a sadistic game, the vast majority of people will agree with the following statement: a person basically differs from a thing by a certain *inwardness*, which means that any attempt to subject him to an external constraint is an actual desecration.

But this common stand remains very ambiguous for the simple reason that, in general, we know neither where to locate this inner dimension nor how to define it. As a matter of fact, even if man develops an acute sense of his dignity when he is subjected to degrading treatment—or when he knows it is being inflicted upon others with whom he identifies—even if he spontaneously claims his inviolability against injustice, he cannot provide a basis for his claim.

What has the little boy, who suddenly discovers within himself a space, inaccessible to his mother, that he is determined to defend, in fact done to make it inviolable? Nothing. He is not the origin of his own being, he was brought into this world without wishing it; he is constantly nurtured by his mother's tender care and he receives all the elements of his subsistence from the external universe. How can he say *I* and *me*? What authorizes him to make use of these personal pronouns and to stand as an autonomous being? Once again, nothing. And yet, his realization is irreversible and will accompany him all his life, like the imprescriptible justification of the rights he claims.

If we do not wish to dispute the value of his experience, we will have to acknowledge that the inviolable inner dimension just revealed to the boy is a *vocation* to be fulfilled, and not an already acquired good. All the prefabricated elements he bears within, which are not from him, will have to undergo a radical transformation, so that the dignity of the person may be actualized in him. He is returned to himself, so to speak, in order to recreate himself, *by freeing himself from anything that might prevent him from being the origin of the self through which he asserts himself.*

This self-conquest, which we are all called upon to achieve, is what is most difficult. Many people neither know nor care about it. Most of the time, those who do are not aware of its goal and the way to attain it. Our fierce opposition to the encroachments of others on our freedom is in sharp contrast with the pathetically feeble desire to build ourselves. This is most probably because we rarely perceive the necessity to mould ourselves anew, in order to demand, in all honesty, the respect of others.

This blindness is almost natural. Indeed, if it is easy for us to defend our dignity in relation to others when we believe we have been offended, where shall this dignity lie when we are alone, face to face with ourselves? Where and who is this "I" who appeared so sure of himself in front of others? It escapes us as soon as we try to grasp it.

In *Macbeth*, which to me is Shakespeare's masterpiece, the playwright moves us deeply by communicating how difficult it is to reach this inner self of ours.

The main character of this tragedy is, as you know, Lady Macbeth, ambition personified. Her only goal is to attain the highest rank and enjoy the honors attached to it. In Scotland, where she lives, the highest honor is to wear the crown. Since witches have predicted that her husband will become king, she is consumed with the desire to hasten the fulfillment of this omen. There is only one obstacle: the reigning king. If he disappears, the throne will fall to Macbeth by right and she will be queen. Under her spell, Macbeth murders the king, his host, and lays the crime on the guards at the door of the royal chamber. The true murderers accede to the throne according to their plan. At the height of her glory, Lady Macbeth revels in the homages paid to her, relishing the kind of divinity that supreme power implies for her.

But in order to consolidate the benefits of his first crime, Macbeth is forced to commit a series of other crimes. These can no longer be concealed, and the usurpers are unmasked. The truth is revealed, and soon Lady Macbeth reads nothing but hatred and contempt in the eyes of the courtiers, who are waiting for the right moment to overthrow the murderous couple. She is the first to understand this: no one believes in her royalty any more. How could she believe in it herself, since it was from the eyes of others that she derived the image of her greatness. All her dreams collapse and she is left with nothing.

The external world she wanted to conquer and possess escapes her. And for her, the inner world does not exist and can offer her neither a refuge nor the chance to recreate herself. She has no access to her innermost self, buried as it is under a passion-driven ego, completely turned outward and with which she has totally identified. Disconnected from the two facets of being, she can no longer survive anywhere.

So she goes mad and thinks she sees on her hands the blood of the victims sacrificed to her ambition. Blood on her hands, not on her conscience, which could be the first step toward a liberating repentance. She wears herself out desperately trying to rub off the incriminating stain. "Out, out, damned spot!" But it persists and, no longer able to stand the sight of it, Lady Macbeth kills herself.

Can the distance from the outer self to the inner self be expressed any better than in Shakespeare's remarkable tragedy? Just when we assert our *inviolability* against interference from others in our innermost life, it rises up against us because of our very incapacity to dispose of it. More than by satisfying all the demands that actualize our dignity, truly making it a universal value where others can find their own good, as they enter its field of light, as others must respect it, we can only attain our dignity by respecting it. It is not a possession we can clearly identify as ours in order to keep others from having access to it, but rather a space of generosity, created by total self-divesting, a space that is open to anyone who perceives it, inside oneself, through the love that emanates from it.

Thus we are led, in the wake of the great Shakespearean tragedy, to acknowledge that, inasmuch as it is claimed as the intangible expression of our inviolable self, freedom actually entails a radical transformation of ourselves. It will be achieved by severing all the bonds of possession that constitute, within ourselves, its most formidable negation.

Therefore, although it seems essential for us to admit that ultimately, the basis for the widespread protest we know is in all likelihood a very keen and positive sense of the inviolability of the human person, we cannot help but see that, in general, it fails to recognize its requirements, the fulfillment of which alone can give it real existence and endow it with meaning.

Its most zealous promoters appear to believe that it is enough to sweep away the established institutions, to bring the house down, as they say, for an ideal order to emerge, in which individuals will fully enjoy all their rights. Too often, they forget that the privileges of dignity presuppose its arduous conquest, and that we can only claim them at the expense of radical self-divesting. Thus, by taking for granted what is achieved only at the end of a long purification process, they run the risk of being moved, unknowingly, by the passion-driven spontaneity of their unconscious, more than by a concern for their own interiority. Nevertheless, that is where the autonomy they claim as their due must be set.

The errors they may make, however, must not prevent us from seeing the problem they state and which concerns the whole man: what order is compatible with freedom or, better yet, what order can spring from the inner requirements that structure freedom and that must be fulfilled to make it a reality?

The Gospel gives a very enlightening answer to this question. We shall devote all our efforts to bring it out during this retreat. We hope to go beyond protest, thanks to the positive element that basically gives rise to it and makes it dynamic.

2

Temples of Stone Can Fall in Ruins

The deepest, most sensitive point where every human being connects with his humanity, along with what distinguishes him specifically from every other living being, is that sense of his own *inviolability* on which we focused yesterday. Is is indeed through this sense that each one concretely experiences his humanity: in revolt, if his inviolability is ignored, but fortunately also in friendship when it is fully acknowledged. No gift is more precious than respect for the inner dimension of man, no favor can compensate for its disregard. It is in those secret depths that begins the silent dialogue that gives life to the word, and makes a real presence flow through human relationships.

That is why it is hard to imagine any kind of spiritual action, and especially of religious teaching, that would not aim aim at being received from within, as the answer to a deep personal need that is awakened as it is satisfied.

The sense of incomparable authority that emanated from the Person of Jesus was undoubtedly based on the unique power he had to touch his listeners at the very root of their being, eliciting from them a new vision of themselves.

This stands out very clearly in the three gospel scenes which are the subject of our meditation this morning.

The first one is from the Gospel according to St. John; it is the story of Jesus meeting a Samaritan woman at Jacob's well. Even though we may know it by heart—the sequence of events is easy to remember—we rediscover it every time we read it, because it always manages to get us intimately involved in the ever timely dialogue between the Lord and this anonymous woman who received from Him a supreme revelation (Jn 4:5-30).

It is noon. Weary from his journey, Jesus is sitting by the well. He is alone and so is she. She possibly comes from the nearby town where the young Master's disciples have gone for supplies. With her jug on her head, she has absolutely no idea of what lies ahead, her only purpose being to draw water from the well. Jesus speaks to her: "Give me a drink." Her soul is what he is thirsting for, but how could she guess that? Her soul she knows not. What she sees is that he is a Jew. How can he speak to her after centuries of enmity between his people and hers? She does not refrain from pointing this out to him. His answer is enigmatic, in order to give her the thirst that he alone can quench: if she knew who he is, she would have asked him for a drink. But she bluntly tells him that he has nothing with which to draw the living water he prides himself on being able to give her. He then adds something to his offer: he promises her a water that will permanently quench the thirst of whoever drinks it, by becoming an inner spring of life eternal. Does she pretend not to understand a symbolism meant to make her go from without to within, from the material element to the spiritual reality it suggests? Is she being ironic, even a bit insolent, when she obstinately stays in a realm with no way out? Well, let him give her some of this miraculous water; it will spare her the trouble and fatigue of her perpetual trips back and forth between her home and the well!

However, she will not escape the unforeseen hit that will land her in the net of a love determined to save her by bringing her back to her inner being: "Go, call your husband, and come back." There she is, forced to come face to face with herself. She lives with a man who is not her husband, after five marriages buried in her past. She then attempts to use this ambiguous escape: "I have no husband." Jesus unmasks her cunning lie. So he knows everything she has done. She gives in: "I see that you are a prophet."

Henceforth, she is ready to discover within herself the spring to which he wanted to lead her. She will get to it by way of the old feud dividing the Jews and the Samaritans. Which is the rightful shrine, where must we worship, on the Garizim close by, which she can point to, or in Jerusalem? The answer shines forth in its dazzling originality: "Neither here nor there." In spite of the fact the Jews have the hitherto accepted privilege of an authentic mission, the time is coming indeed, and that time is almost here, when true worshippers will adore the Father in spirit and in truth.

For, understand this, woman, God does not limit himself to a place or a people. The sanctuary, where he truly dwells, must be built within you by opening your heart to this infinite source that He is in your innermost self. You have placed Him up on a mountain, like a distant being, outside yourself and with no personal relationship with you. And, since you were unable to love this person, a stranger to your being, you fell back on what seemed nearest to you, forcing your soul to settle for the dubious happiness to which you were clinging. You will no longer need to lie to yourself, since from now on, you will find within the only love worthy of you.

Indeed, it is to the Samaritan woman that this call to worship "in spirit and in truth" is first addressed. Her sin is revealed to her against a lofty background that exorcises its attraction. She discovers the depths of her soul in the light of the good which alone can fill them. She thinks of the promised Messiah as if she saw the signs of his coming in the new dawn breaking inside her.

In fact, all she has to do is wait. He has come, he is there: "I am he, the one who is speaking to you."

The return of the disciples puts an end to the conversation. But the essential things have been said and already ascertained in the transformation felt by this woman who, for the first time, is confronted with her own inner reality. She is so moved that she forgets her jug on the coping of the well as she runs back to the city to alert her fellow citizens: "Come and see a man who has told me everything I have ever done! Could it not be the Messiah?"

Many believe in him and ask him to stay with them, and many more, having received from him the word that awakens them to themselves, recognize him to be the savior of the world.

This account, centered only on the essential elements, unfolds in a kind of timelessness that endows it with inexhaustible freshness. It is astounding to think that a schismatic woman, involved in an unorthodox relationship, should have been the first to benefit from this incomparable initiation. She had come to fetch the water needed by her household, not in the least thinking of questioning herself. She leaves, having been revealed to herself, taking with her, deep in her heart, the spring of life eternal.

Temples of stone can now fall in ruins, they are no longer necessary. From now on, men are called to discover the sanctuary of the living God within themselves. But this will be at the expense of a radical transformation, of a new birth, which will allow them at last to reach their inner being. This absolute requirement draws an indelible dividing line between all forms of superstition or deceit and an authentic approach to Divinity. A religion of the Spirit, which had already begun to appear among the great prophets of the Old Testament, has been founded for good.

This infinitely delicate pedagogical approach, operating from within, is found again, in a very different key, in the story of the sinful woman from the Gospel according to St. Luke (7: 36-50).

Here the atmosphere is more important than the facts and the words that it generates.

We are somewhere in Galilee. A Pharisee, bearing the very common name of Simon and appearing only in this story, has invited Jesus for a meal. What are his reasons? It is difficult to say. Perhaps he has heard, or someone has told him, of the harsh judgment recently passed by the young Master on the Pharisees for their indifference towards John the Baptist (Lk 7:30). He likely plans to observe the Master and, if the opportunity arises, to induce him to open up an reveal his intentions in the casual remarks exchanged during a meal.

But the unexpected happens. It is not through chance conversation that Jesus will in fact reveal what his host could have hoped to make him say: it is through a life that bursts in on his own.

How did this prostitute, whom Luke does not name, get wind of his presence? How did she dare enter, uninvited, this austere home, ruled according to the law and tradition of the elders? Her appearance alone is an insult to the virtue professed here, even if she does wear proper clothes instead of the frivolous garb sported by those of her trade.

We shall discover the mainspring of this bold intrusion by reliving, as an essentially internal event, the scene that we witness through Luke's account.

Everything happens, indeed, as if Jesus and this woman were by themselves. She sees only her own wretchedness and the one who can save her. He sees only her distress and a burst of hope which throws her at his feet. The purity of the young prophet goes right through her like a bolt of lightning. In his presence, she no longer is this flesh given over to lust that now nauseates her. The look he casts on her gives her back her personal dignity. The world of possession disappears in his light, and she will now love by embracing with her whole being this light that restores the virginal essence of her being. The veneration that keeps her down on her knees, the tears she sheds on his feet as she kisses them, her long hair she lets down to dry them, the perfumes she uses to anoint them: it all unfolds in the transparent love that emanates from him. And Jesus accepts these expressions of reverence through that inner vision that sees the person as a whole, in the glow of her unity, reflected in all her gestures.

Both he and she actually live this encounter so totally from within that they are no longer aware of the people around them, and that these, in turn, experience the perfect interiority of the scene, to the point that they do not question its purity.

And so, it is not so much Jesus' morality that the host Simon is thinking of questioning, but his perceptiveness. Jesus' innocence shines forth for all to see in the radiance of his virginity, and there can be no doubt about it. But, Simon thinks, "if this man were a prophet, he would know who this woman touching him is, and what she is: a sinner."

Jesus, who can read his mind, then tells his host the parable of the two debtors. One owes five hundred denarii and the other fifty. Their creditor cancels their debts. Which of the two will love him more? Simon answers that, surely, it is the one who owed the most. Let him apply his answer to the case of this woman and he will understand her, for she is precisely in the same situation as the first debtor. Her effusiveness is commensurate with the huge debt remitted. She lavished expressions of homage on him—which Simon himself carefully avoided doing —to match the kindness she had received. "That is why her sins, which were many, have been forgiven, for she has shown great love."

These last words recreate the whole scene and raise it to its true level. What they mean is that it is Jesus' holiness that has moved this woman deeply, just as it is the firm

53

belief that only he could purify her that led her to him. And it is because, in his presence, she felt actually liberated from her sins and totally reborn that she expressed her gratitude in the moving gestures that Luke has faithfully recorded.

But we must go a little further. By declaring that her sins are forgiven, Jesus leads us to understand—as he has already done before—that he has the right to absolve her. This is also how his table companions understand his words, and they become indignant. "Who is this man who takes it upon himself to forgive sins?" The woman too must have understood the same thing, but for her, it is the assurance of having been forgiven. She has detected in the young prophet a superhuman quality that allows him to exercise divine power with the greatest ease. It is quite possible that, as soon as she decided to join him, she had a feeling that he was the Savior of the world, in a transcendent sense, and that the total love she vowed to him was the love that a creature can only give to God. In some way, she recognized God made flesh in him, as is possibly suggested in the last words of the episode: "Your faith has saved you, go in peace!"

This story has very deep roots indeed, the kind that bind man to God when man is nothing more than a loving gaze turned to God. The miraculous transparency, at the visible level, of Jesus' encounter with the sinful woman stems from that invisible light that radiates from him, and which she receives in the joy of her rebirth.

If this woman is not Mary Magdalene—her true name is perhaps "She-who-has-shown-great-love"—she is nonetheless one of the most admirable witnesses to

Christ's action. This divine action takes hold of human beings in the depths of their soul by setting them free of their own selves through the revelation of the infinite Good they bear within.

Although the episode of the adulteress, from the Gospel according to St. John (8:1-11), does not originally belong to this gospel, it extends admirably the teaching of the first two scenes that were the subject of our meditation.

This time, we are in Jerusalem within the precincts of the temple. Jesus has arrived at daybreak. He is soon surrounded by a large crowd; he sits down and begins to teach. A group of Scribes and Pharisees then bring to him a woman guilty of adultery. They make her stand before him and say: "Master, this woman was caught in the act of committing adultery. Now, the Law of Moses commands us to stone adulterous women. What do you say?" They are setting a trap to be able to accuse him.

The trap appears to be brilliantly set indeed because the question calls for a yes or no answer. A yes could bring about the hasty execution of the woman before him. A no would mean he is rebelling against the Law. But, in fact, a third option offers a way out, precisely because it is a trap and Jesus senses it right away. In this case, the Scribes and the Pharisees care neither about a woman's virtue, nor about the Law of Moses. Their sole preoccupation is to destroy Jesus by forcing him to choose between two alternatives that hardly represent a valid choice. And yet, here is this woman who must be saved. They are indifferent to her fate: she is but a pretext to them; he is clearly determined to protect her against their hypocritical zeal, to spare her the punishment they could inflict upon her. But he also wants to try to save them from the evil within themselves, from the false justice they boast about, from their blinding conceit.

First, he avoids confronting them. He remains silent; bending down, he begins to write on the ground.

Mauriac suggests, if I am not mistaken, that Jesus is thereby attempting to hide his face blushing with shame because of the cowardice of the accusers, who are using the adulteress to destroy him, and of the disgrace they are inflicting upon her by this ruthless display. Jesus was certainly capable of feeling this twofold compassion and, among all the other feelings he experienced at the time, we can assume that this was one of them.

Whatever the case may be, time passes, and his enemies, determined not to let him get away with it, insist on having an answer. It will be neither a yes nor a no, but a tremendous jolt to their complacent hypocrisy, forcing them to plumb the depths of their being. Jesus stands up and says to them: "Let he among you who is without sin cast the first stone." And, bending down again, he resumes his writing on the ground, this time perhaps to leave them alone to face themselves.

And behold, at the sound of their own conscience, they scatter, leaving one by one, starting with the elders. One cannot imagine a more complete and more silent victory, a more generous one also, or more brotherly, since those who have been defeated have been so by their own triumph over themselves.

Thus, they are saved, as Jesus wished, but so is the woman. Twice saved since she is spared the execution imposed by the Law, and freed from the sin that made her incur the penalty.

Indeed, it is impossible for her not to have been completely shaken, from the moment she was dragged through the crowd before Jesus, to the moment her executioners put an end to their game. Her life and shame weighed heavily on her every second that she waited for a possibly atrocious outcome. She remained hanging upon the young Master's silence, trying to find in it a glimmer of hope. She is struck right in the heart by his words, which refer her accusers to the court of their conscience and awaken her own. It was not before them that she was guilty, but before an authority within herself. And there she is, confronted with this incorruptible witness whose presence, in our innermost solitude, prevents us from deceiving ourselves. A great light shines in her. And is that not what good is, to be in harmony with the mysterious innocence that glows inside us, and to which Jesus has just given a voice?

What miracle could better convince her of this than to see her persecutors leaving silently? For they too have discovered this innner requirement, whereby the good turns out to be a personal relationship with someone who dwells within us, and not just observance of the Law in whose name they wanted to kill her. The woman cannot believe what she sees. They are truly gone. This new world, on the threshold of which she is standing in amazement, is thus very real, since they were unable to resist the powerful truth that rules it.

She finds herself alone with Jesus who questions her: "Woman, where are they? Has no one condemned you?" —"No one, Lord."—"Neither do I condemn you. Go, and from now on, do not sin again."

How could she not be radically purified by such an absolution, and protected forever from herself by this divine encounter? She goes her way, wondrously fulfilled, since she has discovered deep in her heart, as did the Samaritan woman, the Spring of life eternal.

And here we are, deeply moved ourselves, carried along by the current of interiority that flows through this incredible triptych: in it, we understand, from real-life situations, Jesus' incomparable capacity for identifying with those human beings apparently least concerned about their own spiritual life, a power so well expressed in the words of an outstanding exegete: "He is at home deep inside others."

3

"My Life Shall Wholly Live,
as Wholly Full of Thee"

That inner touch, that gaze penetrating our very being, so forcefully expressed in the three gospel stories, can be seen in two examples taken from Christian experience.

The first, relatively recent, is from Koriakoff's book *I have placed myself outside the law*.

Koriakoff was a Russian journalist, born and educated under the Soviet regime. He had absorbed its ideology without any resistance and was a convinced Marxist Leninist; as a result, he was an atheist in good faith, as could be expected within the system that provided him with all his *Weltanschauung*[1]. The mobilization of the population at the time of the German offensive in 1941 tore him away from his profession. Thanks to his bravery, he was promoted from private to the rank of captain. While on leave in Moscow, he met up again with an old librarian, a friend of the family and still a Christian, who gave him a New Testament. He immersed himself in this book that was

---

[1] *Weltanschauung* : vision of the world.

totally unknown to him, and was deeply moved. A true encounter took place between him and Christ who soon became the center of his life. His recall to the front prevented him from officially joining the Church. The only way he could affirm his new faith was by trying to behave in conformity with his unexpected and amazing discovery. He strove—inasmuch as his rank gave him the power to do so—to protect civilians, especially women, against the acts of violence to which they were exposed.

His army corps made a lightning advance, from Russia to Poland and from Poland to Germany, which it reached in the last month of the war. Although they knew it was a losing battle, the Germans fiercely fought on. In the area where Koriakoff's company was engaged, the outcome of the battle remained uncertain: one minute the Russians were winning, the next, it was the Germans. One morning, when the Russians had the upper hand, Koriakoff saved two young German women from attempted rape. In the course of the same day, the Germans regained the position occupied by the Russians and Koriakoff fell into their hands.

He was brought to the German camp and was received by an officer who struck his face so violently that his glasses fell off. The officer said to him: "You are one of those Soviet brutes who violate German women." A German colonel witnessed the scene, unmoved. In the midst of all this appeared a German farming woman. She pointed to Koriakoff as the Russian officer who had saved her two daughters that very morning. She had barely finished her statement when the colonel bent down, picked up Koriakoff's glasses and respectfully handed them back to him.

This infinitely small gestures reaches a level of utter greatness: it is like a surge of humanity in someone who, up until then, had been trapped within his prefabricated ego. Thirty seconds earlier, this colonel could certainly not have imagined himself capable of such deference, nor of experiencing such a need to make amends, he, a German, toward a Slav, sub-human in his eyes; he, a colonel, toward a captain; he, the conqueror, toward a defeated man.

If this soldier had suddenly been led to express such respect, it was because he had turned his attention away from himself. All the dividing walls in his consciousness had collapsed; he had been transformed in the depths of his being. He no longer saw Koriakoff as an enemy or a stranger, but as a man whose dignity, brutally insulted, had just been revealed to him through the woman's testimony. He immediately felt solidarity for this dignity, the basis for which, as he had discovered, was the same as his own. Moreover, this dignity was one with his, and lay in the same fundamental sense of his own worth that identified him with his prisoner. So much so that he could not reach this sense of worth within himself unless he could respect it in this man who depended on him. It is by virtue of the sudden awareness of this identification that his gesture of amends sprang out of total self-negation: from inner self to inner self, from the German colonel's innermost being to the Russian captain's. At that moment, there were only two souls merged together in the breath of the same *presence*, a presence that breaks down all barriers in the radiance of its light and love.

This incident deeply moves me precisely because of its apparent insignificance. In a flash, as I have already noted, we witness the birth of a human being an individual who is suddenly torn from his limitations, his prejudices and his pride, in a word, from all his inner constraints. He thus attains true freedom in this self-liberation when he meets, in another human being, the infinite presence on which man's inviolability is founded.

Nothing can teach us more simply, in an equally subtle experience, how the inviolability in Gottfried Keller's little boy[2] must be complemented in order to have any meaning. On this subject, we have asked ourselves how man, who defends his *dignity* against others with such passion, and who has often shown himself capable of facing death rather than contempt, how then he can affirm it when he is alone with himself. Indeed, what is the basis for his dignity, how can it be defined and maintained when there is no longer a need to defend it because there is no one to contest it? Without a doubt, most of the time we shun this solitude that would force us to answer these questions : before an audience of imaginary spectators, we pursue, to our own advantage, a debate we instinctively avoid pushing to the limit. But that only proves that we are incapable, on our own, of justifying to ourselves the respect for our honor that we demand from others. Our prefabricated ego leaves us totally powerless in this regard.

We must therefore rise above it in order to provide a solid basis for our most fundamental claim. That is the whole question. A question with no solution unless that

---

[2] See above, p. 38.

same unexpected event, as told by Koriakoff, occurs in the wake of the three gospel accounts already reflected upon: the encounter, within ourselves, with the presence that makes us go from a narcissistic monologue to the dialogue of love, through the transmutation of our possessive ego into a self-sacrificing one. It is through this event, and through it alone, that our innermost self becomes a universal good: it can be accepted by others without their feeling limited by it, and it will spontaneously command their respect without having to claim it. This is tantamount to saying that the birth of God in man is the condition for the birth of man to himself.

St. Augustine offers us the most magnificent confirmation of this in a text which, in its own right, is a masterpiece that one never grows weary of admiring. "Late I came to love you, O Beauty, so ancient and so new; I came to love you late. You were inside and I was outside, rushing about, frantically searching for you like some monster let loose in your beautiful world. You were with me, but I was not with you."[3]

We cannot express, only sense the full meaning of these sentences. They are all the more striking as they spring from a prayer that was not meant to instruct, all the more persuasive as the words they use belong to the most universal language. These words are doubtless chosen and arranged in such a way as to dramatize the contrasts which deepen Augustine's regrets for having failed so long to recognize what was nearest to him. But he was enough of

---

[3] St. Augustine, *Confessions*, X, xxvii.

a great artist and a great thinker not to have to strive for effect, which would have been incompatible with the emotion showing through these lines; it is this emotion that manifestly guided his pen in the same way that it grips us deep down.

As he writes, does Augustine remember the precise moment of his conversion some fifteen years before? It is certainly implied as he recalls the misery that preceded his conversion and that is now seen in the light of the radical change that followed. How, indeed, was he able to know that he had been *outside* for so long, if not because one day he entered *inside*.

Obviously, the whole passage we have seen hinges on these two words, *intus* (inside) and *foris* (outside). They shed light on each other by their strong opposition. We are either within or without, there is no middle way. This entails an essential discovery, for it is not a matter of entering a house, but inside *oneself*. How can one reach this *self*? And that is precisely the problem that tore Augustine apart until he was able to express it, that is, until he found the solution which allowed him to formulate it in clear terms.

When his long and laborious search suddenly comes to a fruitful conclusion, one thing becomes immediately evident to him: until now, I was *outside myself*. Until now means until my thirty-third year, with all my past as a student and professor, all my readings and all my meditations, all my aspirations to good and all my passion for a happiness founded in truth. And, we might add, with all his genius that makes him one of the greatest thinkers of all times, with all his powers of expression which raise him to the rank of the greatest writers.

It is true that he was enslaved by his sensuality which he did not manage to control and which was not in keeping with the lofty aspirations of his spirit. Also, these aspirations could hardly take root in the sensuous self that ruled him but whose dark accomplice he was. They were a luxury, like cut flowers that will inevitably rot in a vase that cannot provide them with a nourishing soil. Augustine was painfully aware of this contradiction that put him at odds with himself. But, no matter how hard he tried, he always came up against this barrier of darkness which stood in the way of his unity as a person.

His experience, lived on the level of his genius, is what gives so much weight to the word *foris* that rings out like a cry of liberation in the light of his conversion: *I was outside*, totally incapable of reaching my own self.

As far as I know, no one has ever perceived or expressed so keenly and with such force the *exteriority* of what we consider and defend as our most inviolable self while, in reality, *we are subjected to* a prefabricated ego. Its subterranean impulses often drive us to get stuck in irrational positions, which, without our knowing it, belie that inviolable space in which we claim to take refuge. *Foris: outside*, this little word sheds more light on what we are than the countless psychological analyses accumulated throughout history.

And that is because no one could have used this word with the meaning it has here without first living the experience that it presupposes, without undergoing the radical transformation that gives life a new center of gravity, without discovering that he can only find his true self in a *relationship* with another, who is really within himself. When the whole being is rooted in this relationship, a new vision is born that perceives all that came before as something outside oneself.

The *intus*, which is opposed to the outside and situates it, describes the "Beauty so ancient and so new" behind whose features Augustine met God. It might be interesting here to dwell on this aspect; it reveals the artist in the mystic who sings his love because, conceivably, he is fulfilled as much in his sensitivity as in his mind. But this would require us to develop the subject unnecessarily for the purposes of our talk.

We must focus all our attention on the *intus*, the essential attribute of divine Beauty. It is at the center of the Augustinian experience: the *interiority* of God. This discovery does not appear to be the fruit of a dialectic that would climb all the levels of being, from the visible to the invisible, as Plato does in *The Banquet*. It is rather the result of this obvious fact: Augustine's own *interiority* is the outcome of his encounter with the "Beauty so ancient and so new." In other words, God is the one who creates his *intus*, who awakens him to his "inside", who propels him into the heart of his innermost self, and through whom he is born to his self. He finds himself at last in the mysterious Host who reveals Himself as the One who *gives him to himself*, who liberates him from his self by transmuting his possessive ego into a self-sacrificing one: in short, the One who makes him go from the *given* that subjected him to the *giving* that fulfills him.

That is why he can only express himself in terms of wonder as he recalls what he has received. God has healed him of his deafness and blindness. He breathes Him in like a fragrance, he hungers and thirsts for Him, he longs for his peace, certain that by clinging to Him with all his might, he can cry out: "My life shall wholly live, as wholly full of Thee." Elsewhere he calls God "the Life of my life" and he declares him to be "deeper than my deepest being and higher than the loftiest part of me." We could go on forever quoting such effusions that link us directly to his heartbeat.

We must remember that this lyricism constantly flows from Augustine's underlying perception of the *ultimate identity of being and love*. First, in man, whose existence becomes transparent to himself only in the act of giving himself to this infinite Good, hidden inside him, which alone can lead him to himself.

This throws a revealing light on the problem of freedom. If we are not entirely subjected to our instinctual drives, as is apparently the case with animals, and if we do have a choice which really involves our responsibility by making us principle and source of our decisions, we immediately begin to see that we must, in some way, become the origin of our own selves in order to meet this condition of freedom. If, indeed, we yield the helm to our prefabricated ego, our decisions will emanate precisely from the unconscious drives that converge in it. In other words, the possibility we have of making choices implies the possibility of *choosing ourselves* by refusing *to be subjected to ourselves*. Ultimately, this freedom claimed so passionately and celebrated in such laudatory terms acquires a meaning only in *self-liberation*. Also, political freedoms can only be founded in the respect for the decision-making power of someone who is destined to be the source of his own self, by creating an unlimited inner space of light and love which will make him a universal good.

But how can one truly be one's own origin, how can one rise above what one is, but one has not chosen to be? And to become what? How can we create this inner space where others will find their good? The Augustinian experience provides the answer: all this was given to me when I met the infinite Presence within myself. It "emptied" me of myself, because it reached down to the very roots of my being, tapping all my capacity for love, a love that It alone could fulfill. Then I was nothing more than my own impetus toward It, toward this Presence in which I found my true center of gravity by shaking off the narcissism that held me down, pinned to my limitations, and immersing myself in its vastness. This is how I learned that being is fully realized in the transparency of love: when one is nothing but giving, one ceases to be subjected to oneself. But such a total gift can only spring from the encounter with the perfect Good. To It alone can the gift be offered, just as It alone is capable of receiving our gift *from within*, because It is Giving, and yet without wanting to possess it. That is why I, not being free *from* myself, was unable to be free *within* myself, until the day of my encounter with Him through whose Presence I was born to myself.

Provided this paraphrase mirrors faithfully Augustine's experience, we see that, basically, it is the same thing to say that he recognized God by attaining his own interiority—going from without to within—or by achieving full freedom through self-liberation.

Rather than being someone who dominates, limits, commands, threatens and punishes by imposing upon us from the outside, God appears, in this perspective, as someone who carries us along from within toward our true self. Here again, Augustine is our best authority. What indeed do these words mean: "You were with me, but I was not with you," if not that God was waiting for him deep inside himself—like "the silent music" of St. John of the Cross—without his noticing it or ever feeling compelled to acknowledge His presence, of which he became aware only by discovering his own interiority.

Nothing contrasts more with the arguments Marx uses to reject God. For Marx, God is the principle of a radical *heteronomy*, of a total dependence that alienates me from myself by preventing me from creating myself while I fashion the universe in man's image. The problem is precisely that Marx uses argumentation. He starts from a *concept* or an idea of God that contains everything that he abhors and, naturally, he can only reject this idol. Augustine, on the other hand, starts from an *experience*: he actually lives the marvellous change that rescues him from inner enslavement and creates the *autonomy* that truly makes him the origin of his own self. It occurred at depths that Marx could never have suspected, since he himself had not experienced this transformation of his whole being into love, the essence of our freedom.

That is why, in the transparency of the offered self that is born in him, Augustine cannot fail to perceive God both as partner in the nuptial relationship referred to by St. Paul ("I promised you in marriage to one Spouse to offer you as a chaste virgin to Christ" [2 Cor 11 :2]), and as a father whose only concern is to bring his son to take charge of his life, so that it will flow from within himself and not be borne like a yoke.

If Marx and Nietzsche (and Sartre in their wake) saw in God a denial and a violation of our humanity, it is because they did not really know man in his deepest being. Undoubtedly because they failed to question their being at its very source, they remained prisoners, to some degree, of an ego which did not originate from them and which therefore could not be the foundation of their inviolability. Their vast culture and prodigious talent could not teach them about an experience they did not have the chance to have.

The inexhaustible fecundity of the Augustinian *intus* and *foris* stems precisely from the fact that they are linked to an actual experience, that they are inconceivable without it, and that they have opened a door which can never be closed. They reveal, in a definitive way, our original exteriority and the impossibility of overcoming it without meeting within ourselves a Presence "deeper than our deepest being." Whatever we may call it—Augustine calls it Beauty—only this Presence can lead us to ourselves, as the essential partner in our liberation.

We hardly need to stress the pastoral implications of such a discovery. Who would refuse God, in the name of autonomy, if he came to see, in the silence of his own self, that such a refusal is in reality a refusal to be one's own origin? This refusal deprives our inviolability, our dignity and our freedom of any kind of foundation and meaning. But, of course, since no words can take the place of experience, the only valid testimony would be that of our own liberation.

We have become convinced of it by noticing the emotional and educational impact that Koriakoff's story and Augustine's "confession" both had on us, precisely because they reach *inside* us, where man is born within himself. This they do by revealing to us, in the light of the *intus*, the God who has no *outside*, who waits for us without ever coercing us, and whose encounter makes Augustine cry out in wonder those ever-amazing words: "My life shall wholly live, as wholly full of Thee."

4

Levels of Knowledge

Two testimonies from scientists, who do not profess to be Christians, seem to express a spiritual experience similar to that of St. Augustine on which we have just reflected, indeed similar enough for us to draw a comparison.

The first one is from Einstein. I quote: "The most beautiful and most profound emotion we can experience is the mystical feeling. It is the seed of all true science. The person to whom this feeling is unknown, who can no longer marvel at things and stand in awe before them, is as good as dead. To know that what is unfathomable to us really exists, that it is revealed in the highest wisdom and the most radiant beauty which our dull faculties can comprehend only in their most primitive forms—this knowledge, this feeling is at the center of true religion [...] The cosmic religious experience is the strongest and noblest mainspring of scientific research [...] My religion consists in a humble admiration for the superior, boundless spirit that is revealed in the slightest details that we can perceive with our frail and feeble minds. This deeply emotional conviction of the presence of a superior and powerful reason which is revealed in the incomprehensible universe, that is my idea of God."[1]

The second testimony is from Jean Rostand: "What would carry scientists and sustain them if not the strange *passion to know*? 'In spite of their shortcomings and vices,' Charles Richet used to say, 'all scientists have the same soul; they all make a cult of truth for its own sake; they are all prompted by a common thought: love of the truth hidden in things.' The cult of truth for its own sake... Indeed, these truth lovers do not think of the consequences, the possible applications of what they might discover or, if they do, it is simply because they are evidence of their involvement with reality. What they aspire to, what alone in their eyes can *justify the act of living*... is simply to reach *what is*. Their love of truth for itself is pressing, irrational, irrepressible, uncompromising. They love it—as one always loves—because they are who they are, and because it is what it is. They love it to the point of considering it an honor, and almost a delight, to proclaim the truth when it displeases them. And that is why they do not accept, nor do they suffer that, for any reason, for any cause or for any ideal, however lofty it may appear, the truth be distorted, or even that anything be simply added to it. They serve the truth with a passion unimpeded by scruples, convinced that the zeal they have for it can never be excessive, and happy to put at its service the passion, enthusiasm and fervor which, every-

---

[1] Quoted from Lincoln Barnett, *The Universe and Dr. Einstein*, with a foreword by Albert Einstein. American Reprint Co., Mattituck, New York, 1950, pp. 117-118.

where else, are its enemies. They know that truth is difficult, that it is fragile, that, like Chestov's God, we risk losing it as soon as we think we have grasped it. They know that man cannot approach it without mastering himself, that it is not what gives contentment or comfort, that it is never found where there is shouting, as Vinci used to say, and almost never where there is speaking... *Love of What is, and simply because It is*! Love and not plain curiosity... For they think that *what is* surpasses all human language, and that there is more sense, more grandeur and poetry in that little word than in the noblest of epithets."[2]

In this hymn to "truth for itself", so passionate and so fervent, we can sense that, for his part, Jean Rostand carefully avoids naming God. Later, we shall have the opportunity of asking ourselves why.

In spite of this small reservation, it is no less obvious that these two testimonies concur on this: they express an actual experience, a real-life event in which each of the two authors is totally involved: involved in a *personal relationship* with the object of his research. This relationship, both the origin and the end of the research, inspires in them an attitude of respect, humility, admiration and love. No scientific observations, no proof, no line of argument support these statements, which nevertheless commit their whole vocation as scientists. For them, the proof lies in a universe in action in the depths of their being, a supposedly external universe they nevertheless

---

2 Jean Rostand, *Peut-on modifier l'homme?*, pp. 145-147.

perceive as the bearer of a truth that surpasses them as it fulfills them. They too, in their own way, move from the outside to the inside, attracted by a Reality which increasingly becomes their supreme reason for living.

But we could doubtless say as much, to different degrees, about all the philosophers, scientists and artists of all times. Their works remain very much alive insofar as they continue to make us aware of the presence that "amazes us and strikes us with awe", through the countless expressions of art and science that make this world a better place for the spirit.

It is thus a kind of religion, both permanent and universal, that inspires all the masterpieces of the spirit. We acknowledge them as such precisely because they are "the voices of Silence" that bring us back to our own interiority.

Hence, we should never fail to appreciate all that the arts and sciences imply in the way of spirituality among those who devote themselves to them, as well as those who are able to understand them. For Einstein and Rostand, that is what religion is apparently all about. Many of our contemporaries are content with experiencing, before the cosmos, that "mystical" feeling of which the great physicist speaks and which, by the way, may well be a natural prelude to faith.

The Church obviously cannot object to the "joy of knowing" that Pierre Termier has celebrated so magnificently, since it has always professed to love intelligence and to want to pray "over beauty." Nor can it be suspicious of the contemplative mood created by the liturgical chanting born of its tradition, and the polyphony of the greatest

Christian artists. What Brémond calls "religious feeling" implies this silent sense of wonder, the object of which is experienced through the purified fervor of the subject. And so we see the greatest mystics spontaneously resorting to poetry, that is to the music of language, to infuse words with the vital impulse of the Love (*Agape*) that moves them.

By a strange paradox, some scientists and artists, who would shrink from affirming a personal God, seem at times to have a more profoundly personal relationship with the reality that fascinates them than certain theologians with the God whose attributes they abstractly present. This is a particularly sensitive point since it bears upon the presentation of divine revelation. Revelation cannot fail to take hold of somebody's life and have an impact on it at least as great as that of the mystical intuitions that nourished the fervor of people such as Einstein or Rostand. Now, a certain professorial way of holding forth on the mysteries of the faith may make them appear as a system with no roots in real existence, to which specialists devote their efforts as to an interesting dialectic; they may even defend it fiercely on occasion, and not without possessiveness. This sometimes creates the impression that they are speaking of God as an object that can be known by using the appropriate technique, without necessarily commiting in a personal way to Him.

Undoubtedly, the academic aspect of this kind of initiation to theology does not in itself preclude, in its proponents, the existence of a truly authentic inner life, but it is likely to place the most serious debates on the level of scholastic discussions.

On this subject, I recall taking a course on the physical premotion (or predetermination) of a free act, which was meant to shed some light on the mystery of predestination. Naturally, the principle that God is the absolute First Cause was constantly reaffirmed, followed by all the "therefores" that one could possibly draw from it: therefore, He knows everything by himself and in himself; therefore, He loves himself and everything for himself; therefore, He possesses everything by himself and in himself, and can receive nothing from anyone; therefore, He is perfectly happy by himself and in himself, and nothing can alter his happiness; therefore, He knows his chosen ones, not by learning from them the way to salvation they have elected, but by deciding to give to some an intrinsically and infallibly efficacious grace which inevitably leads them to choose salvation; therefore, He knows those who are not chosen and who will be damned by the very fact that they do not benefit from such a decision; in view of their salvation, they will receive only sufficient —and not intrinsically and infallibly efficacious—graces which will not save them; God's happiness will in no way be affected by this: the damned will glorify his justice as the chosen will glorify his mercy.

These consequences were so closely linked together that a great debate followed this question, humbly asked by a colleague: could not an imperfect act of contrition be made under the impulse of a sufficient grace (as opposed to an intrinsically and infallibly efficacious one)? The ensuing polemic shook the entire order to the point of forcing the unfortunate questioner to resign and be exiled. Our professor maintained with utmost sincerity that he was endangering the fundamental principles of the faith.

By adding one more "therefore", we could undoubtedly have concluded from this series of deductions that each individual's salvation is ultimately his own personal concern since, in any case, the glory of God will be revealed as much by his eternal unhappiness as by his eternal bliss.

But are we really on Gospel ground? Does this kind of reasoning, inexorably unfolding, open us to the mystery of Redemption? Does it prepare us to live the agony and the crucifixion of Jesus? Does it lead us to commit ourselves totally to this mystery of Love, the fullness of which is so movingly symbolized by the Sacred Heart? Can God be reduced to a principle that belongs to objective logic, something that we would not even apply to a human being? To a theorem from which all the implied corollaries could be definitely deduced provided the premise was known?

This is a good time to review basic epistemology by briefly examining the ways in which we know reality and the various levels to which they are suited.

First, we are inundated with external and internal *sensory knowledge*: we have a concrete perception of our external and internal environment with an affective and subjective coloring of countless shades. It varies according to our organic state, our sensuous appetites, our individual or collective prejudices and the impulses from our unconscious that feed them—where our childhood history plays a considerable role—according to our sex and age, the climate and the rhythm of the seasons, the behavior of others, far and near, and our relationships with them at all possible levels; according to our sympathies and antipathies, the information we have and the power of our imagination which determines its impact on us; our successes and failures in a variety of contexts. All of these elements create a tremendous potential for passions, the center of gravity of which is a prefabricated ego. The ego seeks to assert itself through this network of energies and interdependent physical and psychic elements, a network that defines the ego's universe as it adapts, whether it wants to or not, to the universe of others, which is always more or less part of its own. There is always a risk that conflicts and rivalries may arise, and some day explode in crime or war.

Through *scientific knowledge*, we reach another level. It aims at pure objectivity by examining every phenomenon according to a well-defined experimental method. The rigorous application of this method will lead all competent researchers to the same results. This *systematic* unification of all research is relatively recent, Galileo (1564 -1642) being acknowledged as one of its principal initiators. The creation of a single and universally accepted language makes this unification an event of enormous significance. Thanks to this universal language, it has become possible to express every discovery in a formula that has the same meaning everywhere, and to subject it to the test of the same calculations and the same instruments. This allows scientists the world over to use it as the starting point toward new discoveries. The result has been an inexhaustibly fruitful international collaboration, and the trip to the moon was a spectacular example of how marvellously efficient it is.

In spite of this prodigious success, we must not forget the *limits* intentionally implied in scientific language, precisely in view of guaranteeing its universal character. If the Russians and the Americans, the Chinese and the Spanish, the Indians and the Italians, the Egyptians and the French, if scientists of every nation are able to speak and understand this language, it is on condition that they leave all their personal options at the door of the laboratory. The individual doing research must abide by only one goal: making the phenomena he is studying intelligible by going back, as far as possible, to the point of origin from which their development can be explained in terms of a necessary chain of events. But he never goes outside the realm of experimentally—that is materially—verifiable data.

In their personal lives, scientists will naturally have to make choices and take positions which will differ greatly from one person to the other, and even within the same individual. But they will remain faithful to the scientific method only by never allowing their personal options to interfere with their research. In this area, they do not have to defend their nation or their race, their social class or their political party, their philosophy or their moral code, their religion or rejection thereof. The intrusion of any personal commitment—outside the one they have made to absolute objectivity in a field experimentally verifiable by all—would compromise the universality of the language which is the *sine qua non* condition of that very objectivity. Ultimately, this means that science, insofar as it remains truly objective, can offer no answers to any specifically human problem. The positions that scientists inevitably take on questions of vital importance to our behavior are a matter of personal commitment, and they cannot cover themselves by referring to their authority as scientists, an authority they do not have in such questions.

Therefore, they must submit themselves to a rigorous ascesis. First, they must be as objective and impersonal in their observations as a computer. Then, they must become aware of the limits deliberately set on experimental science so as not to turn it into a philosophy. Finally, they must acknowledge that objects, defined by the method as materially and necessarily verifiable, in no way exhaust reality and cannot offer a complete explanation for it.

That being said, we can only marvel, our hearts filled with gratitude, at everything that science teaches us, as it constantly broadens our view of the universe; at the many ways in which it makes our lives more bearable by putting new energies at our disposal; above all, at the universal language it alone succeeded in creating, a language with precise limits, and yet one that brings about a fruitful dialogue among all those who understand it.

Unfortunately, in its search for the first principles of being, knowledge and action, philosophy has not managed to create such a universally accepted language. It comes close to science, as we have just defined it, when it restricts itself to reflecting, in scientific terms, on the meaning and methods of scientific investigation. When it tackles its own specific subject matter, for which, by the way, definitions vary according to philosophers, philosophy moves away from science by the very fact that it cannot be subjected to the testing procedures which define scientific objectivity. The result is a philosophical pluralism that conceivably comes from the primary, possibly complementary, intuitions through which each philosopher first perceives reality. Thus, it is not easy to define objectivity in the vast number of *Weltanschauungen* offered as philosophies, all the less so as the problems raised and the solutions put forward, like the question of our beginnings and our end, have a greater impact on the direction of our lives. It would seem that, in this area, individual experience and personal choices influence the support one gives to one view rather than another.

Finally, I think we can agree on *interpersonal knowledge* as the supreme level of knowledge in the natural order. It is rarely the subject of specific studies and is not generally considered as knowledge that would interest epistemology. It certainly cannot be classified among what is generally referred to as the social sciences, which can claim the title of sciences only by studying human phenomena as facts subjected to some form of determinism and, therefore, by respecting the limits inherent to the scientific method. Interpersonal knowledge, on the contrary, is transobjective, that is, it concerns what cannot be an object in a human being, what motivates his refusal to be treated as an object, in other words, the essence of what he is.

But, as we have seen, this essential element, so clearly voiced in this refusal, is very difficult to define. As a rule, it is so intermingled with subjective passions that it appears only at rare intervals and may sometimes seem to be non-existent. However, the fact that no one accepts to be treated as an object means that human beings want to be acknowledged in that essential element—even though they are often unaware of its existence—acknowledged in their own dignity, which they themselves frequently do not respect.

This has already been abundantly emphasized: through their specific worth and the inviolability of their conscience, human beings rise above mere existence. They are destined to fashion their own selves—instead of being subjected to them—and this transformation entails all the possible stages from zero to infinity.

Interpersonal knowledge aims at the reality of what we are in this life, a reality always in the process of becoming; this becoming, by our supreme vocation, our very movement and direction, is leading us toward the totally fulfilled personality in which is founded the respect we claim for our humanity, that humanity we sense obscurely deep inside ourselves. Such an aim naturally presupposes a very keen awareness of what is most profound in a human being, a perception always alerted to that "inside" where, from "something", we become "someone." But it also requires that we *commit ourselves*. For if we hope to perceive correctly and on a long-term basis this inner reality, in others as well as in ourselves, our egos must step aside before the undiscovered worth that it hides, while we turn ourselves into unlimited space to welcome it.

We can see that interpersonal knowledge is thus a knowledge that *radiates love*, and reaches its object all the more deeply as this love is more generous. It discovers it, not by observing it, but *by assuming it*, by living it, with the sole concern of awakening or confirming, in others as in itself, the interiority that constitutes it. Obviously, it is not sure of succeeding when another is involved, since it can only meet him provided its gift is accepted, that is, meet him through the offering he himself becomes through self-liberation. *Reciprocity* may be non-existent at first, then come to life and grow, and finally reach the same level of love. It is perfect when the innermost being of one shows through the innermost being of the other, in the mutual exchange of an infinite Presence that excludes possession.

Clearly, in order to discover the true face of man, one must be prepared to pay the price.

This became vividly clear when a divorced woman admitted to me that now she could meet her ex-husband with total calm and indifference. And yet, she had loved him at the time of their marriage, and he had meant a lot to her. His infidelity gradually eroded her attachment to him. Consequently, she saw him in a new light. One day, she stopped seeing him: he was nothing but a face in the crowd, someone she could meet on the street without feeling the slightest emotion.

From this example, we can easily grasp that knowledge and love are indissolubly linked in this approach to the person which is the true goal of ultimate knowledge. On this level, we know as much as we love, and we no longer know when we no longer love. No doubt, this is because the object to be known here is love itself, and love is the very essence of any authentic personality and the source of its radiating influence. Since love constitutes personality, love alone can reach it without injuring its inviolability, because love alone can let us into the depths of another being by making us a part of him.

In the realm of *interpersonal knowledge*, *truth* is the result of a mutual internalization, whereby the light of one person's inner being shines through the transparency of another's, as they are united with the infinite *Presence* that gives each its worth. This is how, at least, truth is experienced in specifically human relationships, more or less vividly, to be sure, depending on the degree of commitment out of which they are born.

Although this truth essentially concerns all human beings, since no real human relationship may be established outside of it, generally speaking, it is experienced in a very obscure way. It is not attested by a sufficiently clear and profound awareness to bring about radical modifications in our behavior. That is why it is so often contaminated by our subjective passions which seek to justify their options as so many claims to or expressions of human values, even if they lead to enslaving or destroying humankind.

However, these discrepancies or abuses do not eliminate the fact that whatever true humanity remains in us is founded on the perception and respect of the inner self which constitute interpersonal knowledge.

Life's most illuminating dialogues (between a mother and her child, between a real teacher and his pupils, between a great artist and his admirers, between very close spouses, between faithful friends) are all effective because of the light that, rising from their depths, shines from one being to the other, and reveals to them the Presence in whom they are united.

This type of communication is not linked to a specific language, as are scientific or philosophical discourses.

But when it does resort to language or when it goes through it, it transforms it quite radically. Words and concepts are internalized: as is always the case in real poetry, they become *someone* when they are energized by the current flowing from soul to soul. Through the kind of confidential, intimate communication that words then transmit, we are freed from their limitations.

We may well ask ourselves whether this interpersonal knowledge, which we called transobjective, remains objective, that is, capable of attaining truth. Let us first note that it forms the basis for all authentically human relationships: between spouses, parents and children, friends, associates, etc. Its premise is respect for human dignity in every individual involved in a relationship arising from cohabitation, education, team work, dealings between races and nations. Nothing is less subjective, if by subjectivity we mean the blindness caused by our passions, which reduces reality to merely what coincides with individual or collective egocentricity, setting itself up as the criterion for all things. Interpersonal knowledge aims at man's human dimension and contributes to its harmonious development by acknowledging the values that it implies. In some way, it "creates" the truth as it discovers it.

It seems to me that these considerations should be kept in mind when we deal with the problem of Revelation. Should Revelation be interpreted within the framework of scientific knowledge, or that of interpersonal knowledge as we have defined it? In short, does Revelation propose to make us know something or Someone?

The question remains unanswered when we say that Revelation is the Word of God. Indeed, is Revelation one-way information, absolute in nature, always imposed in definitive terms, or is it a *dialogue* in which the First Love seeks our love by adapting to us, as must be done in any effective dialogue? Jesus himself directs us toward the second hypothesis when he explains why he speaks in parables to crowds who cannot understand him any better (Lk 8:9-10 and par.), or when he tells his own Apostles on the eve of his Passion: "I still have many things to say to you, but you cannot bear them now" (Jn 16:12-13).

We can thus say that it is a dialogue open to every form of development, in keeping with the growing receptivity of humankind with whom it is started.

The Word of God is spoken at different levels depending on the times and the prophets who pass it on. It is frequently limited, but its limitations cannot be attributed to God, but rather to human beings for whom it is intended. It is often the same for the Word of God as for the words a mother speaks to her little one. With him, she does not use Plato's or Einstein's language, which he would not understand. She babbles with him, following his pace as he explores the world of language. Similarly, God spoke in a babble, as it were, to reach primitive man in his spiritual infancy, and thus lead him, little by little, toward a less imperfect understanding of his divine vocation.

In this perspective, we can say with Fr. Durand that one of the most moving aspects of divine teaching is that it adapted to an anthropomorphic vision of God, one that sometimes gave Him a face quite different from the one that was to shine through the life of the Word Incarnate.

And so, while we should indeed admire the merciful adaptation of the Word of God to the stages of humanity on the move, it is of the utmost importance that we not go back to outdated words or images, as if they were still valid expressions of our relationship with God, when in reality Christ has cast an entirely new light on it. This is what St. Paul urges us not to do by opposing Law and Grace.

As we have seen, St. Augustine's recollection of his encounter with eternal Beauty, from which we have derived such a great lesson, is particularly remarkable in this way: it starts from an actual experience, it entails no limits and is expressed in the language of love, which, by its very nature, is interpersonal. It is an example to be followed.

Man, to whom the Gospel is proposed, must feel that he is most intimately concerned; in it, he must discover the ultimate meaning of his freedom in a boundless inner space, and, finally, meet Someone who can capture and fulfill his potential for admiration and love.

This is not about providing abstract proof of an invisible reality, the need for which is not felt, but about awakening in each one all that is specifically human, until one recognizes in that the call which finds no adequate answer outside of Christ.

"God is spirit and those who adore him must do so in spirit and in truth." Thus Revelation (*acceptio cognitorum*) is a communication from Spirit to spirit bearing fruit through faith, hope and charity in the light of the Holy Spirit. This does not prevent Revelation, conveyed through inspiration *(judicium de acceptis)* in Holy Scripture, from being objective and infallibly true in what it formally teaches through all the literary genres that express it. But that is compatible with a progressive development of the History of Salvation and a more or less profound understanding of its meaning and purpose: these depend on the spiritual quality of the people who transmit or receive the sacred trust.

5

The Eyes of the Heart :
to Be Born Again in Order to Know

Sophists, who taught in the days of Plato and Aristotle, prided themselves in being able to demonstrate anything thanks to a verbal virtuosity that allowed them to nimbly switch sides on any debate. This misuse of discourse, abundantly pursued since then, clearly shows that reason can easily be swayed in any direction if it is not rooted in a being freed of his own self. A stand based on passion will always find arguments to justify itself from premises it will bend to suit its point of view. This means that there is no pure reason, outside of reason purified by radical self-divesting in the subject whose reason it is. Hence the ambiguity of what we call rationalism, which reduces reality to what science, in any given period, can grasp of it, forgetting the intentional limits that condition it.

A yet more serious confusion results when an inadequately purified reason attempts to interpret the revealed message. It will then unavoidably tend to study from the outside the most intimate message that can be given to us, either to determine what it cannot accept, or to impose its understanding of it as the only orthodox one.

Jesus, more than anyone else, came up against the barrier of this horizontal logic as he met with the fiercest resistance precisely among certain men of learning. These were locked in their own system, outside of which, in their eyes, there could only be error and blasphemy. He was often confronted with such oppositon which, on occasion, he condemned very sternly, but never did he bring to light the root of the problem as clearly as in his discussion with Nicodemus. Undoubtedly, as we shall see, this was because the person he was speaking to was sufficiently well —disposed toward him to benefit from the lesson.

To this "Master in Israel", who comes to him during the night and respectfully congratulates him for the "signs" he is fulfilling, Jesus gives this abrupt answer: "No one can see the kingdom of God without being born again" (Jn 3:3). *To be born again in order to know*: how could the interpersonal nature of our relationship with God be better expressed? And yet, that is precisely what is dangerously lacking in those religious people who spend their lives scrutinizing the Scriptures and collecting the sayings of the Fathers, commenting them, possibly adding their own interpretations. They do not have a relationship with God that liberates and transforms them enough to allow them to go beyond the letter. They do not perceive the sacred texts' own secret movement towards a completion that transcends them. Thus, in the name of blind faithfulness, they will absolutely refuse change and keep stubbornly to a rigid view of God that will irremediably relegate Him to the level of human beings with all their limitations.

On this subject, Fr. Lagrange reminded us, in his little book *La Méthode historique*, that certain Christian exegetes did not sufficiently discern, in the Old Testament, the invitation to supplement it implied by the fact that it was unfinished. They too wanted to find in it the whole, final Revelation.

"By dint of exaggerating the doctrinal importance of the Old Testament as it relates to us, the perfection of the Jewish faith and the scope of its views on the Trinity and the Incarnation, we come across, without even realizing it, the very stumbling block—natural evolution—that we try to avoid. Of course, it is quite unintentional. We strongly and unduly stress the intensity of divine action and we erase any dividing line between Judaism and Christianity. Through Jesus' revelation, humanity enters a truly new phase of its religious life. Judaism [...] rejects such a close to its history because it does not seem to be a natural outcome: God intervenes and new things happen. What surprised Christians and appeared divine to them was precisely the fact that the prophecies had been fulfilled in Jesus in a totally different way from what could have been foreseen. What really matters [...] is that Jesus himself bears witness to a doctrine that was to save the world. For, if Jesus had been nothing but a synthesis of the ideas of his time, the Jews would have obediently followed him; just for that, there was no need for a prophet. Jesus is not the last link in a chain: he is the flower suddenly bursting from the plant that was hiding it; when it blooms, the tree dies."

This quotation aptly brings out the novelty of the New Testament as suggested by its very title. We can certainly understand why Jeremiah would pray for the annihilation of his enemies (Jer 17:19-23). Nothing could be more natural in his situation, but it is the spirit of God that we spontaneously recognize in Jesus' prayer for his executioners.

We see once more that the divine dialogue, specifically designed to be in tune with the receptivity of the human subject, will take place at different levels. These differences were clearly shown by Pope St. Gregory in his homily on the disciples of Emmaus: "The Lord appeared to two disciples who were walking along the road, speaking about him, although, in fact, they did not believe in him. But he did not show them a face they could recognize; the Lord was thus revealing, on the outside, to the eyes of their body, what they were seeing inside, in the eyes of the heart. Deep inside, they loved and they doubted, and so the Lord was present to them on the outside, but he was not showing them who he was. While they were speaking about him, he revealed his presence to them, but since they doubted him, he hid the sight of his face from them."

Is there a better and more succinct way of saying that God reveals himself only insofar as He can be grasped to the recipient's advantage when He intervenes, even if it means that he will have to reveal himself more fully when the eyes of the heart will be able to receive a greater light? Besides, this is what St. Gregory states a few lines further, when he attributes the fact that the disciples recognize Jesus in the breaking of the bread to their charity toward a "stranger", forced by their pressing invitation to accept their hospitality: "As they listened to his teachings, they were not enlightened; it is by carrying them out that they saw the light."

The lesson is always the same: interpersonal knowledge can only grow essentially at the expense of a transformation of the knowing subject: we know inasmuch as we love.

This observation, which is true in the case of one's actual encounter with the Word of God, cannot be adequately applied to the objective development or doctrinal progress of Revelation. The prophet is not necessarily a saint, even if his message is ultimately directed to holiness. The charisma with which he is endowed makes him an entirely valid instrument of communication for others —individuals or the community—and this, even if he is unable to fully understand and live the message he delivers, even if this message causes him to become hardened, as with Caiaphas in the *Gospel according to St. John* (11:49-52). Conversely, the content of the message can be inferior to the personal quality of the prophet, like a concession designed to avoid greater evils, as is divorce according to *Deuteronomy* 24:1 (cf. Mk 10:1-12).

God is Spirit and He speaks to our spirit. But our spirit is slow to awaken, all the more so as it is part of a community whose temporal destiny and prophetic mission fall under one law, a religious law, as in the case of the people in the Bible. The divine message, which must deal with every eventuality, adapts to reality in whatever way is necessary to have a hold on it. Intermingled with contingencies, it is not always sublime.

In his treatise *De divina inspiratione et veritate Sacrae Scripturae*,[1] Fr. Vosté wonders: what doctrinal heights do the Chronicles, Esther, Judith, the Song of

---

[1] Second edition, pp. 20-21

Songs,[2] or Ecclesiastes reach? What are the persuasive virtues of the major part of the Pentateuch, of the books of Joshua, of Judges, of Kings? He does not hesitate in maintaining that St. Thomas' *Summa theologica* reaches greater heights than any other book of the Old Testament. These thoughts from an exacting exegete confirm our idea of an infinitely patient teaching, whereby the divine Master comes down to man's level and leads him, step by step, higher and higher, towards an increasingly perfect knowledge of Himself and His plans, a knowledge that will attain full completion only in and through the Word Incarnate.

So we do not insult the "Word of God", which finds its highest expression in the Word Incarnate, when we distinguish its different levels—by recognizing that its limitations are due to man himself—nor when we go from the less perfect levels to the more perfect ones. That is precisely what Jesus was asking of the Learned men of his time when he suggested to Nicodemus that he be born again in order to know.

But I do not wish to dwell on this any longer, for I am eager to move on to the mystery of the Holy Trinity, Revelation's summit, and, in the words of the Gospel, "the pearl of the Kingdom."

It is faith in this mystery that essentially characterizes Christianity and makes it the most profound and enlightening answer to our questions and the aspirations of our hearts.

---

[2] *Sic*: amazing!

As we have already acknowledged, we are all originally tainted by our possessive ego with which we have identified since childhood. Even before we could think, we used the words *I* and *me* for this cluster of determinisms made up of our heredity, our temperament, our environment, our language and childhood history. And we have kept on doing it without questioning ourselves, without noticing that we were labelling a prefabricated entity with this deceptively personal tag: "I-me". Our blindness has induced us to amalgamate with this ego, to which we *are subjected,* values that can only be acquired by *overcoming* it. In the name of our ego, we have demanded inviolability, dignity and freedom, which vest it with a character of *false absolute*; the idolatry that Hitler and Stalin fostered for a certain image of themselves is a terrifying example of this phenomenon. Without going that far, we can all detect in ourselves a form of narcissism that makes us gravitate endlessly around ourselves.

But can this be otherwise if, as Hesnard maintains, our basic instinct is the need to enhance ourselves in our own eyes and in the eyes of others? On a deeper level, is it not because we sense the presence of a real absolute within ourselves that we fix our interest on this unique entity—non-interchangeable—that we are to ourselves? That is undoubtedly the heart of the problem. Because we do not know on what to base this absolute and where to find it, we confuse its voice with the pressing call of our untamed passions. As a result, these passions are erroneously sanctioned, and our possessive ego cannot help but become intoxicated with its own greatness.

But it is an illusory attempt since this greatness implies a comparison with others, who must perforce be at the bottom of the *pyramid* while we place ourselves at the top, at least in the hierarchy inside which we measure ourselves. For people to go along with this and play the game, they will have to be won over, bribed or compelled to accept, and we can never be sure that a rival will not rise to challenge our primacy. Unless, of course, we merely imagine our superiority and savor it in our private dreams. Still, in order to believe in it, we will need a small circle of admirers to reflect it. In any case, this pyramid is built from the outside, and the image of ourselves that we seek in it can only ruin any plan of achieving inner greatness.

Does this mean that we have to give up any thought of greatness and reduce life's activities to the bare necessities of survival? That is out of the question: it would be tantamount to renouncing our humanity, because it would mean that we show no regard for that sense of our own inviolability which is strong evidence of the absolute Worth hidden within ourselves, even though, as a rule, we are unable to find it and grasp it.

It is precisely to our quest for greatness, irrepressible and yet hopeless, that the *Trinitarian revelation* offers a totally unpredictable solution.

It is summed up most simply and profoundly by St. John's little sentence in his first Epistle: "God is Love" (1 Jn 4:16). He is Love, not only with respect to us and the whole of creation, but in Himself, in his own Being, essentially, infinitely, eternally. And since love can only be love in relation to another that constitutes it ("*Dilectio in alterum tendit ut caritas esse possit*": in order to be charity, love [must] reach out to another, writes Pope St.

Gregory), to say that God *is* Love is to say that his innermost Being implies, or rather consists in this movement toward the other without which there is no love. In other words, God *finds the other in himself*, he possesses, *in himself*, all that is needed for the fullness of love that He is.

We can see that the revelation of God's Trinity is in no way a metaphysical puzzle, an insurmountable test for the intelligence often expressed in this terrible oversimplification: how can three make one? What is at stake here is the reality of a love absolutely independent of any external object and, therefore, entirely contained within the divine being, a love that, in order to be itself, springs eternally from the relationship to the other, which is the essence of love.

In order to grasp fully the meaning of this first approach to the mystery, we must come back to ourselves.

We have just seen that we are torn between the vague feeling of *absolute worth* within ourselves—the only basis for our autonomy—and our powerlessness to grasp it. We relentlessly affirm it against others; face to face with ourselves, we are unable to identify it. That is why, by treating this inner worth as a possession, we sometimes expect it to build up the narcissism in which ego cult flourishes, sometimes to give the green light to our passions in the name of freedom which it confers on us as a privilege. As such, it cannot shed any light on our dealings with others when, no longer on the defensive, we try to strike up an affectionate relationship with them. Not knowing where to find our own worth, how could we possibly discover theirs? Hence, this mixture of lust and interest that usually makes up what we call love.

Again, we note that our ego comes up against limitations that belie its claims. It cannot single out the worth in which it prides itself and from which our passions derive a misunderstood and anarchic autonomy that a-cually increases our enslavement. Our humanity eludes us and we try in vain to discover our true face.

Paradoxically, the Holy Trinity will reveal it to us. Indeed, it presents an altruistic awareness that is the opposite of our narcissistic awareness. In the Trinity, God takes hold of his own being by communicating it, he possesses it only by giving it. Also, in God, the language of self, whereby we constantly speak of ourselves to ourselves, is uttered for another whom it creates. Whereas in us, the self-love that results from our own words traps us within ourselves, in God, it pours itself out into another, exhaled as a breath of life.

Far from being solitary and narcissistic, the self in God springs forth in three subsisting relationships—Father, Son and Holy Ghost—each one embracing the totality of the divine being, in order to give it in the absolute transparency of eternal relinquishment.

"Is there the slightest trace of selfishness in that?" writes Fr. Garrigou-Lagrange, referring to Fr. de Régnon. "The self is only that subsisting relationship with the object of love; it does not appropriate anything anymore [...]. The only selfishness in the Father is to give his infinitely perfect nature to his Son, keeping only his paternity for himself, which still essentially relates him to his Son. The only selfishness in the Son and in the Holy

Ghost is to relate to each other and to the Father from whom they proceed. These three divine persons, essentially relative to one other, constitute the eminent example of the life of charity."[3]

Thus, God is Love in his very being. That is why he is totally *Spirit*, as the Samaritan woman learns from Jesus.

In us, the spirit consists in the capacity to rise above the given, the prefabricated entity—so as not to be subjected to it—by measuring it against the infinite worth we sense in the very space we create when we stand back from our own selves. But almost invariably, the prefabricated, possessive ego captures this power to rise, brings it down to its own level and harnesses its energy for itself, thus greatly increasing the virulence of its impulses. The spirit is then plunged in darkness and no longer able to know itself. However, as if it wanted to take revenge for a decay it vaguely perceives, and carried away in a kind of frenzy, it exalts itself in insane pride, thereby being party to the worst aberrations and truly becoming a spirit of possession.

Naturally, it is then unable to find the *absolute* that troubles it deep inside and to which it is preordained. It finally agrees to its own removal for the benefit of obscure and anarchic forces that well up from the unconscious. In the end, the very spirit that had every chance for liberating us becomes its own most fearsome enemy.

---

[3] Fr. Garrigou-Lagrange, *God, His Existence and His Nature*, translation of the Fifth Edition, 2nd impression, 1941, vol. 2, pp. 183-184.

However, liberation becomes possible again in the light of *self-divesting,* whereby, as we have seen above, each divine person becomes a pure relationship to the other two, through the total giving of self that constitutes it. A *new scale of values* is revealed in this. Greatness no longer consists in the pre-eminence of one individual asserting his dominance over others by restricting them —as in the case of the deified pharaohs ruling over their subjects reduced to mere dust. Greatness consists in becoming unlimited space open to others, thereby contributing to their liberation through one's own. In other words, true greatness is at one with love. We can never stress enough the liberating effect of this transmutation of values, which obviously goes hand in hand with a new vision of God, surely the most precious aspect of the Trinitarian revelation.

In unitarian monotheism, such as Judaism or Islam, where the one and only God is *solitary*, we may be tempted to understand Him through the concept of the pyramid I referred to above. At the top, God will reign supreme over the mechanics of the universe as both source and regulator of its energies, as creator of all that is not himself. We will see him as the highest legislator of the world and of humanity, judge of our behavior and master of our destiny, omnipotence that can come to our help and take pity on us, incomparable wisdom that directs all things through its providence and awesome holiness before which we can only prostrate ourselves. In great religions like Judaism and Islam, these beliefs will often lead to exemplary lives and a truly authentic spirituality, which, at least implicitly, remains open to a greater revelation.

However, if we confine ourselves strictly to the concept of one solitary God, it is difficult to resist asking the following question: outside his relationship with Creation, considered from the point of view of its total dependence on him, who is God in himself and for himself? Does not his absolute solitude destine him to infinite self-love which would disappoint our devotion and make it more difficult for us to accept his power over us? How could this supreme self-complacency, were it indeed the source of his happiness, deserve our trust and respect? In this perspective, we could understand Nietzsche's words: "If there were gods, how could I bear not to be god?" This amounts to saying: why should someone else be god instead of me? As a matter of fact, I know a little girl who thought that absolute and full happiness could not be exclusive and who was naively waiting for her turn to be God.

Trinitarian monotheism prevents such fantasies. It maintains that God is one, but he is not alone. Moreover, he is unique—unique, to be sure, in spiritual worth—because he is not alone, because he forever finds in himself the other to whom he gives himself. He can thus realize, in the depths of his own being, the total giving of self that constitutes the perfection of love, without which his holiness is inconceivable.

But there is still more: the giving within God himself is also the basis for his infinite *freedom*. Indeed, God is not subjected to or imprisoned in his being, as we generally are in ours, since he attains it only through this virginal contact of pure offering, relinquishing his being in order to communicate it. It is precisely in this contact that he reveals himself as absolute Spirit, flowing through the transparent love that he is, a love that never needs to reflect upon itself, without limits or shadows: in God, the self is pure relationship to the other. And, it bears repeating, it is also in this contact that God reveals to us the meaning of our freedom.

When we begin to see the radical self-divesting, whereby being, at the heart of the Divinity, is an eternal communion of love, we shall understand how fundamentally we are enslaved by our possessive ego, and that our first step is to set ourselves free.

Henceforth, the way to liberation is clear: if supreme greatness consists in this self-divesting, whereby each divine person is pure impulse toward the other, our own greatness will be achieved through the same total giving of ourselves that will take hold of our being down to its very roots and "turn it toward its Sun."

Besides, this Sun is hidden deep within ourselves. It is the absolute that we sense in the awareness of our inviolability, but that we have turned into an *object* by expecting it to sanction the claims made by our possessive ego. However, as soon as our ego loses its prestige and ceases to blind us, we begin to recognize this absolute as Someone to whom we can dedicate the offering of ourselves. The more we rise above our "egolatry", the more the personal nature of the mysterious Presence will be asserted—it gradually becomes the center of our very being, as it is both the ferment and the end result of our liberation—and the deeper will be our interaction with It, in which our possessive ego is transformed into an offered self.

This transformation always affects our whole being, just as much as the *self* —on all possible levels—which is its center of gravity. All the prefabricated elements within ourselves and all the acquired ones grafted onto them will thus flow into this altruistic relationship that opens us "to the Friend dwelling within."

What would be an appropriate comparison? A dynamism propelling us ahead? A wave sweeping us away? A momentum carrying us forward? A gaze transferring us into the Other? This last image best suggests the whole being focusing on a single point, from which comes the impetus toward the Other, who "is closer to our self than our own innermost self."

This transformation of our whole being, a decisive one since we go from the given to the giving, from slavery to freedom, from the individual to the person, directs us toward a certain understanding of the intra-divine relationships that constitute the personality of the Father, the Son and the Holy Spirit.

These relationships do not add an iota of being to the divine substance and in no way multiply it. The Father does not beget the Son—who is his perfect image—by bringing to life someone who did not exist, of a similar nature to his own and outside himself, as a human father procreates a child who can outlive him. And, similarly, the Holy Spirit does not emerge from nothingness through the common aspiration of the Father and the Son, whose living breath he is.

The *whole* divine being is consubstantially, that is, identically, completely, equally and eternally involved in each relationship, bears it within and springs from it *in the form of giving* through infinite self-divesting. It is indeed the spirit's special attribute to be able to assume itself without being subjected to its being. God is Spirit. He is not subjected to his being, he gives it; he is free in himself with regard to himself, whereas it is through him that we become free with regard to ourselves.

It is of the utmost importance to consider the mystery of the Holy Trinity as the revelation of the eternal communion of love that gives God his true face, while allowing us to discover our own.

God *is* Trinity. It is what the term *consubstantial* means. It urges us to introduce neither priority nor supremacy among the divine Persons. Everyday language often creates a dangerous confusion between what is suitable for the *Word Incarnate* as such, and what belongs to the Word in God's eternity, by placing the Word in a subordinate position in relation to the Father, something which is totally excluded by the very meaning of Christian monotheism. Once again: God *is* Trinity.

In God's eternity, the Father is not before the Son, nor without the Son, nor greater than the Son. Fatherhood and filiation are two reciprocal relationships flowing, so to speak, along the line of self-knowledge, cleansing it from any appropriation and giving it, as it were, a virginal purity. One *presupposes* the other, filiation presupposes fatherhood as something expressed presupposes someone expressing it. That is why we say that the Father is without origin. But, with respect to the Son, that implies neither pre-existence nor pre-eminence. And the same holds true about the reciprocal relationships "flowing" along the line of self-love, between the Father and the Son, on the one hand, and the Holy Spirit on the other.

These clarifications, quite standard, were meant to remind us of the pure interiority of the "living flame of love" that burns at the heart of Divinity. We can forget them as soon as we have understood them, and go back to the main point, which is to *live* this mystery that sheds such a bright light on our own.

Indeed, I believe that we could never have been able to formulate in such clear terms the problem that we are — nor could we have resolved it as fully as we now can —without the light from the Trinitarian revelation.

Our thirst for greatness always oscillates between a paranoid exaltation and a so-called freedom tagging behind all our untamed passions. We needed to contemplate self-divesting, which constitutes divine personalism, to discover that the height of being is reached in love, when man is but a relationship to the other, after he has *shed* his own self completely in order to make room for the other.

Prior to the Trinitarian revelation and, outside of it, even *after*, people who faithfully obeyed the dictates of their conscience undoubtedly achieved authentic liberation. But the Holy Trinity existed before revelation, and it can always work where it has not yet been revealed. Righteous people could certainly live under its influence without identifying its source. That did not necessarily protect them from errors, possibly fatal to others, if not to themselves. Nor should it prevent us from acknowledging the infinite grace that is the explicit communication of this secret of love, hidden in God's depths.

To discover God *at the origin of the life of the spirit*, and to become increasingly aware of it—in actual experience—every time that, in the light of "divine Poverty," we achieve some progress toward self-liberation, that is, after all, much more important to us than whatever we can say about God's intervention in the origins of the physical world, which are still beyond our reach. Knowing that we no longer have to look for heaven beyond the stars, but that we can find it within ourselves brings us wonderfully close to the discreet Presence that awaits us, deep down in our hearts, like "a silent music".

We cannot help being amazed by the fact that Christians have generally failed to recognize the inexpressible novelty of the Trinitarian revelation, and that it has almost no part in their lives. And yet, it could have thrown light on so many human problems that we always seem to tackle the wrong way. No true solution can be found as long as we do not learn from God that, in us as in Him, "*I is Another.*"

6

The Smuggler's Three Novenas

Dogma often gets a bad press. It is accused of subjecting people's thinking to decrees that violate its freedom and impede its progress; of reducing faith to a pharisaic adherence to the letter of Christian doctrine to the detriment of its spirit; of being opposed to the mystical experience which defies expression; of slowing down ecumenism by fanatically keeping up the old barriers and, finally, of not helping to establish justice by its refusal to accept any social or political commitment that does not bear the stamp of rigid orthodoxy.

On the contrary, our meditation on the Trinity has opened up such vast perspectives that we now see this fundamental dogma as the source of the deepest insight we could ever have of God and of ourselves. It is the ferment secretly at work in all authentic spirituality and, ultimately, the foundation of all our freedoms.

If this dogma has not always been seen in that light, it is no doubt because people have failed to grasp its essential truth, yet so perfectly expressed in St. John's simple little sentence: "God *is* love". For Him to be so, not only in his relationship with his creatures, but in his own being, God must indeed have, in himself and by himself, the power to realize fully the giving of oneself to another without which love is not worthy of its name. The intradivine relationships meet this requirement by explicitly excluding in God all elements of self-possession. They attest as well that he has a hold on his being only by communicating it, that his *self* is pure altruism, consisting solely in this relationship to the other in which he renounces his self.

For these assertions to become an inexhaustible source of wonder, we must have experienced, at least occasionally, the utter impurity of narcissistic self-love, a love in which we pretend to be the origin of our own self, taking pleasure in what in fact is a prefabricated ego to which we are subjected. We must also have experienced the limitations of any human love that does not aim at mutual self-liberation: the solution to a problem concerns only whoever raises it. In the present case, the problem is ourselves. We are radically challenged by our inability to find and grasp the self we are constantly talking about and through which we see our universe. Besides, the actual *experience* of the self remains as obscure as its relation to the prefabricated ego that foreshadows it.

The revelation of *self-divesting* which, in God, defines his whole person as pure relationship to the other, is the light shining into our cave. To love in order to be, to give ourselves completely in order to gain freedom, to merge into the absolute we bear within—instead of making it our possession—to establish our dignity and attain true greatness: these are the teachings which result directly from our coming face to face with the secret of divine being. Clearly, they must be *experienced* for their light to shine through, as is always the case in interpersonal matters, where knowledge is proportional to commitment. It is on this condition alone that we will discover that the mystery of God is the key to our own.

Besides the Trinity, all the other dogmas—in which the apostolic testimony is also made explicit under the guidance of the Holy Spirit—naturally present the same requirement. All of them, indeed, according to Fr. Pinard de la Boulaye's apt phrase, are "directions of thought" that can be borne out at different *levels,* depending on our degree of commitment. Moreover, all of them have their source and center in the revelation of God's Trinity, and they aim, as the Trinity does, at bringing out in us that infinite self-worth that will turn our life into a universal and imperishable good.

In order to help us understand the importance of commitment in understanding faith, we shall now relate two experiences in which *eschatology*—the doctrine of death, judgment, heaven and hell—becomes clearer through the stages of a very touching personal progression.

The first actually happened and I can guarantee its authenticity. A smuggler, who did some trafficking between two borders across the Alps, and who did not hesitate to use his gun against anyone interfering with his operations, found a piece of paper in the snow one day, at an altitude of 4000 meters. He picked it up and was struck by the words printed on it: *"Perpetual help ".* What could this term mean to a man like him? The only protection he had ever known was bold violence on his part. He read on and discovered that the paper outlined the program of a novena to Our Lady of Perpetual Help. Until then, in spite of a Christian upbringing, he had been fiercely opposed to any belief, and he never failed to punctuate his fits of anger with the worst obscenities. And yet, he felt mysteriously driven to begin this novena as the words of the prescribed prayers began surfacing from his memory. After nine days, he came to a hopeless realization: he was nothing but a criminal, irremediably and deservedly doomed to hell. He felt the sheer horror of this hell which Paul Althaus defines admirably as "an irremissible absence of God in an irremissible relationship to God".

Although he felt that all was lost, he started the novena over again. At the end of it, a ray of hope began to glimmer like a star barely visible in a stormy sky. "Maybe", he would say to himself, "I'll get off with a few billion years in purgatory." After the third novena, he had overcome the fear of punishment by thinking of God whom he had offended. He began to see that he was responsible for his personal relationship with him. He had to provide an answer. He had not just broken a law, he had hurt Someone whose forgiveness he had to obtain. But how could he believe in forgiveness if he did not believe in love? That was the problem: he had closed his heart to love by fiercely defending his solitary independence which had become like a prison. By entrenching himself in self-possession, he had created his own hell: God was not the one condemning him to it. To acknowledge this was already a way of opening up to the Presence whose light was dawning upon him. His resistance was melting away in this encounter which liberated him from all constraints, and he surrendered to the grace through which he had found himself. When he came to confession, after seven novenas, he was so radically transformed, so overflowing with the love he had just discovered, that the priest was overwhelmed, asked him to give an account of his conversion, and heard how an allusion to Perpetual Help, on a little piece of paper, had brought him out of his torpor.

It is difficult to find a better example in which dogma is shown to be a "direction of thought," without limit and therefore one that can be borne out on different levels.

As we have just seen, our bandit *first* discovers the hell of Dogma in a sudden realization of his own *responsibility*: he is not a thing or an object, whose only option is to accept his condition: he is capable of taking initiative, he is destined to mould himself, to choose what he will be, to determine his own fate. As he becomes aware of sin, he understands that it is essentially a refusal to be, and he must accept the consequences of this refusal precisely because of his dignity as creator. If these consequences extend beyond his earthly existence, it is because he can rise above what he was given at birth, as a creature of flesh and blood, to a life "beyond" the reach of death. All this he can *feel*: he has made a mess of his life and perhaps it is too late to do anything about it. He also understands that the moral order he tried to ignore rests on *Someone*. In other words, this order, which concerns the person we are all meant to become, is naturally a *personal* order, and we cannot cheat because its guardian is an incorruptible Witness. Under his watchful eye, our bandit will be what he will have chosen to be, with no chance to hide. He will be judged by his actions: they will exclude him from the order he has rejected, with which he will nevertheless maintain "an irremissible relationship", and that in turn may become the source of endless torments.

But since this is a personal order we adhere to or from which we cut ourselves off by an act of will, could we not restore the situation from which we have deliberately fallen by a reversal of the initial choice?

This question allows us to anticipate a way out. But it only includes one aspect of the problem. This personal order is indeed an *order of love*: it implies essentially a relationship with Someone from whom we part as soon as we claim to follow only our own will. Therefore, it is impossible, without Him, to re-establish the relationship with Him who is good itself. Thus, the second step in our bandit's conversion, following the promise of "Perpetual Help", is marked by the quest and the hope for forgiveness.

However, the point of view is still an external one in relation to the next stages. Our man acknowledges that he has sinned and that he has done so against God. But, for him, God remains the Master whose sovereignty he has failed to recognize and whose judgment he must fear, rather than the Love he has hurt and who nonetheless has never given up on him. At this point, it is concern for his own salvation that leads him to ask to be forgiven rather than attachment to God for God's sake. In the later stages, *internalization* occurs: he discovers God as the hidden Presence within, as Love committed to him until death on the Cross. It is then that his very heart is transformed, in the wonder of rebirth, to the point of completely losing sight of himself. It is no longer for him a question of ensuring his salvation, but of giving himself totally to this Love who gave himself for him, thereby lending human life the same weight as divine life. From now on, evil will be the Agony on the Cross, that moment of infinite loneliness and ultimate desertion, and he will be ready to understand how St. Francis of Assisi could have worn his eyes out, for almost twenty years, weeping over the Passion that was to counterbalance our refusal to love. He will even begin to see that it is God, as it were, who must be saved from hell, which means that, if our *refusal* became hardened into eternal denial, it is his Love that would have failed. Is this not what is symbolized, on the tympanum above the great portal of Notre-Dame in Paris, by Christ's stigmatized hands raised at the Last Judgment as a supreme affirmation of his love? "*Quid ultra debui facere et non feci?*" (What more should I have done that I did not do?) "It is not I who condemn them, but they who reject me". Is this not what Jesus wanted to suggest to the Apostles at the washing of the feet, when he knelt down before them so that they might turn toward the heaven within themselves, that they risked losing by seeking the kingdom of God in the outer world?

What new dimension will the smuggler's existence acquire? He only knew hatred, and now he knows that he bears God within himself, a God he first discovered in the terror of being irredeemably condemned, and whom he meets at last in his innermost being, as a Life that has placed itself in his hands. How could he not put his trust in a call so deeply felt? In any case, it is clear that a *gradual passage from without to within* has reversed the situation: what was first experienced as a terrifying threat to man is felt in the end as a loving fear of God, since we can always refuse to say *yes*, the condition for the coming of his kingdom within us.

Dogma is thus always open to a deeper understanding that stems from a more generous commitment. It remains *true*, analogically speaking, at every stage of the experience it guides, and the direction it gives to that experience will be sustained at different levels. When he realizes his crimes, our smuggler is abruptly awakened by terror. What he feels—a sense of responsibility whereby "the totality of his being is at stake", as Paul Tillich would say, as well as a sense of the eternal consequences implied in the exercise of such a responsibility—gives him an inkling of the greatness he is destined to achieve as a man. It also gives him the measure of the risk he ran in not answering the call, when he gave in to the impulses of his ego, without caring about being the *origin* of his actions. At that stage, God inevitably appears to him as the unyielding guardian of an ontological order he thought he could elude, and whose inexorable embrace he now knows. The progressive stages of his conversion will alter his *vision*: the order of being will be identified with the order of love, and it will touch him *from within* through his freedom, actualized in the giving of himself. And God, who is love personified, will be all the closer to him and all the more internalized as the giving is perfected. God will then truly become, in Augustine's words, "the Life of his life".

His sense of responsibility will not be watered down as a result of this. On the contrary. Becoming responsible for God is not something he can do intermittently: at every moment, his whole being must bear witness to his Presence. But his requirement is the flame of the burning bush ablaze in his heart; it allows him to constantly renew his offering by getting in touch again and again with the Infinite within himself. The dark abyss that threatened to engulf him was nothing more than the other side of the light deep inside in which he is now immersed.

This *experience* of fundamental liberation brings us back to the "original source", the Holy Trinity, where the light of love never fades. And yet, in our bandit, it happened through the revelation of dogma which, at first, shocks our sensitivity the most But this proves that dogma can be experienced at different levels, and that the first level, fear, is exactly that, only the first. It is not a bad idea to experience it once in a while, so that we can be shaken out of our torpor and acknowledge that our choice is what determines our fate: we cannot do just anything because we are not just anybody, because *being* has a meaning outside of which we are headed for *nothingness*, while continuing our "irremissible relationship" with it. For our primitive being—which is not of our own choice—is never taken away from us, it is irrevocably ours. If we refuse to assume responsibility for it, to make it really our own, to enrich it with a new dimension by moving from the given to the giving, it will definitely bind us to an ontological order which can tear us apart if we forego the chance to fit into it.

But we must not stop there. This *order of being* may indeed appear abstract and impersonal, like a theorem. Without prejudice to its reality, it is as an *order of love* (based, in the final analysis, on the Trinity) that it will touch us and suggest the direction we should take to emerge from our primitive self without surrendering to anarchic freedom. The perspective of love will make it possible for us to surpass ourselves in all our actions; by becoming progressively *internalized*, we will at last lose sight of ourselves as we completely merge into the absolute that is the living God within. Our only concern then will be to let him shine through every aspect of our lives.

So that we will not stop at the first level of dogma, that of the popular images of Hell, the story on which we have just reflected contains, in its simplest form, a most precious teaching. It could appear in a catechism as a perfect example of the progression of dogma *within ourselves*, according to the growing commitment of a faith that reflects the "lines of thought" most likely to produce the kind of "homogeneous" development in which its truth will be increasingly clear.

In his novel *The Power and the Glory*, Graham Greene offers a testimony worthy of note in this respect. It shows that considering man's ultimate end from the angle of fear—which is the lowest level of awareness—may have no hold on someone who is perfectly capable of total commitment out of love.

This novel, which was made into a movie, takes us to Mexico where the clergy was severely persecuted shortly after the revolution of October 1917 in the U.S.S.R. The bishops go into exile, priests flee and, in a vast territory, only two priests are left, either unable or unwilling to escape. Both are worse than mediocre, and they have obviously joined the priesthood only to live a life of *dolce farniente*, without denying themselves—discreetly—the least pleasure. To escape the storm, one of them immediately marries his housekeeper, thus finding favor with the government; he is given a pension since, having discredited his ministry, he could never pose as an enemy of the regime.

The other, on the contrary, in a state of shock from the events, discovers a vocation that he possibly never had. When the ship is sinking, the captain must be the last to leave, and when the flock is attacked, the shepherd cannot abandon it to save his skin. These two images will determine his destiny. He will be shepherd of the flock, captain of the ship in distress. He knows he is in a state of sin, but this is hardly the time to look at his own problems. For thousands of kilometers around, he is the only one who can celebrate the Eucharist and minister the sacraments. He will attend to his soul after he has taken care of the souls of others, who suffer from a spiritual famine he has the power and the duty to remedy. This decision transforms his life radically. It forces him into the opposition and makes him an outlaw. He can exercise his ministry only at night and on the run. Food and rest are never guaranteed. He must constantly flee from one place to another in the hope of outwitting the police who get wind of his presence and spare no efforts to capture him. Finally, a price is put on his head. However, all these ordeals seem to roll off him; having decided to play the game, he abides by its rules. He heroically relinquishes his own self without even realizing it. He goes so far as to save the life of a man who spies on him and who, he knows, will despicably denounce him. His only protection is the invincible silence of the faithful who appeal to his ministry: neither promises nor threats can make them talk. As a last resort, the police take hostages wherever they pick up his trail.

The hunted priest sees in this a sign of Providence. He can risk his life—that is in line with his vocation—but he does not have the right to risk other people's lives. God is not necessarily linked to the sacraments He has instituted, however precious they may be, and He can communicate his grace through other means. Therefore, His minister is not deserting if he leaves with Him the flock endangered by his presence. Consequently, he decides to escape to the United States where, at last, he can take care of his own soul. He manages to reach the border and is about to cross it when the alleged spy catches up with him and begs him to retrace his steps to go and assist a dying man. If he agrees, he is admitting to being a man of the Church and he falls into the trap. If he refuses, the attempt will simply have failed. The priest smells a rat. However, if it is true that a dying man is calling for him, he could never forgive himself for not having risked his life. Besides, the thought that his security on the other side of the border probably means a mediocre existence is already making him sick. So he follows the suspicious guide. He takes him to an isolated shack where, just as he has been told, a man, hunted down by the police, lies dying. The priest begins to question him in a low voice: "Are you the one who sent for me?—No!" So he was set up. Unperturbed, he urges the sick man to take advantage of the ministry that he brings to him at the risk of his own life, and not to reject the grace offered at such a price. While this is going on, the police burst into the room and grab the fugitive. A young lieutenant, filled with revolutionary zeal, tells him without further ado that he will be shot the very next day. The priest calmly accepts this outcome which he sees as the crowning achievement of his mission. All he asks from the young officer, whose esteem and friendship he has won in return for his honesty, is to find him a priest who will give him absolution before he is executed. The only one left in the country is his ex-fellow priest, now married, whose wife prevents him from lending himself to this urgent ministry in spite of the lieutenant's pleas. All that the hero of our story can do now is commit himself to the Lord's mercy while he prepares for the supreme purification of martyrdom.

Besides, since he has been devoting himself, body and soul, to the shepherdless flock, he has lost sight of himself to the point that he does not even think of turning his death —from which renouncing his faith would save him— into tragedy. All that matters, he now knows, is not to be an obstacle to the kingdom of God. He has recently bluntly said as much to a bigot who was busy coddling her precious little soul: *"To love God is to want to protect him against yourself."* That is the great discovery that decided his conversion. Everything changed for him when he became insensitive to the danger his behavior exposed him to, but understood that it could expose God to danger. The opaqueness of a selfish heart can only tarnish God's radiant presence whose influence only love can communicate. In his experience, that "irremissible relationship with God" implies our taking responsibility for God. Rather than "an irremissible absence *of* God", which would be his punishment, he experiences the intolerable *refusal to love* that rejection of God—absence *from*— *essentially is. God will never cease to be Love*, even to the creature who would definitively reject him, since this creature would cease to exist if it were not sustained in its very being by God's love. Besides, Hell would be inconceivable if God ceased to love, since there could be no question of refusing love where there is no love.

It is in this perspective that we can interpret the verses Dante reads on the gates of hell: *"Fecemi la divina Potestate, La somma Sapienza, e'l primo Amore"* (divine Power made me, the highest Wisdom and first Love).

At any rate, it seems that we cannot dispute the legitimacy of a Christian experience which, like that of Graham Greene's hero, begins with love and not with fear, without wishing to exclude the legitimacy of the latter.

Indeed, understanding dogma implies all the levels to which love can rise in its unlimited growth, always respecting the line of thought it opens and, in the end, bringing us back to God's Trinity, the Sun of which it is a ray.

From this point of view, we can "tentatively" conclude the following about our ultimate end: our true end is *Someone* who lives in us, whom we are destined to join *immediately*. We can draw our inspiration from the admirable words we have just quoted: "To love God is wanting to protect him against ourselves."

7

God's Heartrending Innocence
and Eternal Beginnings

A father worthy of the name is, according to his means, the natural material providence for his children; he makes sure that all their needs are amply met so that they never feel frustrated. But he would never think of taking advantage of his concern for them, however generous, to put pressure on their helpless freedom and push them into a reassuring imitation of himself, as did a strangely devout man who forced his sons to go to communion every day in order to have an indisputable proof of their good behavior.

On the contrary, a real father, whose responsibility it is to teach self-respect to those in his care, will consider that the supreme gift of his love is to show respect for their consciences. He must foster *from within* the discovery of interiority through which conscience is fully established. He cannot be accused of weakness because he is careful not to hurt them, provided his example of a totally honest life allows the good, which he so wants them to embrace, to shine through his teaching. Rather, we will admire the magnanimous educator who resists the temptation to use his power so as not to distort the values on which the child is expected to build his autonomy.

Can we use this ideal of human fatherhood, that only the most demanding self-sacrifice can attain, as a parable to help us understand divine fatherhood with regard to us?

The excerpt from *De Beatitudine*, used as an epigraph, implies unequivocally that this analogy is appropriate. It was already suggested in St. Augustine's meditations on the *traces* and the *image* of the Trinity in the universe and in human beings, as he looks for the ultimate secret of our origins at the heart of intradivine relationships. If the whole of creation indeed hangs upon trinitarian love, it also derives its meaning from it. Therefore, every creature, like God himself, through its individual network of relationships, in its own way and depending on its level, must ultimately grasp its own being, have a hold on it by communicating it. In other words, every creature must be expected to participate, according to its level of being, in the totally self-divesting love and infinite freedom that are the very breath of divine being. It is indeed as inconceivable that the God revealed in the Word Incarnate could have created a robot universe, as it is that a true father would try relentlessly to turn his son into a robot.

Going back to our parable, God's fatherhood can thus be experienced at the leading edge of human fatherhood, where power merges into love. Seen in these terms, it will express itself by respecting the inviolable freedom conferred on intelligent creatures as the supreme gift of Infinite Love : God wants his creatures to dispose of the being they owe Him—to be able to give it in turn—without their dependence affecting their autonomy in any way. No trace of despotism or paternalism can be found in these *spirit-to-spirit relationships* that God intends to establish with us, as one shares a secret with friends, not with servants. These relationships are in keeping with Jesus'*teaching* to the Samaritan woman, a teaching confirmed by deed in the washing of the feet and written in blood in his agony and crucifixion. This paradoxical independence granted to beings responsible for themselves is vividly expressed by Bergson in these meaningful words: "*God created creators.*"

The mystical experience of a marriage of love with God is further evidence of this, as is compassion which makes us eager to share in the redemptive suffering of the Lord.

All these spiritual directions, emanating from the Gospel, imply grasping God's creative action as an outpouring in the universe of the communion of love that allows the flow of divine being among the three divine Persons. From this point of view, the whole of creation is involved in a mission of love and freedom.

In order to be convinced, clearly one must never lose sight of the fact that it is impossible to really reach out to another human being without acknowledging and respecting the inviolability that surrounds his dignity. Whoever is familiar with this experience knows that it gives a glimpse of both the inner face of man and the sacred aspect of the universe. We often hear ironic calls to humility, inspired by a materialistic ideology and directed against a naive anthropocentricity that insists on giving man a privileged rank in the cosmos. Even if we admit, according to such an ideology, that man is a simple product of the universe, it is no less true that this product is a being full of problems that the universe cannot solve in his place, vested with a responsibility of which the universe cannot relieve him. In reality, this kind of "humility" amounts to a negation of man and it is of no benefit whatsoever to man in the ever-increasing number of steps he must take in order to survive.

How much closer to the point Pascal comes when he writes: "Man is but a reed, the weakest in nature, but he is a thinking reed." And also: "By its expanse, the universe encompasses me and swallows me up like a speck; by thought, it is I who comprehend it." That is, as Brunschvicg explains: "I am contained in the universe and the universe is contained in me."

It might be useful to point out here that it is man who has invented this notion of *universe* with his general overview of space-time that "swallows him up like a speck". It is he who has created history and discovered the long chain linking him to his origins. It is he who has explored the atom, the nebulas and his own unconscious, who has deciphered the genetic code and all the laws of inert matter and living things. It is man who has triumphed over weight and weightlessness, who has domesticated animals and harnessed cosmic energies. It is man who anticipates the probable *future* of his species, according to the decisions it requires him to make, and the future of the cosmos according to the entropy that measures the deterioration of its potential. To emphasize man's insignificance in an infinite space-time is to overwhelm him with his own greatness.

But there is more. Not only does man, with his mind, "swallow up" the universe like a speck, but he also draws from it a whole system of *values* that add new dimensions to it. First, he makes it an object to be *known* that comes to *life* in his mind. He discovers, in its mutability, some invariants that guarantee the certainty and universality of knowledge. He abstracts and codifies its structural norms which allow him to understand it, to act on it and with it, and this, by relying on his inner logic to predict and link phenomena with the astounding precision that made possible man's first steps on the Moon. On a deeper level yet, he draws from the universe the *joy of knowing*. It arises, always *identical,* from any scientific subject through the contact with a *presence* that is always the same, a presence which, through any discovery in physics or mathematics, is perceived like a light suddenly shining in the mind. And at that moment, man experiences the object of his quest as existing simultaneously without and within himself. Finally, at every stage of his research, in every area of the material universe, man is capable of arriving at the *truth.* Truth is most difficult to define but, as a rule, it is felt to be an *absolute* that cannot and must not be attained by cheating.

And yet, we know that new discoveries can always challenge the most firmly established positions—as Einstein did in the case of Newton's law of gravitation—and that there is no final word on anything. We constantly give credit to world-renowned scientists who, after years of unconditional support, disavow some popular theory, as Louis de Broglie did when he finally expressed his doubts about the absolute value of Heisenberg's principle of uncertainty. So where is this truth which Jean Rostand described as the great love of the scientist? "Love of That which is and simply because It is." But how can we ever be sure of reaching "That which is" when Lecomte du Noüy can write about the reversibility of time in quantum mechanics: "This expresses the state of the question at the moment I write (I believe). When this book will be published, I have no doubt that new facts and especially new theories will have come to light. Nowadays, a theory is often outdated in six months."[1] The *progress* of knowledge, indeed, seems to be linked to this uncontrollable acceleration of research which will always prevent us from grasping "That which is". Besides, even supposing that someday we should succeed in making a complete and definitive discovery about some phenomenon, how can we explain this "love" Jean Rostand talks about in the passage we quoted above in its entirety, overflowing with fervor and "devotion"? Is a mechanism of nature worth devoting one's life to it? Unless, as Einstein did, we see in it, as if through a veil, "the infinite superior spirit that is revealed in the slightest details that we can perceive with our frail and feeble minds."

Indeed, that explains it. The absolute commitment to truth Rostand insists on is essentially an interpersonal commitment, a commitment to Someone whose existence we cannot sense unless we "marvel and stand in awe" (Einstein). The Truth is a Person whose "presence" (Einstein) shows through a phenomenon, suddenly lighting it *from within*—at that moment when its intelligibility flashes in the mind—as in an alabaster vase when the

---

[1] *L'Homme devant la science*, p. 122.

lamp hidden inside it is lit. Without at least an implicit reference to this presence,[2] it seems to me that we cannot talk about truth, experienced as such in "the joy of knowing", in experimental scientific knowledge which must constantly advance and yet forever remain incomplete.

A researcher exploring the immeasurable circumference of phenomena is suddenly hit by a ray from the center that links him to the "original source" where the light shines eternally. He is immersed in this light and, as I was just saying about the joy of knowing, in the light inside himself. Then he knows, and he knows that he knows. But what does he know? If he is more than just a technician, if he frees himself from his limitations in the fervor of research, and depending on the level of the research and the range of tools at his disposal, he knows Someone rather than something, as Pierre Termier so powerfully experienced; he knows the meaning of the world rather than the exact nature of the energies that constitute it in all their different forms. That is why it has always been possible, throughout the ages, to arrive at *Truth* as we have defined it, no matter how rudimentary the determination of the way in which to study the phenomena might have been.

Even older than the attempt to explain the universe is the attempt to represent it in volumes or colors, in music or body rhythms, giving birth to *art*. The history of these endeavours is wonderful, and humanity could certainly benefit if it replaced, in our textbooks, the account of

---

[2] This is one of the possible meanings of the Augustinian illumination.

rivalries and wars which show man as a predator on his own species. Art seems to be the result of a kind of marriage between the unconscious, whose drives it organizes, and a perception of the concrete universe experienced as a presence.

Weight and grace, movement and rest, strength and lightness, numbers and imagination, rigor and flexibility, necessity and freedom, light and shadow, fury and serenity, frivolity and contemplation, noise and silence, void and fullness, the inert and the living, the infinite and the finite: it is the confrontation of these opposites, which symbolize our conflicts and the solution found in balance, that brings out their illuminating power. It lights up our unconscious and brings harmony to it; it draws our whole being, secretly unified, toward the Source where the artist himself has found the liberating urge that his work communicates.

For example, if we stand in front of Notre-Dame in Paris and take in the façade in an overall view, the first impression is the perfect balance between the vertical lines and the horizontal ones represented by the two galleries that divide it into three superimposed areas. The cathedral soars up to the sky because it is firmly rooted in the ground: the point is not to renounce this earth, but rather "to let a divine dew make it fruitful". If we look at the apse from a good distance, we will see the whole structure, borne along by the flying buttresses that boldly surround it, start like a huge sailing ship casting off for the high seas. As we enter the cathedral, we will immediately have a feeling of unlimited space, in height and in depth, and in the subdued half-light, the real confines of that enclosure around us will disappear. We can see the wonders of architecture in this ability to make heavy masses appear light, to suggest infinity inside a limited space, and to break the monotony by using complementary opposing elements. And all this to *create a dwelling place for the spirit*, while conforming to the basic requirement that the structure be sound and useful, since its primary function is to provide man with a shelter for himself and his activities.

All the arts possess similar powers of incantation. They evoke a *beyond* that is a *within*; they bring all things back to the same point of origin; they gravitate in the orbit of the same absolute; they make us open to the same presence, and liberate us from our own selves by immersing us in its infinity. The work of art alludes to this presence, and that *allusion* imparts form to it and is like the mark of the creative moment when the artist himself perceived, in some object, what Rodin calls the "Truth within".

We could never exaggerate the importance of this non-utilitarian hold on the world which is apprehended in a contemplative mode. From prehistoric times, it has initiated man to the sacred by internalizing the spectacle of nature and endowing it with a kind of transcendence experienced through the perception of the senses. The neighing horse of the Mas-d'Azil, the galloping horse with bristling hair of Niaux, the boldly outlined mammoth of Pech-Merle, the large fresco of animals in motion of Lascaux[3] testify to this vision which, again as Rodin tells

---

[3] *Le Courrier*, August-September 1972, Unesco.

us, discovers in appearances "the signs of hidden realities".

Of course, art *suggests* this transcendence through "correspondences" inherent to the materials on which it works—without making them explicit—but this is precisely what enables art to penetrate into the depths of our unconscious, as open to symbolism as it is insensitive to discursive reasoning.

It is impossible to express here, even in a cursory fashion, all we owe to architecture, sculpture, painting, music, writing, theater, choreography (and cinema), through the various cultures we have inherited. Our sensibility is steeped in all that art has given us. What we can learn from these brief observations is that art has greatly contributed to *humanizing* the universe by fulfilling, at least in part, what we believe to be the vocation for love and freedom of creation, if indeed it is the work of the First Love. I believe we are justified in thinking that creation lends itself, and perhaps invites us, to this vocation, since man has always considered this way of approaching creation as the most beautiful use we can make of it.

As we have defined it, and insofar as it keeps to its method, which must suspend all personal options, science has absolutely nothing to tell us about the meaning of the universe: it merely tries to understand its mechanisms. However, it is essential to note that, on its own ground, certain basic notions needed to describe those mechanisms have been profoundly modified. Ever since Einstein, time, space and mass are considered as *relative quantities*. An object contracts in the direction of its movement and its mass increases with its velocity. Matter and energy are equivalent to each other: matter is energy and energy is matter; they are two interchangeable temporary states of the same reality. This is what has allowed man to transform matter into energy (light, heat, sound, motion), as he did in a spectacular way when he created the first atom bomb. These "relativities" teach us to distrust any assertion founded on the apparent clarity of concepts and words. Where is this star *now* whose light must travel thirty-eight years at 300,000 km/sec to reach us? How can we *observe* an electron in motion if it is impossible to determine its position and its "velocity" at the same time, if the very fact of "throwing light on it" knocks it off course and changes its "velocity"? (Heisenberg). On a deeper level yet: what is this matter-energy which can be interpreted in terms of waves or particles? What is this universe that Einstein perceived in the end "as one elemental field in which each star, each atom, each wandering comet, each slow-wheeling galaxy and each flying electron are nothing but ripples and swellings on the underlying space-time unity"?[4]

Perhaps all we can say scientifically about the ultimate constituent of the *"material" world* in which we are immersed is that there exists a "mysterious something": its different potentialities are at the source of all physical phenomena, until the final levelling out, foreseen by the second principle of thermodynamics, when nothing more will happen and the universe will die.

---

[4] Lincoln Barnett, *op. cit.*, pp. 31-32, 37, 52, 61-62, 67-71, 121.

No doubt, we belong to this world on the level of living things where it unfolds with maximum complexity. But that does not give us any advantage when it comes to knowing it. We experience the universe subjectively, for the sake of our own subsistence, letting it carry out in us all the vital functions which do not require our initiative and about which we generally think only in times of illness. Our narcissistic awareness is astonishingly blind with respect to our internal organs and the prodigious workings that condition our survival at every moment. We breathe and digest, our blood circulates and our heart beats, our sensory channels transmit signals that put our muscles to work, and we know neither how nor through how many relays this is done. Books tell us about the brain consisting of fourteen billion neurons, interconnected by an even greater number of synapses between which the nerve impulses travel through molecular interactions. Books also describe our body as "a lacunary system [...], consisting mainly of empty space [...]; if the atoms that make up each one of us were reduced to only their nucleus, they could easily be contained in a cube four billionths of a millimeter in size, and that if the nuclei of all humanity were joined together, they would fit in a space of $10\,mm^3$, the size of a grain of rice." Finally, books teach us that, out of approximately 60 million millions of cells in our organism, some 500 thousand millions die each day. This does not prevent us from retaining the same identity throughout our whole life, from the embryonic state to old age, in spite of the constant renewal of the material elements produced by our metabolism.

This perpetual "self-renewal" within an individual's identity leads certain biologists to speak of a *subsisting structure*, the "only permanent reality" in us as in any living thing. This structure, this internal plan for self-building, "this creative program", is it material or immaterial? It can be seen in action everywhere and it governs everything in an organism as long as there is life. How does it suddenly stop being active? How does it die out? Can it possibly re-emerge after having disappeared, as was the case in a famous experiment carried out in 1955 on the tobacco mosaic virus? This power to self-regulate is inherent to all living structures; the fact that it obeys, with both rigor and flexibility, the information transmitted by a nucleic acid (D.N.A.) sheds no light on the "overall and omnipresent action" that presides over the construction, preservation and reproduction of living beings through countless simultaneous and coordinated reactions.[5]

All this to say that the term *material* remains as ambiguous in the biosphere (the living world) as it can be in the inorganic (inanimate) world. This brings us to qualify the *meaning* of *materialism* considerably, by first recognizing it as an attitude of the mind. The visible world, indeed, can be a source of wonder; it may arouse a feeling of respect in the researcher and offer the artist an inexhaustible treasure of images and symbols. Far from opposing it, the visible world can indeed enhance the life of the spirit in the transfiguration, suggestive of a presence, that ennobles both of them. On the other hand, the spirit will materialize the universe if it entrenches

---

[5] Cf. Cl. Tresmontant, *Comment se pose aujourd'hui le problème de l'existence de Dieu; — Le Problème de l'âme.* Jacques Monod, *Le Hasard et la nécessité.* J.-E. Charon, *Récentes découvertes sur la matière et la vie.*

itself in narcissistic self-possession, if pride binds it to the ego's passions which rule the spirit instead of being transformed by it and made its own. The opposition here is thus less between the elusive "stuff" that supposedly makes up the physical world, and the "immaterial" essence of the spirit, than between the *exteriority* of a possessive stance and the *interiority* of a giving one. The *Hymn to the Sun*, that St. Francis asked to hear before he died, does not imply that he was a slave to the "elements of the universe," but that, on the contrary, the world for him had become transparent to the love that consumed him.

When Einstein wrote his famous equation: $e = mc^2$, what was interesting was not so much to know whether his organism was made up of proteins and nucleic acids like any other living creature, but to see his genius encompass all the energies of the universe, and give us a hold on them in such a short formula. We are most certainly rooted in the physical world, to the point that, taking into account its action on us, we can consider it as *our body*—from the hydrogen atom to the most distant galaxies—but conversely, it is no doubt true that the physical world is rooted in us by becoming intelligible knowledge in our mind and thus a pure object of thought. In this light, it has conceivably been entrusted to us so that it can reach, through us, a freedom it cannot achieve on its own.

This sort of Jacob's ladder, formed by the *sacraments*, confirms in its own way the spiritual vocation of the Universe: it borrows from it the symbols which are to represent and communicate the presence and the grace of the Lord, extending, as it were, his incarnation in the perceptible signs that are supposed to make us participate in it. With water and oil, bread and wine, gestures and words, these signs bring about the nuptial covenant between God and the world in a supernatural way. They take hold of the whole being, down to the roots of the unconscious, evangelizing it precisely through their symbolic language which alone can reach it and throw light on it. In their wake, *sacramental rites* invest all reality with the blessing that sets its use with a view to the infinite Good, whose quest is the secret magnet for all our aspirations.

Finally, belief in the *resurrection* is a prelude to the definitive transfiguration of those elements in us that we have in common with the universe. No matter how we define them scientifically, we experience their presence and their weight *in a vital way*, and we feel that we shall never be truly ourselves unless we can internalize them by purifying them in the offering of ourselves. It is by personalizing this cosmic heritage and divesting ourselves of our prefabricated ego that we will have the most convincing foretaste of eternity, which will affect our entire being. If the physical energies that surge inside us can become, today, an integral part of our spiritual life, we have indeed good reasons to believe that some day, our corporal entity can be brought back to life, and possibly the world in which it exists. This is what St. Ambrose suggests when he writes: "In Him [Christ] the world is risen, in Him heaven is risen, in him the earth is risen."

The result of these observations seems to be that "matter", with which we have attempted to familiarize ourselves, is not necessarily a materializing factor, and that, on the contrary, it is able to participate in the loftiest expressions of the mind, which is solely responsible for materialism. Therefore, nothing prevents us from admitting, in principle, that the entire visible world can answer its calling to freedom and love through intelligent creatures—set on this or other planets. This optimistic conclusion, however, does not preclude the opposite possibility: degradation inflicted on the world by the weakness of that very intelligence that was supposed to assume it. *Two partners* are involved in the story of creation, the nuptials in which every reasonable creature works with God to create a universe of love; but, if indeed God's *yes* is eternally assured, the *yes* of free creatures is not. Creatures are not a yes in themselves, as God in whom a no cannot be (2 Cor 1:19); they must fashion themselves into a *yes*. And it is probably through this no on which creatures set their minds that *evil* entered the world.

The presence of evil, as Jean Lacroix recalls in his remarkable lecture at the cenacle in Beirut on "atheism and contemporary thought", has always given rise to an "aristocratic" atheism that "seceded" from common beliefs. It became popular when it took the sentimental turn given to it by some Russian writers of the nineteenth century and echoed by Ivan Karamazov in Dostoyevsky's great novel and Albert Camus' *The Plague*. The innocent, victims of evil, must certainly always be heard, since they are the ones *experiencing* it, and we should not be surprised if they reject a God they perceive as the author of their misery. However, we must understand that the "scandal" of evil only makes sense in opposition to an *absolute* good that must necessarily exist somewhere. The more indignant we are at the trampling underfoot of the *values* which should make man sacred to man, and the more impatient we become with being part of a universe that ignores them, the greater the necessity to find for these values a basis that *transcends* both man who violates them and the cosmos that is indifferent to them. Thus we are led to affirm implicitly the existence of a God (an Absolute) who sanctions them; we inevitably place Him in the victims' camp, against the god we deny because he appears to be their executioner.

This position is complicated by the fact that we do not always make the distinction between the ills caused by man and those that are the result of natural causes. The torture inflicted on little children by their parents motivates Ivan Karamazov's atheism; the ordeal of illness suffered by a dying child is the basis for Dr. Rieux' own torment in Camus' *The Plague.*

It is true that, when ills caused by man become generalized, they tend to appear anonymous, similar to a blind fate, as Gheorghiu suggests so forcefully in *La Vingt-cinquième heure* (The twenty-fifth hour). His wretched hero moves from one concentration camp to another; in the West as in the East, he is never more than a number, an indexed record confined to a category that determines his fate, without any possible recourse. When we cannot blame anyone by name for a tragic situation—involving us or loved ones—we almost inevitably accuse fate or an unjust god. Why suddenly a war that, for years, brings about countless deprivations and abolishes any kind of security? Why did this son or that husband die on the battlefield whereas others came out of it unscathed? Why was this mother wrenched from her home to end up in a gas chamber? Why—and this time in normal lives—did Jacques Thibaud die in a plane crash and Pierre Curie under the hoofs of a draft horse? When you add the absurd to cruelty, it naturally seems monstrous. And yet, we know that war is the outcome of human decisions or miscalculations, that technology entails risks and that it is the price of progress, that a scientist's absent-mindedness is not due to cosmic disorder. It is thus possible to accept the presence of evil by attributing to man alone the misfortunes that stem from his choices, his initiatives or his behavior.

It is not the same for natural catastrophes—like earthquakes, volcanic eruptions, tidal waves, cyclones and floods—which are totally beyond our control. They can suddenly devastate entire regions, as if the physics of the planet had absolutely nothing to do with man and all his creations. Besides, we find the same indifference in the wild beasts that attack and devour man, the insects that destroy his crops or the germs that infect him, which can just as well disintegrate the brain of a genius as that of a mentally deficient person. Faced with such indifference, the order of the world and the order of human values seem all the more intolerably dissociated as man is bound to the world and helpless before its aggressions.

The difficulty is huge and may seem insurmountable. However, if we admit that human life implies an absolute value—a belief from which the objection of evil derives all its strength—sanctioned by a transcendent Absolute, the latter can only agree with us in the protest we raise against an inhuman world. Then, how could He be, at the same time, the creator and the providence governing it?

Far from ignoring this problem, the Old Testament approached it from several angles. Cosmic catastrophes like the deluge (Gen 6:5—9:1) or the destruction of Sodom and Gomorrha (Gen 19:1-29) are considered to be just punishment for moral corruption. But the suffering of the innocent, who should be exempt from trials and showered with blessings in the light of a limited life span on earth, does not lend itself to this explanation. The *Book of Job* rejects it with the magnificent violence of sincerity which appeals, as it were, to God against God; the only answer it receives (incomplete) is an affirmation of a Transcendence that reduces man to silence. Dramatized this way, *under divine inspiration*, the problem could have no other solution, given "the stage of Revelation" (*The Jerusalem Bible*, Introd.) at which the author of the book finds himself.

It is surprising that the remarkable poet who raises the question of suffering does not seem to know the first chapters of Genesis. They represent an apparently more advanced stage in divine pedagogy, whereby man is made God's partner, as it were, in his own origins, since his woes are the result of a *fall* for which he is fully responsible: a deliberate refusal on man's part, the consequences of which had been explicitly foretold to him (Gen 3).

If we read the story of Genesis as an attempt (also inspired) to clear God of any responsibility for the evil seemingly inherent to the universe, we will undoubtedly grasp its most profound aspect. St. Paul drew from it a fantastic vision of creation "subjected to vanity" (by man) and "groaning in labor pains", "hoping to be set free from the bondage of corruption and to enter the freedom of the glory of God's children" (Rom 8:19-23; cf 5:12-21). St. Paul thus established a solidarity between the history of the world and the history of man by maintaining that the first is somewhat dependent on the second; this gives him an uninterrupted, overall view of the evolution of the universe, in which he ascribes to the *sin* of creatures those aspects of creation that appear incompatible with the Creator's goodness.

One last step will take us to the end of this "line of thought" which begins on the first page of Revelation. Without setting aside St. Paul, for whom "living is Christ" (Phil 1:21), contemplating the agony and death of the Lord will reveal its ultimate meaning in the form of an actual event. In order to grasp it fully, we must note that, if God is innocent in the story of Genesis, he does not appear to be involved in it. Man alone bears the consequences of his deliberate disobedience. That is because his relationship with God is still that of a subject with his sovereign: it is not a nuptial relationship in which *reciprocity* is the rule. Jesus' agony and crucifixion bring out the nuptial nature of the creative act by revealing that sin wounds love and ultimately causes the death of God. With most tragic realism, God thus changes sides and becomes a victim, but he never ceases to be creator of this torn universe in which *he is the first victim* whenever one of his creatures must endure unjust suffering. Indeed, we would think it wrong to torture a fly by pulling off its wings and taking pleasure in its pain before killing it. The respect we feel for the smallest insect is evidence of an infinite love which confers on every creature a mysterious dignity, by the commitment implied in the act of creation.

At last, we are back to where we started, when, on the question of God's fatherhood, we wondered whether it could be understood as the infinitely generous wish to awaken in every creature, according to its capabilities, a calling to love and freedom that makes it, in some way, similar to the Holy Trinity.

We have paved the way for a clearly positive answer. God is Spirit and the whole universe is destined to participate in the dignity of the spirit, through the nuptial consent that intelligent creatures have been enabled to give in his name. God *is* Love: he can only want a world in which creatures use being—given to them—to achieve total giving, the very foundation of an authentic father-son relationship: all feelings of dependence disappear in the outpouring of mutual intimacy (cf.1 Jn 3:1). The degree of freedom granted to reasonable creatures, capable of consciously establishing this relationship, is measured against the Cross. Because of this unlimited autonomy, we begin to understand how important is the mediation of creatures and how the universe can be hanging on their consent, as St. Paul suggests in his Epistle (8:19-23). The result of their refusal is God's death—in the Word Incarnate—and the history of man and all other creatures is then shrouded in divine tragedy.

That is the absolute evil at the root of all evils: "*L'Amore non è amato*" (Love is not loved [Jacopone da Todi]). St. Francis, St. Catherine of Siena, St. Teresa of Avila, St. John of the Cross, St. Margaret-Mary, St. Thérèse of Lisieux, all known for their great "compassion", understood this, and they decided to assume part of the divine burden to counterbalance all the refusals to love that crucify the Lord, wherever the "weight" holds "grace" in check.

Pascal, too, heard the call of the Cross, the only answer to the "scandal" of evil which, it bears repeating, is absolute only because of the commitment whereby "the first Love" has bound Himself to the universe, a universe where He can only reveal himself as freedom through our own freedom. "Jesus will be in agony even to the end of the world. We must not sleep during that time." We shall add, "since the beginning of the world", and remain faithful to these words in which Pascal has intimately confided to us the depth of his faith.

Remarkably, it is precisely this mysterious "frailty" of God that struck Claudel on that Christmas of 1886. His boredom had led him to Notre-Dame in Paris with the hope of experiencing some esthetic emotion in the half-light of the nave that exuded silence. He was overwhelmed when he heard God's "*de profundis*" being chanted during second vespers. He was unable to resist this call in which he suddenly recognized "God's heartrending innocence and eternal beginnings".

If the author of the *Book of Job* had known and understood this testimony, he would not have written his masterpiece and opened up an abyss which the Cross alone could fill. Between him and Claudel, there is Jesus Christ, the sacrificial Lamb through whom the death of God becomes part of our history.

8

The True Weigher of Souls

André Maurois wrote a delightful little book, *Le Peseur d'âmes* (The weigher of souls) in which he relates the experiments of an English physician who served in the First World War. This physician claimed he noticed a difference in weight between a living body and a corpse. He concluded that the soul itself had weight, which he planned to quantify through research. In spite of the fanciful nature of his plans, the title of the book is nonetheless very suggestive, and we can draw inspiration from it in today's meditation on the mystery of Redemption.

Jesus, indeed, is the true weigher of souls and, on the scales of his love, he weighs each soul against the weight of his own life.

When we read, in *De Beatitudine*, that God submits to his intelligent and saintly creatures as if each one were his God, we may think that this is a mystical hyperbole pertaining to poetic language and not to be taken literally. And yet, the most ordinary Christian believes that Christ really died for him and for his salvation: a cross standing by the roadside can have no other meaning for him than this immolation made for his sake. We must therefore admit, along with the humblest of faithful, that Jesus has truly written, at the core of history, this prodigious equation: for God, *a human being = God.*

We can only understand this—inasmuch as that is possible—if we acknowledge that the communication of God's innermost being is the very meaning of creation, which inaugurates a nuptial plan best expressed, in human terms, by the phrase *you are me* of the old Hindu ritual. It is by means of this identification that was expressed, in an ancient custom, the consent that constitutes marriage. The same phrase, "you are me", applied to the origin of the world, forms the basis for the redemptive equation—for God, a human being = God—while shedding light on it.

Mystics are right when they consider the mystical marriage with God as the *normal* outcome of a Christian life completely true to its baptismal vocation. This is already suggested in St. Paul's Epistle to the Corinthians, in an excerpt we have so often referred to, where he best expresses his apostolic mission: "I feel a divine jealousy for you, for I promised you in marriage to one spouse so as to present you as a chaste virgin to Christ" (2 Cor 11:2). St. John of the Cross, the mystical Doctor *par excellence*, takes up this theme again in the *Spiritual Canticle*, orchestrating it with all the resources that the loftiest poetry can draw from a most authentic experience. He expresses it in particularly moving words in stanza xxxv, which begins with these two verses:

Let us rejoice, Beloved,
And let us go see ourselves in your beauty.

The commentary adds this clarification: "Being transformed into your beauty [...] I shall be you in your beauty and you will be me in your beauty, because your beauty itself will be my beauty." Again, we find the magnificent equivalent of the phrase "you are me" just quoted.

What we have here is thus, in the most authentic Christian tradition, an interpersonal exchange whereby God lives our life and we live his, in keeping with the fundamental requirement of a nuptial relationship, which can only be sustained by the constant giving of one's person.

So, once more, we find that love is the bond and the ultimate meaning of being, in ourselves first, but also, with our essential participation, on all levels of creation. Since it is impossible for us to reach the depths of our own being, and of others, without being rooted in God, we begin to understand that the universe (of which we are a part) cannot attain its true unity without being connected, through us, to the divine Source. All its joints become dislocated when the love, which we have the responsibility to communicate, no longer gives it form. In other words, the *evil* that we do, just as good, its opposite, has a *cosmic* dimension: it wreaks havoc in proportion to the elevation that would be achieved by the universe through our identification with God. Therefore, *Redemption* also concerns the entire cosmos, as St. Paul teaches us when he affirms Christ's primacy over all things, on earth as well as in heaven (Rom 8:19-22; Eph 1:10; Col 1:15-20).

But what meaning should be given to the word Redemption? (*apolutrôsis:* Rom 8:23; Eph 1:7; Col 1:14; cf. *lutron:* Mk 10:45; Mt 20:28, which means "buying back", freeing a captive by means of a ransom, the ransom here being the blood, shed by Christ, the life he gave, in a word, his death.) Several interpretations, based on the literal sense of the word "ransom", have popularized the idea of a debt, infinite and beyond our means, incurred by sin toward divine justice, one that a Man-God alone could pay. St. Anselm is credited for having given this argument its strictest legal form. It was commonly taught with the basics from catechism. We find it in a note from *The Jerusalem Bible* on Mt 20:28: "Through sin, human beings incur a debt toward divine justice, the death penalty required by law [...]. To free them from the slavery of sin and death [...] Jesus will pay the ransom and discharge the debt with the price of his blood [...], thus dying in place of the guilty." (Cf. similar notes on Rom 3:24 and 2 Cor 5:21.)

Justice certainly requires that atonement for a wrong, whenever possible, be commensurate with the violation. But in the case of a unilateral break-up in a loving relationship, what atonement can the innocent party expect if he persists in loving? The parable of the Prodigal Son (Lk 15:11-32) corresponds exactly to this situation and suggests another way, one which Gandhi himself sensed through his own human experience in which is revealed a most moving sense of redemption. He himself tells us that, every time he was informed, upon his return from a trip, of a serious offence committed by some disciple of his ashram, he would begin by fasting before calling in the culprit. The latter, as a rule, was so touched by the penance the Mahatma had inflicted on himself for his sake that he would spontaneously repent.

Our own experience, on this point, confirms the teachings of this advocate for non-violence. We know that the only chance of defusing an enmity, which our opponent justifies by laying all the blame on us, is to overcome our pride and make the first move. This way, he will be able to conquer his own pride and avoid feeling humiliated before us. All the more reason for us to do so in a seriously jeopardized marital relationship: it is impossible to make up with a spouse, and renew a love to which one's whole life is committed, without shedding the old self and offering one's partner a boundless inner space. Indeed, a rejected lover has no other recourse, if he is to remain faithful, but to love ever more generously the partner who loves no more—even if he should die in the process—so as to find new reasons to love in his totally gratuitous gift.

Is not this generosity, which human love is sometimes capable of showing, a reflection of God's own? Could it even appear were it not prompted by the intuition of an *infinite good* present in love, whose encounter could be jeopardized by the slightest appearance of constraint? Indeed, this good can only be recognized through one's inner liberation, which it alone can bring about and which is an absolute freedom, since it is an *infinite good*. But there is no other infinite good except God himself. Hence, it is God who ultimately induces us to step back—in order to defuse any conflict—and to counterbalance, with the fidelity of our love, all the rejections we may have to suffer. It is inconceivable that God's redemptive action not be in accordance with something he himself inspired. The washing of the feet (Jn 13) permits of no doubt in this respect.

And so evil, I mean absolute evil which specifically constitutes sin, is the rejection or the break of the nuptial bond that God wants to establish with us and, through us, with the whole universe. Evil makes man live outside himself, outside God and outside everything. It quenches the Spirit (cf. 1 Thess 5:19). It turns us into things in a world of things, of which we bear the weight in and outside ourselves. Since our freedom is not actualized in self-liberation, it prevents God from appearing to us as absolute freedom. The meaning of creation escapes us, since we are incapable of expressing toward any part of reality the Love that we refuse to accept in ourselves. Our vision of the world becomes fragmented. Our *origin* is lost in the primeval mists of the first syntheses of amino acids, since we give up the chance of becoming our own origin, today, in the light of a new birth tied to our consent; on the other hand, our *end* is shrouded in the mystery of death, since we fail to equate it with the Presence within ourselves, the only Way to ourselves. Caught between these two uncertainties, our values collapse. We no longer know on what to found our inviolability and our dignity, our freedom and our responsibility. We cannot distinguish clearly good from evil, for lack of a firm reference to an *absolute* which asserts its presence—and intermittently at that—only through subjective passions that monopolize and distort it.

If such is the havoc wrought by sin when its rule is consolidated, the fact remains that, from the beginning—as in a marriage breakdown—sin is essentially a rejection of love, and only love can dry up the source of evil and undo the harm done. Indeed, it cannot be defeated if love is not awakened in the hearts of men, thanks to the faithful

Love that never grows weary of loving them. Jesus offers a transparent model of the *recreating* power of love in his dialogue with the Samaritan woman, one that never ceases to amaze us. Jesus reminds this creature of flesh and blood that she is *also* spirit, by revealing to her the God-Spirit whom she will be able to worship in spirit as soon as she discovers Him, deep down in her heart, as a spring of life eternal. He thus frees her from a law—perceived as something outside herself—that she no doubt violated because she felt constrained and alienated by it—and he leads her to the infinite Good inside herself, as the Love which alone can fulfill her.

In this encounter is recreated, as it were, the nuptial situation which fits the Creator's plan. What Jesus teaches the Samaritan woman is that she can indeed have interpersonal ties with God. The good he is urging her to do is to give of her person: she will be born in this encounter with God recognized as the Love eager to enter into a spirit-to-spirit relationship with her, and who will draw her to him through the *freedom* brought about in her by the Gift that he is.

I believe that we can understand man's mission towards humanity and the universe in a similar perspective. Essentially, this mission entails the responsibility to free creation from the rule of sin—which is the refusal to love —by bringing it back to the nuptial level where, at last, it can be fulfilled. This amounts to a new genesis, "more glorious" than the first, nevertheless realized only *at the cost of his own life*.

Why at this cost? We already began to answer this question when we noted that, on the level of human love, it is only through self-sacrifice that the faithful partner may hope to win back the heart of the unfaithful one. Furthermore, such a renewed conquest has to do with the *supreme dimension of being*, since it is the very person of the loved one that must be induced to commit again to the relationship he has broken. The one who still loves must reach the other in the depths of his being, while respecting his inviolability through total self-denial. Here, we touch upon a mystery of creation: it has its roots in the self-divesting in which divine charity is eternally realized.

However, human love is not the last resort. Even if it fails to revive a relationship, all is not irremediably lost. In Elizabeth Leseur's diary, found after her death, her husband discovered the bond she had wanted to create between him and herself. And this bond, which was God, was indeed established when he converted thanks to the posthumous encounter. Undoubtedly, as long as she lived, she offered up her suffering for him, hoping for the conversion to happen; it would have been a consummation of the love of Christ, who had died for him as well as for her. Her wish was not to be fulfilled in her lifetime. She certainly had a part in the conversion and she played it heroically, but his return to God, so ardently implored, did not depend on her alone. She knew this, and she aspired to be nothing more than the instrument of grace, of which she was not the source.

Christ, on the other hand, is the very last resort. Just as his humanity lives on in the Word, so is the whole universe destined to live on in his humanity, to be one with it and, through it, to be linked to the Divinity in a nuptial bond. This nuptial bond, as we said, is the only one that fits the Creator's plan, since it is the same Charity that

God pours out and through which he relinquishes himself in the flow of intradivine relationships, principle and end of all things. But the universe assumed by Christ as Word Incarnate is a universe *disintegrated by the wound of sin.* How can it be "fulfilled" by Christ, as Bérulle would say, without his whole person counterbalancing with love all the rejections that have contributed to depersonalize and disfigure it? It is not enough for him to "preach" and exhort to conversion the world he has wedded in the very same relationship that binds him to God: he must commit his whole being to it, emptying of his own self, as it were, in order to recreate it by giving himself to the world with all the love that he is. This is what St. Paul leads us to understand when he says that Christ, "who knew no sin", was *"made sin* [by God] for our sake, so that in him we might become the righteousness of God." (2 Cor 5: 21)

No words could express the mystery of Redemption more profoundly and more succinctly, and at the same time (as we shall see), shed light on the mystery of the Incarnation, to bring us back in the end to the mystery of the Holy Trinity. The Trinity's eternal communion of love wants to spread to the whole of creation, in order to enable it to take charge of itself through those creatures who are endowed with intelligence and freedom. In fact, as soon as they were able to make choices, these creatures rejected the nuptial status offered to them. Countless generations have ratified the *first refusal to be one's own origin*, thus preventing the human species as a whole from being born of the spirit and the universe from being elevated, through the spirit, to what should have been its natural culmination. Death, the consequence of the original refusal (Rom 5:12), is first a spiritual death. We can say that it is the death of God in man, as truly as God is the Life of our life when we are in a state of grace. If man can so easily kill man, is it not because this solidarity with God has been broken and, as a result, man's face has lost what made it sacred?

Needless to say, the death of God in man does not affect God in his eternity. God cannot lose anything because he has always given everything, and his life is precisely this infinite Gift that he is. The fact remains that this failure, caused by man's deliberate absence, is the most disastrous catastrophe from the viewpoint of His love, as will be revealed by God's personal intervention in our history through Jesus Christ. God's love persists in its will to reach us—such is the very principle of creation.

Indeed, in the Word made flesh, eternal Love takes a visible form, and the death of God in us is expressed in a real death, whereby the "depths of God" will be manifested in a tangible way.

From this human death of the Creator, we immediately learn that the *Good* is Someone who proves to be the Love forever offered to our love, who sacrifices himself out of love for us, so that, at last, we may become love in his Love. We had initially thought of good as a law imposed from the outside, threatening our autonomy and hampering our freedom; in order to assert our independence, we allowed ourselves to be enslaved and we indulged in all the despicable acts of our uptight, strangely resentful narcissism. And now, we see the error of our ways and our cruelty in the Love wounds of the crucified Lord in his agony; at that moment, *Evil* appears as the death of God, in a refusal to be inextricably implied in the refusal to love.

Jesus, the Word Incarnate, who forever stands in solidarity with God, man and his entire universe, is struck head-on by humanity's constant rejections of God, who is disarmed by his own love in the face of human freedom, relentlessly bent on self-destruction because it fails to recognize the self-denial that would fulfill it. And so, Jesus, the "Prince of Life", dies of *our death*; of the same sordid inner death that is repeatedly brought into our lives by the instinctual drives to which we give in. He dies of this death to deliver us from it and give us the nuptial status, where our *yes* is expected to seal God's eternal *yes* in us. He was "made sin" in his absolute innocence in order to abolish the reign of sin within us and in all creation at one with us.

At the very heart of history is thus written in blood the equation of *sacrifice*, which reveals and restores our greatness, a sacrifice in which Jesus offers and is offered up: he is both priest and victim, the God who forgives and the God who is immolated, not by virtue of a legal sentence that would have made forgiveness dependent on this dreadful atonement, but because the Word made flesh that he is subsists in eternal self-divesting; he only aspires to communicate himself to us, and assumes us as we are, committing his sovereign freedom to set us free from our willful enslavement.

Mystics who offer themselves up as victims in order to participate as fully as possible in the Passion of the Lord spontaneously rediscover this twofold identification: with God, over whom they lament because he is the unloved Love (Jacopone da Todi), and with human beings who "un-create" themselves by refusing to love him. These mystics also discover that only giving of oneself totally and freely can break down, *from within*, intentional hard-heartedness. Such resistance can only be overcome by the generosity of love that is ready to accept it, as Thérèse of Lisieux, yet a child, had already understood when she implored with all her soul that Pranzini be saved.

The remission of sins does not just clear our debt and let us off without punishment, but it marks the resurgence of divine life in a being freed of itself and ready to welcome it. That explains these magnificent words about the Holy Spirit in a liturgical prayer: *ipse est remissio omnium peccatorum* (he himself is the remission of all sins).

These words fully apply to Christ the Savior by also underlying the *interiority* of his redemptive action, which aims at recreating in man his nuptial freedom, and that will turn him into a creator again in a universe he is destined to make sacred by his love.

When we say "man" in the singular, we must not forget that Jesus' redemptive action concerns each individual man, but that it is multiplied by billions of billions of billions of individuals, without ever ceasing to be personal to each, from the beginning of history to the end of time. Indeed, universality of love results from each individual heart being embraced in its uniqueness. When we think that the Lord assumed each and every human being this way, in his deepest essence, and that he did it in the short span of a career cut off on the threshold of maturity (humanly speaking), we cannot imagine the burden which the "weigher of souls" took upon himself, since he valued each soul as dearly as his own life.

Such a gift reveals something deeply moving about the greatness of our own life, which, however, is unrelated to the use we make of it in our daily existence. The mediocrity of our lives, as one of Proust's characters would say, has been "raised to the level of an institution". It is true that heroism is rare, but it is generally paid the tribute it deserves. Fr. Kolbe's gesture in Auschwitz is universally admired. A certain sense of "the human Everest" lives in the hearts of most people and makes them unanimous in recognizing true greatness, which is probably more frequent than one might think. Selma Lagerlöf and Mary Webb have found noble traits among the lowly, traits all the more striking as they are due entirely to the person and not the situation. The interest aroused by art —music in particular—is also evidence of a longing for transcendence, which implies a denial of the mediocrity to which everyday life is doomed. And yet, the Cross that holds the entire universe in a divine embrace has not been generally understood as a call to greatness, in spite of liturgy's *mirabilius reformasti*.

If Jesus has restored the dignity of human nature and made it still more admirable than when it was created, it is surely so that it can find "overflowing life" anew (Jn 10:10) in the depths of divinity.

Many Christians have not experienced this plenitude, no doubt because they have not discovered the nuptial relationship that is at the source of creation, and that Christ has the mission of restoring. In their eyes, sin was simply a transgression of divine law, worthy of eternal punishment, which Christ spared us by clearing, through his sacrifice, the insurmountable debt we had incurred. The condition, of course, was that we appeal to his mediation through the means of salvation he has instituted and that, henceforth, we abide by God's commandments. Such an over-simplification of Redemption could certainly not inspire the verses of the *Spiritual Canticle* that ring with heartfelt love. From this viewpoint, we would be, in our relationship with God, like a couple who, setting love aside, would base their relationship on the obligations of husband and wife set down in common law.

Clearly, love makes more exacting demands than any law could ever formulate, since it commits the whole person *from within*, under the impetus of freedom seeking its fulfillment in self-denial. The emotion expressed in the *Spiritual Canticle* could only well up in a soul emptied of itself to welcome the infinite Presence, which alone can fill it; it is afire with the fullness of love, made palpable in words that are "bearers of life."

Therefore, it is better not to dwell on a legalistic interpretation of Redemption. The Good is Someone to love, who can die, and indeed who did, because of our refusal to love. "Jesus will be in agony even to the end of the world; we must not sleep during that time." We have already heard Pascal's call and, following his inspiration, we have added: "Jesus is in agony since the beginning of time", in order to enfold all of history in the embrace of the Cross and discover the meaning of the human adventure in that equation, written in blood, that made us equal to God.

The Lord adds a new dimension to our intimate ties with him in the following statement, which shows his personal commitment in whatever aspect of our lives is most likely to touch us: "Whoever does God's will is my brother, and my sister, and my mother" (Mk 3:35). These last words never fail to amaze me: '*is my mother*'", meaning that *divine motherhood* is offered every soul, according to the Venerable Bede's interpretation (in another context): "Conceiving the Word spiritually by listening with faith and by doing good, begetting and nourishing him, so to speak, in one's own heart and in the heart of our neighbor." The image of motherhood is even more moving than the nuptial image, which must not, of course, be excluded from that higher love that contains all others. It summons us to lavish our most attentive care on the divine Life that wants to be born of us, as it were, and be the ultimate secret of our innermost being, the heart of our heart.

One cannot express more movingly the extent to which our consent is essential for the advent of God in our history and that of the universe, if indeed His true face is to be revealed: God as the Spirit that appeals to our spirit, in the virginal inner exchange in which our freedom is realized.

This brings us back to the ineffable dialogue of the Annunciation: Mary's *yes*, in the unique and unparalleled gift of her whole person, makes her the Mother of the Lord and our mother. It is to this mother that we shall entrust, with filial devotion, the *yes* we must become for Christ to be born in today's humanity.

9

Silence for God

According to an apparently unfounded etymology, the French verb "connaître"—to know—is "co-naître", as Claudel used to write it, that is, "to be born with". In other words, we become what we know by a kind of identification whereby the knowing subject takes the immaterial "form" of the known object and recreates it within himself, in order to experience it from within by integrating it into his own life. In itself, this identification poses no difficulty as far as objective knowledge is concerned, since it does not involve any personal commitment. For instance, what molecular interactions in the brain condition memory? This question is as yet unresolved, but its solution depends entirely on the experiments that an ever-advancing technology will very likely make possible. However, it is quite another matter when it comes to interpersonal knowledge which concerns the interpenetration of inner beings, inviolable in themselves, who can reach each other only through freely accepted mutual communication.

Then, knowledge essentially entails a commitment and varies according to the degree of the commitment, as universally evidenced by married life. The commitment itself naturally depends on the inner requirements that each spouse brings to the marriage. The important thing is that they be maintained approximately at same level. Too sharp a difference makes a genuine encounter of the two impossible, and soon the spouses will be strangers to each other. Ideally, these requirements should evolve together at the same rate, and each spouse should constantly enrich the other by fulfilling changing needs.

In the case of our knowledge of God, which is eminently interpersonal—God being Spirit—the difference of levels appears insurmountable a priori. How can we possibly reach with Him the nuptial level we have discussed at great length, considering what we are and what He is? At the conceptual level, it seems impossible, and apophatic theology will logically conclude that we can only know of Him what He is not. Through personal experience, we feel, along with St. Augustine, that He is closer to us than our own innermost self and that he is truly the only path to ourselves. It is in Him that we know ourselves, just as we reach others in their innermost being only by sharing with them in His Presence. In a sense, He is thus more easily knowable to us than we are to ourselves, for he is the Sun of the intelligible universe making reality visible to our mind. However—and this is where we find the commitment required in any interpersonal knowledge—His light reaches us *effectively* (as one inner being is internalized by another) only insofar as we are open to the Gift that He is—by transforming ourselves in countless stages—just as our self-liberation testifies to the very real change occurring in us.

At this point, there emerges a difficulty, too rarely emphasized, that I will attempt to bring out. If knowledge of God were confined to individual experience, each one could testify only to whatever he had experienced up to the moment of expressing it, without being able to assert anything beyond what he had actually lived. This was certainly true in the case of Socrates, Plato or Aristotle; they could not refer to a divine revelation which would have surpassed in insight anything their genius, together with their virtues, could have attained. On the other hand, whoever has the benefit of a supernatural revelation, handed down by a tradition that has given it an elaborate canonical form, may be tempted to take advantage of it without personal commitment on his part. This is evident in the tragic conflict that pitted Jesus against the doctors of Law and the priests who will eventually plot his death.

This temptation will recur, in an infinitely more serious form, at the heart of Christianity, precisely because its doctrine and requirements are sublime. People will defend or preach the *Gospel*, without feeling really concerned about the rebirth that Jesus talks about to Nicodemus (Jn 3:3), and which implies a radical transformation of oneself. They will possibly limit themselves to the letter of the sacred text as to an eloquent theme for Sunday sermons that fits well into the ritual functions they must carry out. If they want its message to impact more directly on life, they will introduce political and social stands in it, even dogmatic and moral ones that meet the expectations of their audience or address the personal problems that obsess them. In some cases, the Tradition they champion becomes completely identified with their own way of understanding it; in others, they will distance themselves from it to be at the leading edge of progress. One way or the other, they will relate the divine Word to their own temperament, ambitions and resentments, in a word, to their own passions and subjective perceptions, the very things from which the Word is supposed to set them free.

Heaven forbid that I should pass judgment and condemn these biased positions that compromise the universal nature of the Gospel. They are inevitable if one forgets that knowledge, here more than ever, is linked to a personal commitment which, according to the Word of our Lord, should mean being born again. Undoubtedly, the authority of the Church's magisterium, in its *irrevocable* decisions, is not tied to the virtue of those who exercise it. In carrying out their official mission, they can only reaffirm, with the help of the Holy Spirit, the apostolic testimony with which they are entrusted. But for their testimony to be received "in spirit and in truth", they must live it by fulfilling the requirement of self-liberation that it entails. Otherwise, the message will inevitably be bent to suit the determinisms that enslave us, and the ferment it was meant to be in our lives will be neutralized.

This is a matter of *level of being* and it deserves our most careful consideration. We act spontaneously in accordance with what we are. In order to act differently with the same spontaneity, we have to change what we are, change our very being or, what comes to the same thing, we must find ourselves at a deeper level. When we live at the surface of ourselves, superficial currents sweep us along with all the foam they carry. When, on the other hand, we reach deep down to the center of our being, where our life takes root in God, His presence heals us of our narcissism and we are born to true freedom.

This return to the "Spring of life eternal," essential to a full understanding of faith, can come about only in the regular practice of *silence*. The purpose of this long preamble was to make us aware of its necessity.

I found silence in the Benedictine monastery where I completed my high school education; it was like a wonderful gift that made this abbey the homeland of my soul. I found it again in Paris, among the Benedictine nuns of the rue Monsieur during the years I had the privilege of being their chaplain. There, I witnessed the miraculous appeal it had on so many writers and artists who came to their chapel to breathe it in; for them, this simple place, at the heart of a vast, noisy city, had become a shrine of the spirit.

On this subject—should I have the slightest chance of being heard—I would beseech the contemplative orders, who yearn for "meetings and workshops", and who have hastened to do away with their enclosure in order to open up to the world, to remember that their mission is to open the world to God, by living so intensely of his presence that it may become "an all-consuming fire".

Indeed, the silence in which God reveals himself to our innermost being can only be lived as a secret of love. It implies a process directed by the need to lose sight of ourselves in order to become truly free, until we are but a gaze turned towards Him. Ultimately, in silence, our whole being becomes focused on God and is unified in divine light. In silence, we are cleansed of the prostitution wherby we use words to mimic a perfection that is but a mask without a face. Silence allows us to hear, deep down, at the very root of our being, the *musica callada*, the soundless music which, for St. John of the Cross, is one of God's most moving names.

"To be without speaking is better than to speak without being", wrote St. Ignatius of Antioch (Eph xv, 1). Nothing is closer to the truth, but how dazzling a Word is he who fully *exists*, thanks to the silence he keeps within himself! However, such a masterpiece, the source of all others—every masterpiece is born of silence—is the most difficult thing to achieve: before all else, we are noise in our psyche, essentially made up of that *cosmic ocean* we call the unconscious.

At times, it seems to me that one of the most eloquent vestiges of evolution, in the biological sense, happens to be this subliminal universe whose chaotic power is stirring deep down within ourselves, in the tumult of a colossal fermentation. All kinds of forms can emerge out of these depths, from the most delicate to the most monstrous, thrust up by a force constantly under pressure that can explode in any direction. Art and science, invention and adventure, civilization and barbarism, war and peace, love and hate, virtue and crime, serene contemplation and unleashed frenzy, each, in turn, draw from this huge reservoir of energy the behavior instructions and impulses that prompt us to create or destroy in a sometimes abruptly alternating pattern. Such is the essence of human drama.

This drama is aggravated by the fact that we are generally unaware of being led by our unconscious and the prefabricated ego which, to a large extent, is its product. We are thus quite naturally tempted to stand by the impulses of our unconscious as if they truly expressed what we are. Morality has taught us to contain and control them, and rightly so, but it does not provide us with the means to do it. That is why St. Paul, in chapter 7 of his *Epistle to the Romans*, must sadly take note of his failure, a failure which, by the way, is most enlightening. First, it is a matter of *being* and not of doing. We have here, once again, the nuptial requirement. If the good is Someone to love, it is by becoming someone that we will love him, that we will be able to give wholly of our person, which is what love is. If I only keep my passions at bay, that instinctive part of myself that I repress will remain outside the order I impose on it, without ever making it its own order and its own good. It will thus continue to be what it is, rebelling against the constraints placed on it. Soon, exhausted by the struggle, which in no way undermines the opponent's strength, I will begin to wonder what sense there is in fighting against myself, something that will ultimately appear to me as a rejection of my own reality.

What I must do is let the new order penetrate the depths of my being, and transform all the noise of my untamed passions into music. This will awaken in them a sense of *self-sacrifice* that will impart to them the freedom of the spirit, thus enabling them to feel as *their own* the infinite Good who shall illuminate them, like a sun suddenly rising at the bottom of a cave.

The necessity of reaching deep down in order to completely divest our being of its own self—thus assuring it of the benefit of radical purification—is all the more vital as the impulses rising from our unconscious may be explained by events buried in early childhood. These escape us completely, as the book *Autobiography of a Schizophrenic Girl*, among others, teaches us. I shall refer to a few aspects of this book and also to *Symbolic Reali-*

zation: A New Method of Psychotherapy Applied to a Case of Schizophrenia by Marguerite Sechehaye. Mrs. Sechehaye treated and cured the author of the diary, whom she named Renée.

At three months, Renée was supposedly suffering from gastritis. A strict diet was prescribed on the basis of this false diagnosis. In reality, the baby was being starved to death. A sensible grandmother saved her just in time, took complete charge of the child and lavished care on her until the age of eleven months. Back with her parents, the little girl was torn apart by the absence of her tender caretaker and lived in an atmosphere totally lacking in understanding. After the birth of five children, Renée being the eldest, the father abandoned the family who became totally destitute. At the age of five, Renée experienced the first symptoms of schizophrenia: the stages of the developing illness are related in her diary. She suddenly found herself before a dislocated, mineral world, unreal, barren and hostile. At fifteen, the disorders reappeared and became even more serious. In order to keep her place among normal people, she struggled alone, as best she could, against this terrifying disintegration of her world. She developed extremely aggressive tendencies that she turned against herself and that eventually took the form of orders to destroy herself (by fire in particular), orders she resisted with all her might. She finally gave in and placed her right hand on burning embers. Caught in the act by her office manager, who immediately notified the physician from the Council for the Supervision of the Mentally Ill, Renée was finally confined to a mental institution and placed under the care of Mrs. Sechehaye who had already started to practice her "analytical psychotherapy". A great ordeal began for Renée: fear, a feeling of universal guilt, of being forbidden to live, the temptation to commit suicide and the refusal to eat led her, amidst the distortions of reality, to complete autism. She remained walled up in this state, unable to communicate with others through standard language. She invented her own, infantile or incoherent, which no one understood.

However, one element in her behavior caught Marguerite Sechehaye's attention. The only food Renée was allowed to have under the "system" her psyche was subjected to was apples, provided she could pick them herself, still living from the life of the tree that produced them. Following an angry outburst from a farming woman who did not take kindly to her petty thieving, the significance of which she clearly did not understand, Renée referred to them as "Mama's apples", pointing to the psychoanalyst's chest.

In a flash, the therapist understood the link between the apple and mother's breast. She gave a section of an apple to the young girl who was leaning her head on her shoulder, and said: "Now, Mama is going to feed her little Renée. It is time to drink the good milk from Mama's apples."[1] This *symbolic realization* had a miraculous effect. Suddenly, Renée seemed normal again. Presuming too hastily that Renée was totally cured and insisting that she behave as an adult, the psychotherapist induced a

---

[1] Renée, *Autobiography of a Schizophrenic Girl*, with analytic interpretation by Marguerite Sechehaye, translated by Grace Rubin-Rabson. Signet Book, New York, 1970, p. 70.

relapse worse than all the previous ones. But the method which had been successful the first time still held all its potential. Thanks to the symbolic behavior with the apple, to which were added a plush tiger and a monkey, a rag baby doll and the "soft green half-light" of a room shielded from noise where the patient could find the "prenatal paradise she longed for", a lasting cure was achieved at last, with much patience, sound intuition and boundless love.

We see in this case, exemplary in all its aspects, that a trauma, going back to the age of three months and totally unknown to the young girl, had been imprinted on her unconscious as the mother's rejection of the child she was starving, a rejection which rose to the surface of Renée's consciousness only as the torment of being forbidden to live.

No one can know directly the childhood traumas which may perturb, more or less seriously, the adult psyche. By telling us of the devastating effects they can have, the *Autobiography of a Schizophrenic Girl* makes us aware—there lies its main interest—of the importance of our unconscious and of the need to "evangelize" it, to explore it from the bottom up, as it were, in order to harmonize its most secret impulses.

Marguerite Sechehaye appropriately reminds us that it cannot be reached by abstract language. We must speak to the unconscious in the warm, flesh-and-blood language of symbols, resonant with affective overtones, a language that can move us by evoking "correspondences" suggestive of infinity, where freedom can fully expand.

This detour leads us back to *silence*, the *sine qua non* condition for a liberating encounter with the Lord in the depths of our being. Perhaps, through Renée's tragic experience, we now see more clearly that silence must be internalized; it must penetrate the deeper layers of our psyche and ultimately become the silence of love, when the presence of the Beloved becomes the very breath of life. It seems therefore desirable that our silent meditation aim from the start at taking hold of our entire being, and not be reduced solely to a discursive "exercise" on an edifying theme. The cathedral is the jewel box for a morsel of bread. It lives of this morsel, the star to which its forest of pillars leads our steps. But, conversely, it is this morsel of bread that has created the cathedral's boundless space, its soaring vaults, its fiery stained-glass windows. The infinite life contained in the *eucharistic presence*—where, fortunately, God's silence compensates for all our chatter—has fashioned, through the faith it nourishes, this huge vessel of stonework setting sail for eternity; it is this infinite life that reveals to us our eternal goal by giving our journey on earth its ultimate dimension. Symbols thus express, in a way perceptible to the senses, the spiritual impulse that transfigures the "material" it works on and which reverberates in the most secret recesses of our sensibility.

It is essentially the power of symbols, which Christ raised to the dignity of sacraments, that the defenders of the sacred icons wanted to protect, for the sake of faith, during the iconoclastic crisis of the eighth century. They sensed, and rightly so, that piety must not be disembodied, at the risk of creating a dangerous tension between an untamed unconscious, given over to its impulses, and a type of prayer structured on concepts and imposed by a decree of the will. Authentic spirituality demands a creative silence that, in the end, leads to the pacification of all our powers of being and living; this silence can only be born out of an approach to the sacred that imparts its mystery to each one of these powers, as a fulfilling presence.

The effective means of bringing about and achieving such an approach vary according to the situations and the needs that arise from them, according to the times, the cultures and traditions. Happily, modern technology allows us to hear every kind of music, gaze at every masterpiece and relive every discovery right in our own bedroom. Each one can draw from this common treasure whatever elements are necessary to complete his particular spiritual regimen, and thus achieve that state of total silence, which is both the most perfect balance and the most radical act of self-divesting. Indeed, it is by constantly reconquering silence that we truly liberate ourselves and become capable of hearing—in St. Ignatius' words— "the mysterious clamors unfolding in the silence of God." (Eph xix, 1)

10

Jesus, or "Divine Poverty" Personified

In the *interpersonal* dialogue that Revelation is, we have seen that God adapts to humanity, accepting its limitations inasmuch as that is necessary to prompt man to go beyond them, just as a loving mother starts by babbling with her child, while helping him to gradually discover a world which must grow with him. From this viewpoint, revelation may indeed entail some imperfect notions and institutions, which must be ascribed to God's infinitely patient pedagogy that takes man at whatever stage of knowledge he is and leads him to a higher one (cf. Gal 3:24).

These imperfections were all the more unavoidable as Revelation does not pertain to speculative knowledge, as do a professor's teachings to his students, but rather to nuptial knowledge based on commitment and proportional to it. Besides, since man will always be limited in some way, Revelation will be too since it will have to adapt to him. This is all the more true as Revelation normally concerns a *community* whose spiritual progress is generally slower than that of an individual who can grow according to his own specific needs. Let me add that, as a rule, Revelation (in the Old Testament) governs all aspects in the life of the clan or nation as well as of the individual, subjecting all "temporal" matters to "religious" dictates. Observing them all, all the time and under all circumstances, would be nothing short of heroic, and simply cannot be expected of ordinary people (cf. Mk 10:1-12 and Mt 19:1-8); in fact, these dictates provide for some important concessions. If the same conditions had continued to prevail, Revelation could never have reached an unsurpassable and definitive level, since human limitations would always have restricted the ways in which God reveals himself.

The fact that Christianity presents itself precisely as that unsurpassable and definitive revelation presupposes that a radically new event occurred which redefined the problem.

That event is summarized in the short sentence of St. John's Prologue: "The Word became flesh" (1:14), which in everyday language means: "God became man."

The faith of simple people, which I admire the most, adheres spontaneously to this statement, and yet it is most difficult to explain in conceptual terms. It took four centuries, that is until 451, to find a sufficiently balanced wording for the mystery of Christ, by which people lived and died. The difficulty is no smaller today when countless studies in exegesis challenge the statement itself before they even attempt to tackle its meaning. To what extent are problems concerning the texts of the New Testament related to problems of meaning? It is hard to tell. There is no doubt that these texts come down to us from the early Community which, on the whole, stood by them, recognized its faith in them, and referred to them whenever it had to explain and defend it. The principle of "the new order, which is eternal life" (Cf. Ignatius of Antioch, Eph xix, 3), was that of a *God revealed in human form*. In all likelihood, it is the extraordinary nature of such a claim that has attracted to these texts mountains of critical commentaries which the theologian must sort through, and which do sometimes help him to understand them better. Hence, it is on the *meaning* of this fundamental article of our faith that we shall focus our attention.

From the outset, we face the question underlying our meditation: of what God are we speaking, and to what man? "A mind that lives and evolves because it attempts to discern God, whose latent presence it perceives within itself", as Etienne Gilson said about St. Augustine,[1] will naturally carry on its quest according to "the law of interiority"[2] that governs it. In its obscure and intimate experience of the presence of God, the mind will strive to dispel the obscurity by seeking a light expected to rise from within. Indeed, it knows intuitively that God is "inside" (*intus*) and that he escapes us insofar as we are "outside" (*foris*). By going deeper into his contemplation, man cannot fail to find God as the door that leads to his own depths. For it is God who makes man aware of his own self. And what is more, it is to God that man owes his own self since his "self", in its irreducible uniqueness, can only emerge in the silent dialogue in which it is exchanged for His. In short, God always initiates the

---

[1] Etienne Gilson, *Introduction à l'étude de saint Augustin*, 2ᵉ éd., p. 349.

[2] *Ibid.*, p. 94.

presence and man the absence, as Augustine suggested when he said: "You were with me, it is I who was not with You."[3] God is always *already there*, hence he will not have "to come down from heaven" "to put up his tent in our midst" (Jn 1:14). Rather, it is in man that the radical change, implied in the mystery of the Word made flesh, will have to take place.

Before attempting to clarify the nature of this change, we should note that an "Augustinian" mind will spontaneously be led to reflect on the Incarnation when contemplating its own depths, where the experience of God and of self brings the strongest enlightenment, together with the joy of discovering the ultimate answer that both reveals and fulfills a secret aspiration.

The "Augustinian" mind experiences the intimate presence of God as pure interiority with respect to our exteriority, as absolute closeness with respect to our remoteness, as the beyond within ourselves that gently draws us in. On the other hand, a mind that does not start from this inner presence, that externalizes transcendence, perceiving it as an unbridgeable gap between God and his creature, as the beyond outside ourselves, runs the risk of being "shocked" by the idea of God becoming flesh[4] and of finding it difficult to "assimilate". For such a mind, God entering history and revealing himself personally in human form would constitute an unthinkable "defile-

---

[3] *"Mecum eras, et tuum non eram"*, cf. St. Augustine, *Confessions*, X, xxvii, 38.

[4] Couchoud in de Grandmaison, *Jésus-Christ*, II, p. 193.

ment" of divinity, "not only contrary to the very essence of God, but also an affront to his august Majesty."[5]

These two trends may be symbolized by the attitude of the Samaritan woman (Jn 4) before and after her encounter with Christ. Before, she sets God in a sanctuary outside herself, the place of worship *par excellence*. After, she discovers God in the depths of her being as a spring of life eternal.

These differences in attitude are of considerable importance, on the one hand, to understand the various reactions to the affirmation of the Word Incarnate and, on the other, to present this mystery in such a way as to integrate it into our lives, as a wonderful answer to needs it brings out while fulfilling them.

But the great light, here more than anywhere else, is the Holy Trinity; as revealed by and in Jesus, it introduces us to God's innermost being and changes all our ideas about him and, ultimately, about ourselves.

The temptation to turn ourselves into gods ("If there were any gods, how could I bear not being god!" exclaims Nietzsche) presupposes that we perceive God essentially as a power capable of coercing us by crushing our autonomy. Hence the image of greatness that can only express itself by dominating others, using their dependence as a pedestal. Our natural desire to be great, contaminated by this image, inevitably develops in this direction as a craving for power, of which Jesus alone has radically

---

5   Jean Bodin, *VIe siècle, ibid.*, II, p. 168.

cured us by revealing that God's inner life is an eternal communion of love. Once again I will say that, with this intimate revelation from our Lord, it has become possible for the spirit to be fulfilled as it understand itself. God is God, that is, supreme Good and eternal Love, because he achieves the absolute self-divesting that gives him a hold on his being in the very act of communicating it. When we learn this, we immediately begin to see the error of narcissism and its corrupting influence, and we acquire that sense of freedom which will emancipate us from it.

A totally new notion of greatness comes to light in this infinite giving, which is God himself, something we are meant to imitate in ourselves by interacting with him. At the same time, we sense that this total communication of self, the essence of intradivine relationships, is at the origin of Creation. Indeed, creation can only be, in God's own image, an offering of love in a transparent existence freed of itself. Once we discover that such is the vocation of our spirit—the crowning achievement of creation—we may conclude that it is entirely contained in this call to infinite love, as suggested by St. Paul in the eighth chapter of his *Epistle to the Romans* (19-22).

We know only too well how rarely we achieve such total self-divesting that can only result from accepting unconditionally the gift of God, who is always present in the depths of our being. Yet we notice that it is in these moments of self-liberation that we best know God and experience him most strongly as the supreme and innermost reality within ourselves. Besides, nothing prevents God from increasingly becoming the Life of our life.

We note once again, at this turning point in our talk, that God plays a *personalizing and liberating* role in our spiritual life: it is by this role that we know Him as an irrecusable presence, since it is attested by our transformation, which is always strictly dependent on our contact with him.

Moreover, can God the "Spirit" be revealed in any other way than by ultimately becoming an event that changes our life and internalizes it insofar as we accept his coming? What would have become of Christ's message without Pentecost, without this baptism of fire that set it aflame in the hearts of the Apostles?

Starting from these reflections, it seems that we can look at the essential aspect of the Incarnation and have some chance of being on the right track. The idea that God could change is excluded, and his presence is already offered to every human soul, most of the time without its knowledge, as a "spring of life eternal", for God is always *already there*. Therefore, what is completely new about the Incarnation is a change, uniquely profound, that affects Jesus' human nature, in both the personalizing and liberating aspects which characterize divine action in ourselves. As a result, Christ's unique nature becomes the unsurpassable and definitive revelation of God.

Let us note straightaway that this revelation (which is Jesus) bears essentially on the Trinity and, therefore, on the interpersonal relationships at the heart of Divinity. By the way, Jesus affirms them as one who is himself included in them. He speaks of what he lives, he *is* what he reveals. But how?

179

Cardinal de Bérulle admirably sums up traditional Christology in his exhortation to live *in, through* and *for* Jesus, words which are all the more moving as he himself is involved in what he says: "And we must look upon Jesus as our fulfillment, for he is and wants to be, in the same way that the Word is the fulfillment of his human nature. For, just as this nature, considered in its origin, is in the hands of the Holy Spirit who draws it from nothingness and deprives it of subsistence, gives it to the Word so that the Word may invest it and make it his own, surrendering to it and completing it with his own divine subsistence, so are we in the hands of the Holy Spirit: he rescues us from sin, binds us to Jesus as spirit of Jesus, issued from him, acquired by him and sent by him."[6]

What emerges from this text is that the ability to lead a fully autonomous existence (= hypostasis or personality), what we call subsistence, is not realized in Jesus, on the human level, as an enclosure within his human nature which is personalized precisely by the subsistence of the Word, who totally invests it with his power. But the subsistence of the Word is the *infinite self-divesting* that makes him pure relationship with the Father. Therefore, what is communicated to Jesus' humanity is this supreme self-divesting which is also supreme freedom. His human nature is lifted and carried away in the perpetual wave that sweeps the Son into the Father's bosom. The "I" that speaks to us through his lips is subsisting relinquishment, or "divine Poverty" personified.

---

[6] Henri Brémond, *Histoire littéraire du sentiment religieux en France*, vol. 3, p. 79.

We see here, more clearly than anywhere else, the significance of the question: what God are we speaking of? Jesus' divinity is rooted in the Trinity through the personality of the Word in whom his humanity subsists. "The Word communicates to human nature, not his being by nature whereby he is formally God, but his being as a person whereby he subsists in his divine nature."[7] Thus it is as a subsisting relationship, in which "he no longer appropriates anything", that the divine self, through Jesus' humanity invested by him, enters into our history.

Nothing could shed more light on our own selves, for our autonomy, as I have said so many times, is ambiguous. In principle, each one of us, deep down, depends only on himself. That is why our ego secretes its shell with flawless art. But, as a rule, this eagerness to preserve our identity subjects us to our passions, geometric center of all our servitudes. In the name of our dignity, we relentlessly defend the deterministic forces which contradict it, and we confuse the life of the spirit with our ability to manipulate concepts that justify our biases. But how could we have known that the spirit is the power to be our own origin, by becoming radically free of our own selves in the translucent offering of all that we are? How could we have escaped the narcissism whereby we pay homage to ourselves with the being we were given before we met with subsisting self-divesting, which is divine personalism?

---

[7] Ch. V. Héris, *Somme théologique*, III, q. 1-6, *Revue des jeunes*, p. 252.

Jesus' humanity, invested with the Word's subsistence, is "realized" as Bérulle says, by this supreme relinquishing of self, this infinite self-divesting (constituent of intradivine relations) whereby it is radically expropriated of itself and made the witness and the "sacrament" inseparable from the divine self that personalizes it. It is thus the Life of the spirit, in its "eminent model" at the heart of the Trinity, that enters into the world with Jesus in whom "Poverty", which is God, really becomes flesh.

If, from the outset, the meaning of the creative act is the communication of God, this communication is truly, fully and unsurpassably achieved in the actual birth in time of the Word Incarnate, an event which rightly divides our history in two: before and after Jesus Christ.

If I have succeded in making myself understood, it becomes evident that the mystery of Jesus can be understood in different ways, depending on the light in which we see it. We can view it against the Trinity as a background, so to speak, starting from this eternal communion of love in which life springs forth in the infinite self-divesting of reciprocal offering. Or we can perceive it starting from a God whose transcendence is conceived in such a way as to make Him the great Separate One, who could not "dwell among us" "without defiling himself".

God is charity and charity reaches out to another to be itself. *"Dilectio in alterum tendit ut caritas esse possit."* That is the whole point. It is this charity, burning at the heart of the Trinity, that assumes Jesus' humanity and totally divests it of itself, communicating its own movement to it in that eternal filial relationship that personalizes it.

This "absolutely gratuitous gift from God to Christ's humanity"[8] concerns all mankind and the whole universe. Any grace implies a mission, and the more grace abounds, the more the scope of the mission expands. When grace is infinite, the mission has no bounds. Christ, whose human nature is completely given over to the Word in whom it subsists, is also entirely open to creation which "came into being through him" (Jn 1:3, 10). "He is at home inside others" and his mission is precisely to make them children of God (Jn 1:12) by freeing them from themselves. He is ecumenical in the very structure of his being. His receptivity, his capacity to accept us is equal to the twofold self-divesting, divine and human, of the love which the Apostles were amazed to discover when he knelt down to wash their feet. He is giving personified, and he wants to inspire us to give, and make us universal by breaking down, from within, the barriers that our possessiveness constantly erects in and between ourselves.

St. Paul has brought out this ecumenical aspect in the person and action of the Lord by maintaining that He is the second Adam (Rom 5:12-20; 1 Cor 15:22, 45-49). For Paul, Christ is the principle of a new creation where grace is overabundant, where death is overcome at the same time as sin, where we become members of one another by becoming members of Christ, where nothing can separate

---

8 Ch. V. Heris, *Somme théologique*, "Le Verbe incarné", I, p. 254.

us from the love of God, who adopts us as his children in Jesus.

This new creation is proclaimed in the virginal conception of Jesus, born of the Holy Spirit through Mary's contemplation. The human species is thus transcended and all individuals are mobilized to serve it through sexuality. It is the person in us that is affected by this event, as each one is called to free himself from the "flesh and blood" determinisms (Jn 1:13) and to turn himself into the center of a universe which, through his offering, is given a new beginning. Each individual will thus become a common good by contributing to the liberation of others through his own liberation.

We have already noted, I believe, the ambiguity of the term *universal*; it can designate either *mankind as a whole*, as in "universal postal union", or *a personal worth,* which develops in the recesses of the spirit and can be passed on to every person as something that enhances his own innermost being.[9] In this sense, it means a greatness we must be or become in order to create it in others, for it is transmitted from within to within, from inside one being to inside another being, just as a master's knowledge awakens that of his pupils inasmuch as it shines in him.

Christ's universality is to be understood in this sense. It concerns the depths of each one's being and aims at making each man universal by the gift of His presence

---

[9] This is what we mean when we say, for example, that Michelangelo is a universal genius (architect, sculptor, painter, poet).

offered to each; and this, by abolishing the inner boundaries that imprison him inside himself and set him against others.

I felt this most vividly in Byblos, as I have often told, in the presence of a skeleton kept in a broken jar where it had been lying, curled up like a fetus, since about 3,500 before our era. What link could there be between this human being, of whose existence these bones were a reminder, and myself contemplating them? That is the question which kept me by these remains (which have since disappeared). Was it a purely biological link—a sense of belonging to the same species—like the link we could imagine between a live lion and the carcass of one of its distant ancestors? Or was it a personal link uniting both of us in the same spiritual adventure, thus making us contemporaries, as it were? This question made me aware of how narrow our living space is—a space in which the only beings that matter are those we need to be happy—and also of how immensely difficult it is for us to put ourselves on a universal plane in a way other than an abstract and theoretical one, requiring no true commitment. It is then that the figure of the second Adam appeared to me as the only answer that could support the claim of a personal and ever-living link between all generations. Jesus, indeed, is not just a link in the chain of successive generations, but rather, it is He who holds the whole chain together and gives it unity by directing all of it to realizing the same plan. And that is precisely why his birth is out of the ordinary, coming to the world as he does from the supernaturally fruitful virginity of the second Eve.

This reminder, through a skeleton, of Christ's universality made me sense once again the infinite *self-divesting* that enabled him to gather us all, from within, into a vast spiritual body, vitalized by the flow of his presence and unified by the communication of the absolute freedom that he is.

If I use again the term self-divesting, it is because it seems the most apt to introduce the mystery of Jesus in our lives. Indeed, we do not have to scratch the veneer of our apparent virtues very deeply to come upon *our subjective passions* (individual or collective), the most widespread and dangerous form of the spirit of possessiveness. We think we are what we appear to be in the words and attitudes that reflect the position we hold or adopt. We proclaim lofty principles, covering ourselves with their universality, supported and applauded by its supporters; we resort to winning slogans, we flatter those whose arbitration we seek by stirring up old ghosts that revive old animosities; we may pose as victims or heroes and, in the end, we are involved so deeply that we can no longer step back. However, all the noise betrays a fundamental flaw and reveals the prejudices and choices of our unconscious: it is the unconscious that invents those *false absolutes*, in the name of which we wage our battles, and that mobilizes the false absolutes of the opposition, also generally set on the level of instinctual passion. These antagonisms, raised to the level of absolutes, generate all forms of violence and war, as attested by our sordid and cruel century.

When I speak of false absolutes, I do not mean to deny that there are just causes which must be championed. I am simply pointing out that these inevitably deteriorate when they are taken over by subjective passions (individual and collective), which prevents them from leading to true *universality*, only attained through total self-divesting.

A contemplative sister said something which still echoes in my head like a last judgment: "I have no private life." And that was true; she had reached the stage where she no longer had anything of her own. But, by these standards, who is Christian? Set against such silent greatness, expressed with such simplicity in the words "I have no private life", all the disputes inside the Church appeared so vain and futile. This example takes us back to the heart of Christianity, all the way to the trinitarian self-divesting, through the divesting of Jesus' humanity in which it is revealed as a person.

Thousands of books have been written about Jesus, about his divinity (for or against). And yet, rarely has it come to light that it is essentially subsisting relinquishment (and thus infinite freedom) communicated to his humanity as its personal center of gravity, as its true and unique self, in total relinquishment of itself, and that it can only take hold of itself through the relationship which constitutes the personality of the Word in which it subsists.

Since our spirit is dulled by the least hint of self-complacency, since it is obscured by narcissistic self-possession, we can only marvel at the sight of Jesus in whom we find the supreme model for the life of the spirit. In him, the true absolute is revealed as pure self-divesting in the virginal transparency of infinite altruism.

And so, in "God's humanity", we learn who we can be, and discover the path of "poverty" that will lead us to ourselves.

If the mystery of Jesus does indeed mean essentially what we have tried to explain, we can see that ecclesial meditation and mystical experience have greatly contributed to the understanding of the texts in the New Testament, where this mystery is first expressed. These—especially the Gospels and the *Acts of the Apostles*—present Jesus's transcendence through the actual *historical* events in which it was revealed. They make its contingencies and ambiguity perceptible to us. For his disciples, Jesus bears all the hopes of Israel (Lk 24:21; Acts 1:6); for his enemies, he compromises them (Jn 11:49-50). However, Jesus said enough about it for his disciples to be able to transpose the "kingdom" to within themselves, but only after the resurrection, once they had recovered their serenity shattered by his death, and in the Pentecostal fire. They could then proclaim his kingdom as a reality that affects all human beings in their personal relationship with God, through the mediation of Christ, Son of God, who dwells in their hearts by the power of the Holy Spirit (Eph 3:16-17). From the beginning, Jesus' divine transcendence is thus expressed in reference to *trinitarian monotheism* which it reveals and on which it is founded. Ecclesial meditation will first apply itself to maintaining the full integrity of these two terms: only one God, but with plurality of consubstantial relationships in his innermost being. It will then strive to maintain the full integrity of Jesus' humanity and to reject the intermingling of the two natures, divine and human, united in the person of the Word made flesh.[10]

---

[10] Note the remarkable phrase in the Creed said to be by St. Athanasius (fifth or sixth century): *Unus autem non conversione divinitatis in carnem sed*

This colossal amount of intellectual work that, with the help of the Holy Spirit, culminated in the first definitions of dogma, was essential to clarify the mystery of Jesus, which profoundly renews our vision of God and of ourselves. No doubt, the council of bishops who defined the dogma did not necessarily understand the full impact of their confessions of faith and the demands implied in the creed they were promulgating. A wonderful new light was nonetheless shed on the mystical experience, familiar to some of them, by these providential clarifications of the ultimate meaning of *agape,* or charity, which is God: in him, being is identified with love in that eternal self-divesting which personalizes God, Christ and, finally, ourselves through him.

This is what we sense, vaguely and intermittently, when, turning our gaze away from ourselves, in the midst of the silence where all things breathe, we meet "the Beauty so ancient, yet so new" that St. Augustine discovered as the "Life of his life."

In these first steps towards inner liberation—possibly experienced by Rimbaud when he wrote: "I is Another" —we begin to see that a relationship with God is somehow the source and the ferment of our becoming a person. The mystery of Jesus helps us to better understand these sketchy intuitions, and at the same time confirms them: in Jesus, humanity is truly and totally assumed by the divine personality and "realized" to the fullest by subsisting self-divesting, whereby the Son becomes an eternal

---

assumptione humanitatis in Deum. Christ is "one," not by the turning of Divinity into flesh, but by the assumption of humanity into God.

offering to the Father. As such, his humanity is capable of communicating to us the absolute freedom vested in it, which, through it, becomes the focal point of history, drawing us into its radiant relinquishment.

This must be what Pascal felt during that night of November 23, 1654, when he offered up "his total submission to Jesus Christ", in whom he had discovered the "greatness of the human soul" with such "certainty" that his wonder could only be expressed in these words that will never cease to move us: "Joy, joy, joy, tears of joy!"

11

Being Oneself in Another

The chapel of the Medicis in San Lorenzo, where some of Michelangelo's most beautiful works are preserved, is the setting of a particularly precious memory for me. One morning, a friend and I sought refuge there to rest for a while, exhausted as we were from having visited so many museums. We no longer wished to see anything; our eyes were saturated with the profusion of masterpieces in this Mecca of fine arts. We sat in front of Lorenzo's and Giuliano's tombs, alone and silent, happy to find a place to soothe our weariness. That did not prevent me from casting my eyes over the group of sculptured figures that fit harmoniously in this space just large enough to contain them. Little by little, the *beauty* emanating from the sculptures, internalized by the pervasive mood of reverence, swept through me like a presence that gently liberated me from myself. Its hold on me was so peaceful that it left no room for exaltation. I was completely engrossed in that sense of wonder, losing sight of myself, and my very admiration was separating from me in order to adhere to the beauty, for it and through it, as if I were becoming myself in it. I suppose everybody, at some time or other, has had a similar experience and felt the joy of *being oneself in another*, one who is a transcendent reality and yet within oneself. Such an experience is an encounter with the sacred, and in it, one discovers freedom as liberation. It may also provide an image of the Trinity and spark an intuition of the Incarnation, two mysteries in which the wonderful paradox of being oneself in another is eminently realized in different ways.

Going back to the Incarnation we have just discussed, we can ask ourselves how the total and constant hold of the personality of the Word over his humanity was experienced in Jesus' *human* consciousness. Some texts in the Gospel clearly confront us, in biblical language, with the divine Absolute. They would be incomprehensible if it were not God in person who spoke to us. They are the texts in which all human relationships hang on the sovereign word that disposes of everything. Jesus dictates our behavior which is a matter for his judgment (Mt 5:20-43) as it concerns communities (Mt 11:21-24; 23:37-38; 24:1-2), as well as individuals (Mt 7:21-23; 25:31-45). He forgives sins (Mt 9:2) and raises the dead (Mt 9:18-25), as he will do on the last day (Jn 6:44). He demands an unconditional love to which all other loves must be strictly subordinated (Mt 10:37-39); he proclaims the individual (Mt 25:31-46; 26:24) and collective (Mt 21:33-43; 23:33-37) sanctions entailed by the rejection of his message and his person. He towers above all of history; he was before Abraham (Jn 8:55), before the beginning of the world (Jn 6:5), and he will return at the end of time (Mt 25:31-32; Lk 17:22-37). In a word, all of Yahweh's attributes rightly belong to Jesus in the fullest sense. Other texts describe him as inferior to the Father (Jn 14:28): he does not know the date of the last day (Mt 24:36) and he is not authorized to assign the coveted first place (Mt 20:22) to the sons of Zebedee; above all, he is sent to the darkness of his agony and the tortments of crucifixion in spite of his earnest plea that he be spared "the cup" (Mt 26:37-44). In short, according to Bérulle's expression, he appears limited and dependent like a creature "drawn from nothingness". The first group of texts is rightly said to reveal the divine person that he is; the second group reveals the human nature subsisting in the Word of God. And yet, it is the same person who speaks and acts in both cases, and the second group reveals the person no less than the first, for his human nature never asserts itself in its own right, having no "self" of its own and always being entirely under the hold of the divine "self".

How can we then explain the relation between the texts "of majesty", written in biblical language, and the texts of "abasement" written, so to speak, in evangelical language? It seems to me that we can better understand it by starting from the principle that every grace must be *earned*, at least after it has been received. Indeed, it cannot bear fruit as it should unless it is implemented, as it were, by a consent proportional to its greatness. Now, no grace can be compared to the grace of union, which communicates to Jesus' humanity the subsisting self-divesting that constitutes the Word's personality and the supreme freedom that it is. Throughout Jesus' career, his humanity will thus be called upon to express this infinite relinquishment —that makes the Word pure relationship to the Father— until the *"léma sabachthání"* (Mt 27:46) inclusively, when "divine Poverty" will attain its most heartrending expression. That is why, even in the texts of "majesty", we must read the most perfect humility, the most complete effacement of Jesus' humanity into Divinity, of which it is a "co-instrument" and which it always reveals in everything it experiences.

The fact remains that, in Jesus, the torment of his agony and the cry *"léma sabachtháni"* seem difficult to reconcile with an absolutely clear consciousness of the hypostatic union (in person) of his human nature with Divinity.

An Irish Dominican, Fr. MacNabb, whom I had the privilege to hear during my stay in London, greatly clarified this point in circumstances particularly worthy of being recalled. Some Anglican theologians of decidedly "modernist" leanings had asked themselves the question:*"Did Jesus Christ have the consciousness of his divinity?"* Their answer was: "It is not certain, based on the texts at our disposal, that Jesus Christ had the consciousness of his divinity." Fr. McNabb then took up the challenge, with all his faith and charity, and wrote an article found in his book *From a Friar's Cell* and which I am reconstructing from memory.

As they grappled with their problem, our Anglican friends in fact raised four questions; they only dealt with one, behind which the other three were hidden. If we abide by the Christian Tradition that, from the beginning, affirms the divinity of Jesus Christ, they are, in order:

1) Was Jesus, in *his divine person*, conscious of his divinity? The answer leaves no room for any doubt: yes, he was, infinitely and eternally so.

2) Was Jesus, in *his human nature*, conscious of his divinity or, to be more specific, of the union in person

(hypostatic) of his humanity with the Word eternally begotten by the Father? Here is where three questions emerge:

a) Since, even in this life, Jesus' human soul enjoys the *beatific vision* in a perpetual face-to-face with God (*Christus est simul viator et comprehensor*), there is no doubt that it perceives, as revealed in this vision, the mystery of the Word made flesh, the secret of his own life.

b) Furthermore, since Jesus' mission is to propose this mystery of the Word made flesh (that he is) to men, by teaching them, in human language and for their conduct here below, that "God so loved the world that he gave his only Son, so that whoever believes in him may not perish but have eternal life", again there is no doubt that, on the level of his mission and of the *prophetic knowledge* that it implies, he was conscious of being what he was proclaiming to be.

c) But we must admit that, in Jesus, there was another kind of knowledge, neither divine nor beatific, nor prophetic, but *experiential* pertaining to the natural order and originating from the senses. This knowledge is not in itself designed to discern clearly and immediately supernatural realities; through it, Jesus was open to the discovery of the world around him; it allowed him to assimilate the language and the culture of his milieu, to experience wonder, the surprise at meeting friendly faces or the sadness and indignation when confronted by hypocritical opposition and sordid plots of which he was ultimately to be the victim. In a word, it is through this experiential knowledge that he lived *temporally* the eternity in which he subsisted, all the while carrying out his mission in stages and remaining sensitive to the novelty of events: even though these had been foreseen in a vision that encompassed all of time, they preserved, as they became actualized, the sharp edge of unfolding reality.

And everything leads us to think that Jesus' experiential knowledge, although of a natural order, was habitually made sharper and more subtle by the light radiating from the higher spheres of his being, and that such a prodigious enlightenment put him perfectly in tune with all his activities of a specifically supernatural order. But the possibility that there might have been a split at certain moments —and in particular during his passion—between the higher levels of his knowledge and that of the senses is not excluded. And it may very well be that, precisely in this experiential zone, he no longer had the feeling of his hypostatic union (in person) with Divinity.

By acknowledging the possibility of this last hypothesis, Fr. McNabb subscribed to the Anglican thesis when he said: "We can admit, along with our Anglican brothers, that Jesus, at certain moments at least, was possibly not conscious of his divinity." His statement infers that this was so on the level of his experiential knowledge (which alone held their attention), in the same way as, when we say that Mary is the Mother of God, we infer: according to human nature.

I believe I have accurately summarized Fr. MacNabb's thinking which had struck me, both by its depth and its charity, at the time I read his book. I shall now attempt to comment on it as briefly as I can. The easiest way of putting ourselves in a position to understand it is by noting that our own knowledge entails different levels, and that a certain split between them is almost natural. Every man is mortal. Who does not know this truth and is not convinced of it in the abstract, that is, when it does not concern him personally? It is then, as Heidegger constantly emphasized in his extraordinarily powerful phrase, "an accident which happens to others." But come the day when this truth changes for me into an event, and it will take on an entirely new look, if I am conscious of it and if I remain passionately attached to life. That is what happened to the priest whose assistant I was at the beginning of my priesthood; to his question: "Is the end coming tonight?", I had to answer: "Yes". With awesome lucidity, he added: "I would have liked to work some more", painfully aware of an imminent and totally unforeseen end to his life. It is the same when we learn about the death of loved ones. We always knew, of course, that death could take them away. But the telegram bearing the news brutally puts us before a *fait accompli*. In another area, a similar break can be seen in scrupulous people between their guilt feelings and the motives which could reasonably justify them. Reason, indeed, if they could hear it, would free them from their torments, but the problem is precisely that their perturbed sensitivity is impervious to its logic.

Could we suppose an analogous situation in Jesus' humanity during his passion, obviously on the level of his experiential knowledge? Could we imagine, if we take St. Paul's words literally (he was "made sin for us"), that he experienced a kind of scruple on an infinite scale, the weight of which would have made him *feel* responsible for and guilty of all the sins of humankind, while on all other levels of knowledge, he would have kept the clear vision of his perfect innocence? And yet, this illuminating evidence could not in any way benefit his sensitivity, entirely in the grip of the dark universal evil he had to vanquish by accepting all of its consequences. In total solidarity with God as the Word Incarnate that he is, he sees himself repudiated by men, hunted down by all the rejections with which they repay his love—throughout history—leading directly to his crucifixion. But, in total solidarity with human beings, identifying with each one of them as the new Adam that he also is, he feels engulfed in the darkness that emanates from sin, spurned along with it by divine holiness, overwhelmed by the impression of having been forsaken. And this feeling is all the more unbearable as it is precisely his obedience to the mission received from the Father (Jn 14:31) that sets him up on Golgotha, accursed by heaven and earth, deprived of any place in which to exist.

If this interpretation is admissible, we can assume that Jesus' death was brought about *from within* by the coexistence inside him of the absolute holiness that he was with the infinite guilt he experienced, rather than by the atrocious wounds of the crucifixion. This idea is familiar to me. I have already stated that Jesus' death is a unique death. It does not result, as ours does, simply from the spontaneous breakdown of the biological compound that we are, when we lose the ability to draw from cosmic energies what we need to renew our own. Rather, death seems to contradict the very structure of his being, which is a source of eternal life. It answers to a supernatural reason, it is part of a mission, it is willingly accepted, in a word, it is death by *substitution*. Hence, it does not do away with immortality in Jesus, which is co-natural to him, so to speak, and which his resurrection, also *from within*, will reaffirm as the only normal state for "the Prince of life", as Peter calls him in his speech from Solomon's Portico (Acts 3:15). This sometimes brings me to say paradoxically that, if we consider the structure of his person and not the demands of his mission, it is Jesus' death that is the great miracle, while the resurrection is natural to him, as it were, (and thereby unique).

Whatever the case may be, the traditional distinctions recalled by Fr. MacNabb help us to see, at least partially, how Jesus might have lived the hypostatic union with the Word of God in his human consciousness. They allow us to reconcile the consciousness of his divinity to the temporal development of his humanity on the level of experiential knowledge, and make possible the suffering, barely conceivable, that brings the death of God into history. We ask the Mother of the Lord that Jesus' sorrow be imprinted in our hearts:

Sancta Mater istud agas,
Crucifixi fige plagas
Cordi meo valide.[1]

---

[1] Holy Mother, we pray,
Etch your Crucified Son's wounds
Deep in our hearts.

12

Conquering Oneself :
Overcoming Death in One's Life

The funeral of our venerable Cardinal Tisserand, that
we are about to celebrate, invites us to meditate on death.
Death first appears as the inexorable fate that strips us of
everything. It is, nevertheless, programmed in our biology
from the moment of our conception. Living organisms,
and this is especially true of human being, rely heavily on
their environment to survive. The baby growing in its
mother's womb breathes and is nourished through her.
Once it is born, it is directly dependent on the external
environment which surrounds it: on the air it breathes
and, after it has been breast-fed, if possible, on elements
of mineral, plant or animal origin for food, shelter against
bad weather, or clothing to compensate for a climate,
determined by the sun, which is unsuited to its internal
temperature. All these loans from the environment are
available to everyone, at least in principle, in the "depart-
ment stores" of our technological civilization, but not
without danger, the price we must pay for technology.
Besides, they can only be assimilated through infinitely
complex physiological processes. The organs needed for
this assimilation age quickly. They gradually lose precision and flexibility, and they collect waste that eventually

poisons them. Soon, they barely compensate for their deterioration or they proliferate in a disorderly way. Finally, their connections become obstructed, and the system whereby the supplies of the outer world are integrated into the substance of the living organism breaks down. Our umbilical cord—all the different abilities to assimilate and eliminate that connect us to the nourishing earth—is cut, and this is what constitutes physical death. Our body becomes a corpse as soon as it is no longer able to draw from the universe the energies it requires every single moment to survive. When we look at a dead person, we are struck by its inertia: the corpse before us is no longer operating inside the circuit of life, it no longer has roots in our world.

That does not mean that the person ceases to live in a sphere of existence other than the one to which our vegetative functions connect us. Indeed, the death of a human being must correspond to the *multidimensional* reality of his life. Let us take a simple example from everyday life. As a rule, when we sit down to eat, we are satisfying our most basic need. However, this does not prevent us from placing a greater value on the presence of friends around us than on the meal itself, which is above all a celebration of our joy to be with them. Our death must be exceptional in the biosphere, as is our life which has several dimensions. If death poses a problem for us, it is because our life itself is a problem. If our life reveals transcendence, it must also be found in death.

The strong sense we have of our inviolability, or of the inviolability of persons with whom we can identify—when it is trampled underfoot—is obviously not a visceral emotion, any more than the pain we experience over the moral degradation of a loved one. It is not by feeling the skull of our fellow humans that we can detect their dignity, but by becoming aware of an infinite worth, identical in them and in ourselves, which, to be actualized in reality, depends as much on them as on us. Indeed, man has the power to add an essential dimension to his animal nature, a dimension which gives him a human face and transforms him from something into someone. It is through this dimension that we establish those relationships that come from the heart and in which we pour forth our esteem, our trust and admiration. Except in the case of illness, where our sympathy and help are specifically required, we are not interested in our friends' breathing, digestion or other automatic neurovegetative functions. What appeals to us in them is precisely what is beyong anonymity, the quality of which they are the origin and which constitutes their personality.

And so, in contrast with other living beings, whose lives are entirely programmed by their instincts and who cannot overstep their limitations, since they are incapable of questioning their existence, we have to answer for ourselves. We can choose to be subjected to what we are or to recreate ourselves; we can assert ourselves through a prefabricated ego rooted in our subjective passions, or rise above our inner servitudes as a new self, founded on self-denial and shaped by the offering that it is. In the first case, we are reduced to one dimension and we opt for *death* by yielding ourselves up to the interplay of cosmic forces active in our being. In the second, we opt for a *super-life*—the specifically human demension beyond life—by directing these untamed energies to an end that transcends them, thus fulfilling them in a new dimension of being. All the problems escalating in an alarming fashion throughout the globe come down to this option: death today or super-life today, life *beyond*. If *each one of us* does not become aware of the radical change that must be brought about inside in order to *be*, he will not be. Unconscious impulses will inevitably prevail over the demands of an increasingly uncertain morality, and society will step in to solve the problems: it will propose, while waiting to impose, massive solutions which the individual, deprived of his dignity as creator—his only dignity —will passively accept.

We can appreciate the truth of this diagnosis as we watch the frenzied campaign being led in India (a part of the free world?) to restrict the family to one or two children. The only means ever discussed are contraceptive methods or surgical sterilization. An appeal to personal discipline, if my information is correct, is not part of the public welfare program that the government is desperately trying to apply by every possible means, except that one. And this is only one example; India is far from being the only country pursuing a demographic policy reduced to this dimension.

Once more we note that it is incomparably easier for man to use his mind—which should reveal to him his true greatness—to conquer space and measure its vastness than to conquer himself and vanquish death in his life. And yet, that is what must be accomplished, day by day —by discovering our inner space, infinitely greater than the other—in order to root immortality in our experience and prepare ourselves to turn our death into an *act of life*. That is what Blessed Fr. Kolbe did in Auschwitz to the admiration of the whole world. To die *freely*, after having suffered dreadful tortures, in place of someone who could only have *endured* a death he was not ready to face, what better proof of a life lived daily, through self-offering, in a dimension of eternity, a life that now subsists in itself, freed from the organic servitudes of which it takes leave so serenely! And the whole camp, including the guards, understood that Fr. Kolbe had achieved greatness of life in death, death overcome every day of his career through heroically faithful love: for "love is mightier than death."

Of course, the great majority of human beings do not live their lives on such a level, and death comes to most of them as an event that is not integrated into their personal history. In general, they have pushed the thought of death aside, as a threat to their happiness and activity, and it takes them completely by surprise, assuming they are lucid enough to be aware of its approach. As for those left behind, if they had close ties to the deceased, they feel the shock of this severing all the more painfully as they too, most of the time, carefully avoided envisaging its possibility. They are torn by a separation they experience as a mutilation, and their faith, if they are believers, slowly leads them to resign themselves until, as the saying goes, time will have healed all wounds.

However, they will discover "seeds" of hope and consolation by trying to bring back the memory of those "starry hours", as Zweig calls them, in which they had a true encounter with those they mourn, when they shared their souls in a communion of their innermost selves. As they relive these moments of supreme happiness, they will realize that they attained together an infinite Good whose presence shone through their mutual dispossession, in that space that each one completely emptied inside to let the other in. They will understand that it was the presence of the same *God* in each one of them that was the very breath of their tenderness and the eternity of their love. Then, they will know that He remains the bond, and the living place where they can always find their loved ones again, in that heaven inside themselves, which is the God within. For, as Pope St. Gregory says, *"Caelum est anima justi,"* heaven is the soul of the just. Thus, it is by going deeper into our union with God that we can make eternal our greatest affections and save them from death, which has no hold over what is founded on Him. Indeed, it is in God alone that we can go beyond our reciprocal limits and reach one another without disappointment and hurt. Eternal life is at the heart of "real life" (Rimbaud), like a super-life (Mounier), in which we emerge from the cosmos in the original freedom of a new creation.

In any case, only in God do we come together.

From all the preceding reflections, we can conclude that, because we depend on supply sources outside ourselves, death is a process unfolding from the time of conception in the womb. This process *dominates* our entire life—which is nothing but a reprieve—until the umbilical cord tying us to the universe is cut, unless we are born again to a super-life which, as it develops, diminishes the hold death has over our daily existence.

Every death normally results in this break with the physical world—that is the common element—but each death is different depending on the choice one has made for oneself. As Rilke says, each one dies of his own death. Death can be an apotheosis, like St. Francis' death, streaming with paschal joy: it seems to herald the triumph of the resurrection, so powerfully suggested by Gilles' *Requiem*.

Up until now, the mystery of the resurrection had benefitted from an altogether natural yearning to see once more those we have loved—and lost—just as we knew them, so that we would be able to recognize them. I wonder to what extent this feeling will survive the generalized practice of cremation. The difficulty lies perhaps not so much in admitting the possibility of resurrection as in trying to imagine it. If the spirit cannot assert itself adequately in the course of our earthly existence without permeating all our organic powers, communicating its freedom to them, what will become of most of them when they no longer serve a specific purpose?

Astronauts have familiarized us with the indisputable fact that our organism is strictly adapted to our earthly habitat. Breathing on the Moon, which, apparently, has no atmosphere, would have been impossible for them if they had not brought along a supply of oxygen. In order to colonize planets other than our own, we would probably have to undergo physical transformations that would profoundly alter the aspect and the shape of our body. Supposing that this were possible, how would we define and where would we locate the essence of a human body capable of such changes? Our Lord himself leads us to this question when he states that "when they rise from the dead, they take neither husband nor wife" (Mk 12:25). If reproduction is excluded, we can assume that so are all other physiological functions tied to our earthly condition. What then remains of this physical entity of ours, "sown a natural body, raised a spiritual body" (1 Cor 15:44)?

We can try and get some idea of this by remembering certain privileged moments when our inward gaze was pure enough to perceive another in that one point where his whole being is concentrated in his own light, where the only thing we apprehend in him is the fullness of his presence transparent to God. The body is then truly, entirely and solely the concrete manifestation of *someone*, in the mystery and dignity of his spirit, and that someone is never more authentically human. We can thus imagine a body that would retain its *essential identity* while losing the organs which are necessary only because of our dependence on the physical world: provided we remember that what is important in a human body is precisely its humanity. Humanity is something to be conquered—our body too must be born again—and it can only be seen if the body is looked upon without lust. In order to determine what specifically constitutes the identity of a human body and what will rise again, if we are to really speak of resurrection, it seems to me that we must take into account the very different aspects that our body presents in our *experience*, depending on its degree of humanization and the quality of the gaze that comes to rest on it—we see what we are worthy of seeing.

If we keep in mind that "matter" may appear as mass, energy or radiation, could not our corporeal identity manifest itself in different forms (mass, light, heat, sound, movement)—whatever would be appropriate in the circumstances—supposing naturally that, in a "spiritual body", "matter" would retain the fundamental properties that it is now recognized as having. This provides us with a new reason, of a scientific nature this time, for being extremely cautious when we speak about the condition of a "glorified" body. In any case, we note that the risen Christ indeed appears in different forms, depending on the reactions he means to provoke.

If we remember the fact that our body, already here below, reaches the peak of its humanity and of its reality by making itself known as the concrete manifestation of *someone* in the mystery and dignity of the spirit, I believe that the glorified body must, at the very least, eminently possess all the physical reality implied in such a manifestation. That can only induce us to sanctify our bodies, by respecting and fulfilling their eternal vocation in our daily lives as a prelude to their resurrection in glory. The sacred liturgy will remind us of the promise of this resurrection during the funeral ceremony of our venerable brother, Cardinal Tisserand, whom we will entrust to the love of the Lord, as we recall the words that nourish our hope: "He is not a God of the dead, but of the living" (Mk 12:27).

13

Mary : Truth in a Dream

What Aeschylus or Shakespeare could express all the dimensions of the drama contained in just a few lines by St. Matthew concerning Jesus' virgin conception? "Now the birth of Jesus the Messiah took place in this way. When his mother Mary was engaged to Joseph, but before they were together, she was found to be with child from the Holy Spirit. Her husband Joseph, being a righteous man and unwilling to expose her to public disgrace, decided to repudiate her in secrecy. But just when he had resolved to do this, an angel of the Lord appeared to him in a dream and said: 'Joseph, son of David, do not be afraid to take Mary as your wife, for the child conceived in her is from the Holy Spirit'" (Mt 1:18-20).

What a miracle of modesty and restraint we find in this transparent account in which the greatest love is revealed through two silences tragically faced. The case of the unfaithful fiancee is settled by the Law with the harshest of sanctions. Joseph rejects the legal solution straightaway. Mary cannot be guilty. Nevertheless, the physical evidence is there, and the certainty of her innocence cannot do away with it. Is not sending her back quietly to her family, who must not find out, the only way of protecting her without adding pain to the outrage she must have suffered? She will understand, from his attitude, that he has not stopped believing in her and that his silence is the supreme homage of his trust and respect. Why, indeed, insist on a distressing explanation that could neither change an irreversible situation nor motivate a decision he has already taken in the sole light of his love? Giving is more complete when it needs no reason other than the gift itself. But why does she not say anything? She must sense all that is going on inside him, feel his suffering. Besides, does she not need him to protect her secret, the meaning of which he misunderstands? But the secret belongs to God; he has involved Mary in this unique maternity, and he alone can testify with full authority to its supernatural origin, by directly enlightening her husband's heart. She waits for God to determine the outcome that will answer Joseph's silence, without her having to break her own. And, indeed, during that anguished night, when their fate must be decided, Joseph receives in a dream the heavenly message that unveils to him the divine mystery being enacted in her. He will be asked to play his part in this mystery by taking Mary as his wife, for she will give birth to a son whom he will name Jesus. We can imagine the wonder this incomparable couple must have felt as their love was reawakened out of their joint silences, after a night of torment which would normally have led to their separation.

In just a few utterly simple lines, the evangelist relates the genesis of the second Adam and of the new creation that will be born of his love.

This genesis begins with a marital drama, with a human love all the more seriously threatened as it is unique in quality. It is saved only through total self-divesting, as if to root it at the heart of the Trinity by stamping it with the mark of divine poverty, the first Beatitude. But, conversely, by giving the divine mystery a human weight, this drama roots it in our history which it will transform by revealing and renewing its meaning. Indeed, Jesus' virgin conception recapitulates history as a movement toward the Spirit. As a result, what matters is not to multiply individuals, under the impulse of the flesh, into countless fleeting generations, but rather to create persons who *each* attain an identical universal worth that can unify all human beings in a common purpose, one that lies within themselves, and thus to make all generations contemporary. (Therein lies the real demographic problem.) The extraordinary birth of the new Adam, through the workings of the Holy Spirit, foreshadows and forms the basis for the timeless role he is to play by begetting all of humankind again in the virginal embrace of crucified love. Without posterity of the flesh, Jesus gathers all the generations together in his triumph over death: by continually promoting humanity-as-species to humanity-as-person, he is the ever-living bond uniting them in a *super-life* where they can join and merge in the endless present of the communion of saints.

In relation to Jesus, Mary is eminently concerned by this virgin conception that takes place inside her: it is the fruit of her freely-given consent to the angel's call in the annunciation, and, consequently, it signifies the participation of her whole person in Jesus' mission. It cannot be reduced to a natural parthenogenesis, like the one Yves Delage probably dreamed of in his famous experiments, notably on female rabbits. He entertained the hope of achieving someday, even in the human species, fertilization that would exclude any male element. If we were ever to succeed, Mary's case, so to speak, could not be explained as an event anticipating on such an achievement. Her case is altogether different, something we can tentatively describe as a maternity of the *person*. By contrast, ordinary motherhood is first set at the level of (human) *nature*. On the one hand, most of the time, it is an instinctive impulse that, through the interplay of natural mechanisms, brings about conception; on the other hand, all the mother can hope for is that the child she has conceived will be in full possession of his human nature, but he is a stranger to her. Besides, being purely virtual, his personality remains totally unpredictable.

On the contrary, Mary's motherhood is the result of her agreement with divine will in the full light of the spirit; it bears upon the *person* of Jesus, named in advance and designated as the one who will be holy and who will be called the Son of the Most High, the Son of God (Lk 1:31-38). Therefore, it is Mary's person who is directly concerned in the dialogue of the annunciation, and it is through the commitment of her whole person "in the luminous cloud of divine presence" that the tree of Jesse will blossom in her with miraculous fruitfulness. The whole biological process implied in her maternity is set in motion by her spirit, itself moved by the Holy Spirit, and this is precisely what makes it a maternity of the person or, what amounts to the same thing, a maternity of the spirit. It reveals Mary as the *second Eve*. Seen in this inner light, the event appears as uniquely new: it represents the emergence of human nature vested with the subsisting Word that originates in self-sacrificing freedom, which constitutes the Mother's personality. This is vitally important to our spiritual life, if we admit that the spirit is the liberating power actualized in an authentic personality.

The dogma of Mary's Immaculate Conception aptly underlines this essentially spiritual aspect of the virgin conception by stating that, from the very first moment of her existence, the Blessed Virgin is committed to this motherhood that primarily concerns her person; for her person is fundamentally and solely constituted in view of the awaited Savior, and she is capable of begetting him precisely because she has always lived of him.

Mary's relationship to Jesus is one of total belonging; it shapes her personality from the beginning, long before she knows that she is destined to be his mother. As such, it endows her virginity with incomparable depth. It does not consist only in the fact that "she knows no man" (Lk 1:34), but it is integrated into the very structure of her being. If, indeed, Mary's maternity makes her an exception to the law of the species, it is because she bears within herself, and adheres to with all her being, the Good that finalizes the species and which alone can fulfill it by transcending it.

This Good, it is true, is generally perceived very indistinctly. The horror felt by many of us at the sight of bombs pounding Vietnam is all the more vivid as we can put a personal face on the victims. Today, we are no longer exposed merely to global information about masses of people being massacred. Television actually lets us see a grief-stricken mother, a mutilated child, a man dropping dead. Through television, the individual fate of each one of these human beings is a tangible reality, and thus we become aware of the inhuman condition to which their whole existence is doomed. This feeling, however intensely we may experience it, can nonetheless remain vague and be nothing more than the horrified perception of a monstrous insecurity. It may not necessarily lead to the discovery of those values on which is founded human dignity, so tragically ignored in the anonymous hell of total war.

Mary's gaze, on the contrary, embraces all humankind on the level of the absolute Good to whom she will give birth and of whom she lives at the very root of her personality. She sees humanity through the liberation the promised Savior will bring to every man and, in order to contribute to it, she discerns each one in the same way that a mother immediately recognizes her child in a crowd. If Mary herself eludes the species, it is because the species surpasses itself in her love to become a world of persons: her virgin motherhood offers the first fruits of this world in the new Adam, who is the principle of the new creation.

There is no greater love for humanity than one that aims at personalizing each individual, by bringing into play every means so that each may become a universal good and realize the capacity for the infinite that is the prerogative of the spirit. That is the kind of love we must read in Mary's virginity; it bears fruit in the gift of her Son for our liberation. The radiating influence of her motherhood, in its own order, is as far-reaching as Christ's, and it affects everyone equally, in whatever aspect bears upon one's advancement towards an authentically personal life. In Mary, that implies a self-relinquishment that is as radical as her consent to the incarnation of the Word is free, one that makes her the Mother of human beings at the same time as the Mother of their Savior. By giving him birth in this capacity, of her own free will, she participates as fully as one possibly can in the universality of his mission.

Mary's gift of Christ to humanity is the result of the gift of herself to him, from the first moment of her existence. Indeed, it must always be remembered that she is the mother of a Son whose personality is divine, and that maternity for her involves her person first, constituting it, through a certain equation of light, in view of Christ's person. Her maternity ultimately leads Mary's person to the absolute self-divesting which is implied in the eternal relationship of the Son to the Father at the heart of the Trinity.

Through this participation in "divine Poverty," unique in its depth, Mary is born of her Son in her transparent personality, before he takes flesh in her virgin flesh. He is the fruit of a contemplation—that originates in him—which first gives birth *in her spirit* to the Word waiting to become flesh in her body, soon to be his cradle. Dante says it all in these words: *Vergine Madre, figlia del tuo Figlio*[1] (Virgin and Mother, daughter of your Son).

This phrase best reveals the meaning of Mary's Immaculate Conception by linking Jesus' virgin conception to his mother's eminent holiness, the first fruit of the redemption. (*"Sublimiori modo redemptam"*, Pius IX writes in the bull *Ineffabilis Deus*: "Redeemed in a more

---

[1] Dante, *Il Paradiso*, Canto 33, 1.

sublime way".) Christ's grace fell upon Mary so that she might be the suitable mother of this son, the Word Incarnate, as the new Eve born of the heart of the new Adam.

Thus a virgin couple, of that ontological (of being) virginity that has its roots in the transparency of intradivine relations, is at the origin of humanity-as-person, into which humanity-as-species is destined to be transformed, this species to which we are so heavily bound as long as we are not "born of the Spirit".

From this viewpoint, Mary's exemption from original sin is the negative expression of what her (ontological) virginity expresses positively. If we admit that original sin, in the first specifically human act, is the refusal to be our own origin, to relinquish ourselves and be personalized in self-sacrificing love, instead of clinging to narcissistic love, a refusal which, among other consequences, prevents the human species from being promoted to a personal status; if we admit that, then Mary, who totally relinquished her own self from the first moment of her existence, through her unique relation to the promised Savior, is completely dissociated from this refusal that plunges us into darkness. Her only part in it is to work towards setting us free, by uniting to Christ's own yes the *original yes* that he sparked in her as a prelude to her motherhood.

Humanity today, so tragically entangled in its demographic problem because it yields to the impulses of the species, resorts to mutilations to prevent the consequences, rather than seeking to overcome them through spiritual discipline. Compared to that, we cannot help being filled with wonder when, on the threshold of the Gospel, we find in Jesus and Mary such total liberation with respect to the species. It heralds and makes possible the advent of a humanity in which the concern to be one's own origin would finally result in a world of persons.

The new vision of woman, that Mary inspires by her presence in our history, constitutes a vital opportunity to establish a truly free world. What could bear a greater resemblance to the divine generation (of the Word by the Father) in this hierarchy of poverty—that of the Spirit—than a person who gives birth to a person by a radical self-divesting through which she is fulfilled? Woman, fashioned after this model, transcending the species and attracting man by the light of her inner life, might suggest a real answer to the condition of contemporary humanity. She can reveal to man the highest spheres of his own being by embodying the perpetual need to surpass himself. We cannot hope to find a human solution to all the problems facing us as long as we fail to recognize our capacity for the infinite, a capacity that unhinges us when it cannot be actualized in a field of expansion as vast as its potential.

Every child, said a poet, dreams of his mother as immaculate. This dream is so strong that, in spite of all he may know, he forgets most of the time that she is a wife, and he convinces himself that her motherhood was the result of nothing other than her love for him. Without his knowing it, the Blessed Virgin is thus his dream come true.

An adolescent who has the privilege of coming face to face with her miraculous femininity will be endowed with new vision. He will first learn to respect himself because he will sense an imponderable presence that is part of his relationship to himself and which confers upon it a sacred character in the permanent need for love. Evil is no longer what is forbidden nor the good merely a commandment. Someone is simply there to whom we give ourselves as a tribute, in the light emanating from him. I have felt this profound change myself: from the moment the Immaculate Conception comes into our life, walls become stained-glass windows through which the sun's rays sing. *O Virgo virginans*, I like to call you. O purifying Virgin, in one unforgettable second, you were for me the door that opens onto inner liberation, where we attain our freedom in the total self-divesting which is true virginity! And it is by reviving within me this experience, where I recognize your presence, at every decisive moment of my life that you have brought me back on the path of Divine Poverty, which your Son has revealed to us as the pearl of the Kingdom, resplendent at the heart of the Eternal Trinity.

With this cry of infinite gratitude, our talk draws to a close. But we must note yet one more thing. Mary, the new Eve, the Mother of Christ and ours, is also in some way the sign and sacrament of God's motherhood. She reveals his *feminine side*, so to speak, God as the source of all the tenderness one finds in the hearts of mothers and, as such, infinitely more of a mother than all mothers. We must acknowledge, indeed, that most mothers, when need be, are capable of heroic devotion. I can still hear these words from a woman whose son was being taken to prison; in spite of her bitter sense of disgrace, she still protested her love for him by saying: "If his mother doesn't love him, who will?" It seemed that her love was the only tie he had left with life, and that she tried, with all her might, to bind him to it by the passionate gift of herself. It is in such fits of pure generosity that many women rise to motherhood of the person, Mary's motherhood par excellence, thus giving birth again to their sons and daughters in the freedom of the spirit.

By giving her Son to man, the Blessed Virgin—having also received from God the unlimited power to love—embraces all of humanity and the whole universe with immeasurable affection. And it is her motherly tenderness that, better that anything else, can make us feel, as a child feels from his mother, the motherly tenderness of God, alllowing us to pray to him as to a woman, our mother.

Already, in the name of Yahweh, Isaiah prophesied:

Can a woman forget her nursing child,
and cease to love the fruit of her womb?
Even if some may forget,
yet I shall not forget.
(Isaiah 49 :15)

After the personal immolation of the Word Incarnate, we have infinitely more reasons than even the greatest prophet of Israel to believe in God's motherhood and to invoke him as our mother.

When we cry out "mother" with our whole being, this little word can become by itself the prayer that says everything, that asks for everything, that gives everything. Let us not hesitate to use it. Mary's tender love makes it spring naturally from our hearts. Through her, it will shoot up like a rocket, straight to the heart of God, who is more of a mother to us than all the mothers.

14

"Why Wish to Be Something
When We Can Be Someone?"

If a third world war has not yet broken out, it is supposedly because the prospect of an atomic war forces the superpowers to maintain a balance of terror. In case of a direct confrontation, however, they could not avoid one, with an equal risk of annihilation for both sides. This does not prevent them from stocking fifty thousand or one hundred thousand megatons of atom bombs, enough to destroy humanity fifty thousand times over. This situation grew out of the First World War which allowed the founding of the first communist empire, just as the Second World War fostered the birth of the second communist empire. Marxist atheism, sanctioned by power, became a state institution and spread to the satellite countries, as required by materialistic ideology which forms the backbone of the proletarian revolution. By virtue of the tolerance for all opinions that it guarantees as a righ, the "free" world—not to mention the communist parties which automatically support Marxism—has opened its doors to propaganda from Moscow and Beijing. It puts up very littly resistance, especially in view of the fact that it is constantly calling its own existence into question, while cheerfully giving up all the values that would provide it with an absolute to set against the Marxist absolute. It fights Marxism resolutely only when pressing material interests are at stake, while, on the other hand, it contributes unscrupulously to consolidate it as soon as it sees the opportunity of acquiring new markets in the communist countries.

The greatest peril for the "free" world lies in its growing materialism, which coincides with the "decline of absolutes," already pointed out by Bachelard. Accepting everything and permitting everything—for lack of solid principles—except any interfering with the social order from which one benefits: this sordid foundation on which our order is built is bound to instigate revolt among its victims and rejection on the part of those who, if they could, would despise themselves for wanting to gain from it.

There was a time, up to the war of 1914-1918, when certain norms were accepted. They could be transgressed, but only discreetly; they could not be ignored. They had the advantage of protecting the weak, the "sheep" who are legion, against deviations for which they did not have insurmountable propensities. A traditional morality—if not a religion—provided clear guidelines by imposing a *collective* discipline (which was accepted, by the way) that often contributed to making honest people of them. Whatever remains of that sense of loyalty, essential to the normal operation of services vital to our subsistence, emanates from this source. When it runs dry, the free world will disappear, unless there emerges an entirely new awareness among the Western intelligentsia. Its attitude of negative criticism exerts a wide influence on the most affluent and educated levels of society and can, today, thanks to radio and television, sway even the illiterate.

The fact that communist regimes are extremely vigilant when it comes to protecting their ideology, and that opposition carries the most severe sanctions, can serve as an indicator of how the crumbling of its own ideology endangers the "free" world.

But it is not my intention to dwell on this danger; we can learn about it in Jules Monnerot's monumental book, *Sociologie de la Révolution*. While avoiding futile moaning over times gone by—which, by definition, are no more—I am interested in understanding this breathtaking "decline of absolutes," evident even in the Church, in an attempt to discover, as much as possible, the Christian testimony needed by the world such as it is today.

If we say that the world, "such as it is" today, has lost, to a very large extent and as a whole, the *sense of the sacred*—its sacred dimension—it seems appropriate to test the validity of this image of the world we are about to examine. But first, we must ask ourselves what was the significance of the "sacred" in yesterday's world, or what made the world sacred before this notion vanished.

If we looked at this from Bossuet's point of view, we could experience the sacred in public life as the divine foundation of the social order. No society can survive in anarchy: it requires an order and an authority whose responsibility it is to maintain it and, if need be, to impose it. It could not be the authority of one man over other men who, by nature, are his equal. A kind of divine delegation alone can legitimize the power that an individual is called upon to exercise over his fellow men (cf. Rom 13:1). This is precisely how a social order is made sacred. We can safely assume that, in the eyes of Bossuet, this belief meant a guarantee of freedom. As he acknowledged royal supremacy in the temporal order, it was to God he was submitting, and not to a man. The complete liberty he took of reminding Louis the XIVth of his duties toward God in his private life leaves no doubt whatsoever in this regard. And the king, who believed he held his power from God, accepted to be reminded by the bishop that he himself was subjected to God.

Can we detect a similar concept in the divine investiture of the Pharaohs—which Alexander the Great was eager to obtain for himself—or the deification of Roman emperors? Nothing prevents us from thinking that, in both of these cultures, the sovereignty of one individual over all others appeared justifiable and acceptable only on the basis of divine origin.

On a much more restricted plane, the authority of the head of a clan, like Abraham (cf. Gen 14:13), certainly implied a religious basis, all the more undisputed in his case as people knew him to be communicating directly with God. Going back to prehistoric times, we can presume that some way was found to make the group sacred as soon as men had to rely on group cooperation to live and they formed the first societies. Long before people were able to express their individual freedom, they instinctively felt it, in all likelihood, as a threat of anarchy, which had to be prevented by resorting to divine supervision; this would ensure the cohesion of the group through sanctions from which no one would be exempt.

Personal religious feelings, insofar as they existed, could only firmly establish, if not bring to life, this *public* religion which ties the fate of political communities everywhere to a divinity.

This solidarity between divine authority and political power took a variety of forms, but was strong enough to provide one of the charges that led to Socrates' death. Even under Marcus Aurelius, the wisest of emperors, it instigated severe persecutions against the Christians, offset by the banning of paganism under Christian emperors, to bring about the "conversion" of entire nations following the baptism of their sovereign. It built medieval Christendom under the pope as overlord. It imposed the Inquisition as a bastion of faith. It determined Louis the XIVth to revoke the Edict of Nantes. Finally, it incited Napoleon to come to terms with the Church for the sake of his own interests.

But God's covenant with Israel before the coming of Christ, as presented in the Bible, appears to be much more intimate than all these alliances of the spiritual with the temporal, which, besides, are on a different level. We can say that, in this story that begins with Abraham, the only character is the one solitary God who reveals himself to Moses under the famous tetragram (*IHVH*). God alone is the king of this people which exists for the sole purpose of bearing witness to his presence by obeying his commandments. For it has no other Law than the one it receives from divine revelation; this Law, in principle, governs life through a code that encompasses every one of its aspects, down to its minutest details, by turning every rule into a religious obligation. And yet, the people must fulfill its worldly destiny in a land it will have great difficulty in conquering and defending, and of which it will be dispossessed in the end. We see immediately the tension that cannot fail to develop between its spiritual mission and its temporal establishment, and the temptation that constantly leads the people to confuse one with the other. And we can also see that this temptation is all the stronger as the success of the mission depends on the people being established, since the community as such is vested with the mission and it must *last* in order to pursue it. Hence the passionate attachment to the "Holy Land" that rings out in psalm 137, among others, when it calls for the most brutal vengeance against the enemies who have desecrated Jerusalem.

This ambiguous situation will inevitably result in a tendency to *particularize* God and *to externalize* him. A community that acknowledges total dependence on God is naturally inclined to picture him as a superior power: the higher the power, the better able it is to help the community, either by intervening or, if necessary, by coming down to earth from on high in the heavens where it dwells, not without some peril to sinful men (cf. Ex 19 and 20; Ps 14:2; 18:10; 33:13; 57:4; 98:2; 102:20; 115:16; Isa 6). If, moreover, this community is "a chosen people" (chosen for a spiritual mission), it will be tempted to relate this choice to itself—and to use it as a privilege —whenever its temporal destiny is threatened since, as I have just said, the temporal destiny conditions the fulfillment of the mission. The prophets, great champions of fidelity to the covenant with Yahweh, will no doubt remind the people, in terms which still move us today, that the promised salvation is universal; they will repeat that, in the eyes of God, the demands of justice and authenticity outweigh ritual observances. The psalmists, for their part, will develop a personal devotion that still continues to nourish our own. Still, this awareness of being chosen will often stir up in the people a virulent brand of patriotism that will claim the carrying out of God's promises in its favor (cf. Ps 44, 79, 83; Eccl 36), to the point of not recognizing the awaited Messiah, of rejecting him and of insisting on his death to ensure the security of the nation (Jn 11:50).

In spite of this catastrophic outcome, Christians as a whole remain strangely locked into the early story of the peple (truly unique before the coming of Christ), as if the New Covenant, instituted by the New Adam, did not represent a new departure incommensurable with any-thing that preceded it; as if the Law was still the teacher (Gal 3:24), as if their God were no more than Yahweh Sabaoth, the "Holy One and the Rock of Israel", as if the Trinity had not been revealed. In fact, the Trinity counts for so little in their lives that, in general, they have failed to perceive the radical change that it could bring into them; they have simply adopted, as the rule for their morality, the Jewish Decalogue, with its long list of inter-dicts (Ex 20:1-17), without fundamentally imbuing it with the spirit of the Beatitudes, as if the equation written in blood by Jesus' death (For God, man = God) did not modify in any way our relationship with the Divinity.

The result is that, in practice, the majority of Christians have confined their morality to what is forbidden. But we know that the forbidden fruit is the best. "Ah, if only it were not forbidden!" told me a judge particularly sensitive to feminine charms. He was thus naively express-ing the belief held by many that it is prohibition that creates evil by depriving us of what, in itself, could be good. No doubt he did not know that St. Paul wrote from the viewpoint of the Old Self which gives rise to such a belief: "I would not have known what it is to covet if the law had not said: 'You shall not covet'" (Rom 7:7), and that he spoke of the "curse of the law" (Gal 3:13) that decrees orders without giving the power to do what it commands.

For too many Christians, the only thing they remember from their catechism is an inflexible morality, promulgated on Mount Sinai more than three thousand years ago —along with many other dictates we have given up—for a people to which we do not belong, a morality imposed from the outside for no other reason than the sovereign authority of a God, also outside ourselves, to whom we owe unconditional obedience. Not all of them are as virtuous as the judge who, in spite of its appeal, refrained from biting into the forbidden fruit. Their flesh is weak and in the end, acknowledging that they are sinners, they yield to its impulses. Or at least, that is what they used to do. Today, they are learning, sometimes from "theologians," that it does not matter any way. Moreover, what used to be called evil yesterday might well be called good today. After all, morality is always relative to the times and to their way of assessing what human stability requires. The important thing today is to avoid all repression and to recognize everyone's right to happiness, in consideration of which there is no sin any more (and no redemption).

That is where things stand now. The morality of obligations (tied to a *community* on the way to dissolution) has had its day, and now everyone is urged to invent his own. "I have a duty to myself", said a woman as she was leaving her husband and her two small boys to become involved in a new love.

Is there a remedy for this situation, all the more serious as it is changing and imperceptibly slipping toward an attitude of "do as you please"? I firmly believe that there is.

But first, we must admit that it is inevitable, since "the decline of absolutes" tends to blur the line between good and evil. The problem is thus to find an absolute that experience will not be able to challenge.

I think that Flaubert's little sentence points the way to the discovery of such an absolute with poignant spontaneity: *"Why wish to be something when we can be someone?"* He wrote these words in his diary, with a kind of sadness and dismay, after receiving a letter from Baudelaire in which the poet asked him to help him get elected to the French Academy. How can a man devoted to poetry seek a reward other than the joy of letting it well up inside, from a source higher than himself, and giving it the words that will carry, without altering it, the current that will kindle it in others, as Keats did so perfectly in these translucent verses:

And then there crept
A little noiseless noise among the leaves,
Born of the very sigh that silence heaves.[1]

The author disappears behind his work. All that is left in these evocative verses is the Presence one feels in "the silent music" of the rustling foliage. As we hear it, we start

---

[1] *John Keats and Percy Bysshe Shelley: Complete Poetical Works*, The Modern Library, New York, [n. d.], "Poems", p. 1

resonating with it; we sense that there is Someone there whose encounter reveals us to ourselves, freeing us from ourselves. That is how we become someone, thanks to the capacity to "marvel and stand in awe" of which Einstein speaks; we become that someone for Someone we discover deep down in our soul. Many art or nature lovers experience this every time they are lucky enough to feel a sense of wonder through the contact, no matter how fleeting, with the beauty so ancient and so new in which St. Augustine recognized his God. They do not suspect that these privileged moments make them touch, as it were, the very Principle of the Good. To relive this experience throughout one's life in constant self-liberation, by renewing our encounter with the Presence, "closer to our self than our own innermost self," that awakens our sense of wonder: that, in short, is the essence of morality. It thus appears as the actualization of our dignity, which presupposes an original self whose inviolability is founded on an infinite Worth into which it merges to let it radiate. To be something, by contrast, means being subjected to a prefabricated ego, which is a slave to the unconscious, and the ego courts people to seek their approval as evidence of a greatness it is not. In a word, being something is renouncing to be one's own origin while laying claim to the respect due to authentic autonomy.

In his life as much as in his art—one and the same thing—Flaubert had sensed and practiced, more and more rigorously, this self-divesting which is the *sine qua non* condition for liberation. Thus he discovered true morality in his own field, a morality which essentially expresses the requirements for liberation, our only chance of truly being.

Our mind can explore the physical world from the atom to the most distant galaxies. It must now cross the threshold from beast to man by creating within itself a universe as vast as the one outside, which testifies to its own greatness since it is the mind that probes and confronts the depths of the universe. To get bogged down in the beast by exalting the deterministic forces to which we are in fact subjected amounts to a refusal to be, if indeed we consider as specifically human *the possibility of promoting ourselves to an existence anchored in its own freedom, a freedom proclaimed by the self that actually stems from it and that others experience as a universal good that urges them to free themselves of their own egos.* This is precisely what Fr. Kolbe's companions in Auschwitz suddenly discovered; for one moment, the whole camp was lit up by an extraordinary flash of humanity. It is what we look for in works of art, watching closely for that creative moment when the artist, losing sight of himself, recorded in his material the communion with the source, which then spreads inside us. That is what we hope to find in those we admire and to whom we vow our trust and our friendship.

A morality centered on what is forbidden is inadequate because it does not aim explicitly at the ultimate promotion of the self I have just discussed. It imposes types of behavior without caring about the roots from which they should stem. In the words of St. Paul, it is very much like the law without grace (Rom 7:7).

In this respect, it is absolutely remarkable that the same Apostle, dealing with fornication in the *First Epistle to the Corinthians*, does not refer to the law to condemn it, but to the nobility of our bodies as they are the members of Christ and the temples of the Holy Spirit (1 Cor 6:15, 19). He thus brings us back to the divine model, to which we must turn to immerse ourselves into the light of the Holy Trinity. That is where we shall find, it bears repeating again and again, the supreme example for our moral life and the source of all our freedoms.

By revealing this mystery, Jesus has taken us into the *inner life* of God, as opposed to the Old Testament which considers God in his relationship with creation, and not in what he is for himself. Thus, he has taught us not only that God is Spirit (absolutely immaterial), but how he is Spirit in the eternal communion of love that constitutes his eminent holiness. At the same time, he has taught us what the life of the Spirit means to us and how we can achieve it, as God does, in total self-divesting. That old human dream *to be like God*, which supposedly was an indication of inordinate pride, can henceforth be realized in utter humility, since it is by shedding our own self in an unqualified gift of love that we really become like God: indeed God becomes a person by communicating himself in the total self-relinquishment of the relationships within himself, and each one of them subsists as pure relationship to the other two. It is this likeness to God (in that complete self-divesting which is ultimate freedom) that Jesus suggests to the Samaritan woman in these inexhaustible words: "God is spirit, and those who worship him must worship in spirit and in truth" (Jn 4:24).

The two terms—God and man—are both *internalized* in this spirit-to-spirit relationship; man's natural dependence disappears in the *personal* exchange with God: the more man gives of himself, the freer he becomes (of himself). For man's inborn dependence on God was willed (as a condition for his existence) only in order for man to achieve this kind of equality in Love attested by the Cross with unfathomable generosity. This is what the fragment of *De Beatitudine*, quoted as an epigraph, expresses in that magnificent turn of phrase: God "submitted" to his rational creatures "as if each one were his God."

No text could make us appreciate better the difference in impact between a morality of obligation—that comes to mind as soon as morality is mentioned— and a morality of liberation which expresses a need to be, and which, ultimately, is a *mystical* way of life.

Of course, and we could never insist too much on this, there is no question of abandoning the dictates of the Decalogue and granting ourselves ambiguous liberties; they convey a fundamental heritage of human honesty.[2] The morality of liberation is infinitely more exacting than the Decalogue; it asks the totality of ourselves—always and everywhere—in radical self-divesting, the condition for *the emergence of an original self*, equivalent to the new birth that Jesus talks about to Nicodemus (Jn 3:3). Besides, the texts make quite clear the difference of levels between these two moralities. On Mount Sinai, God appears as he might be seen by a *community* that receives the Law from him, whose worldly existence is entirely subordinated to him, and that will be blessed or cursed depending on whether or not it will have been faithful to the Covenant he made with it—blessed or cursed on the

---

[2] Cf. The declarations of innocence in the Egyptian *Book of the Dead*.

temporal plane, of course, for at the time, there is no mention yet of personal immortality. Hence, it is important that the people be forewarned of what its infidelity could cost it by the frightening manifestations of divine omnipotence that make it tremble with fear (Ex 20:18). And the people said to Moses: "Speak to us, and we will listen; but do not let God speak to us, or we will die" (Ex 20:19). This "pedagogical" approach was no doubt necessary at that stage of a revelation that will ultimately lead to the Cross, but which, for the time being, must transform a horde into a nation whose only bond is its "religion". If St. Augustine could use the expression "I was outside" to describe his relationship with God before his conversion, it is easy to understand that a barely organized throng fleeing from slavery, on the way to an unknown destiny, would view God as a fearsome power outside itself which could complete its liberation and ensure its future.

At Jacob's well, on the other hand, what is at stake is an individual conscience that will be revealed to itself as it learns to discover, in its innermost being, the "*spring of life eternal*". In one silent encounter, the Samaritan woman is turned into a worshipper "in spirit and in truth". The kingdom of God moves from without to within; her whole person becomes involved in a relationship that actualizes her freedom, resulting in self-liberation, which is freedom fully realized. The face of the God-Spirit shines through the subtleties of the dialogue at Jacob's well, where a woman learns, and all human beings with her, that she is spirit because she is treated as a spirit.

There lies the radical change that inaugurates the new morality, one that is a mystical way of life. It is not, of course, that God has changed, but rather that in our human world, a unique event has occurred allowing God to reveal himself in his true light at last. It is the humanity of Christ, who "descended from David's lineage according to the flesh", that offered God the transparency he needed to fully reveal himself. Through Jesus, the Holy Trinity entered into human history, and the infinite self-relinquishment of divine greatness showed us the way to our own. Ans so, the dignity we claim, without any real grounds for it, becomes a reality through total self divesting of which intradivine relationships provide the supreme example. Indeed, making the most of what we were given does not mean that it originates from us, nor does it justify the respect we claim for ourselves. It is by breaking down the boundaries of our narcissistic ego that we become an unlimited space in which breathes the universal Good that everyone can recognize as his own. When our ego is transformed into a gift, it becomes, in turn, transparent and capable of communicating the Presence hidden within us, the Life of our life. Thus, in some way, God is born in humanity every time one of us truly frees himself of his ego. That is precisely what makes us "origin", I mean, this communication through us of the Origin in person: it will become part of our own history only if, in the depths of our being, we shed our self in an attitude of virginal self-denial which corresponds to God's infinite self-relinquishment. How often, in the presence of people who obstinately hold on to positions based on their passions, do we not feel that they are letting God die inside them and that "they are putting out the light of the Spirit", thus making us fear we might do the same?

The specifically Christian morality revolves around this divine Center within ourselves. It clearly includes the

Decalogue, but in its positive aspects, which are the immutable demands of liberation implicit in Christian morality, demands that cannot be laid down as laws. This kind of morality brings about liberation by fulfilling the supreme requirement of total self-divesting from which the new being will arise. St. Augustine's *"Dilige et quod vis fac"* expresses it best: "Love and do what you wish" (which, by the way, brilliantly sums up the hymn to charity of 1 Cor 13).

Nothing, to be sure, is more difficult than such a love; it totally precludes any possessive attachment and apprehends being only as it gives it, because, on the level of the spirit, being becomes ultimately identified with love. But discipline is precisely the need to meet with the approval of the spirit.

The spirit wants to be treated as a spirit and it will surrender only on those terms. The rejection of traditional morality probably includes, among other things, the Nietzschean refusal of a rule that seems to violate the spirit. In the eyes of many, it appears as arbitrarily imposed from without, in the name of a God who is himself outside life. It is very important to show that evangelical morality answers the need for liberation implied in our dignity, and involves us in a personal relationship with a God closer to our self than our innermost self, who is Himself infinite freedom.

A human being who suddenly discovers, along with St. Augustine, that God is *within* (and he without) cannot fail to immerse himself into the awed silence of love; from then on, his only thought will be to protect the adorable

Presence within from all the noise he can make, since It can only shine through his relinquishment.

It goes without saying that, when we speak of two moralities—one of obligation and one of liberation—as St. Paul speaks of two covenants and two Jerusalems, one a slave and the other free (Gal 4:21-31), in no way do we mean that the second would allow what the first one forbids. They represent a difference of level, as for instance, a slave woman (Gal 4:23) who would marry her master could still take on the same tasks, but in an altogether different spirit: her work would then express the giving of herself, which would internalize her relationship with her master, now her husband. The Decalogue remains a valid framework to apply concretely the mystical requirements that go beyond its letter, just as the revelation of the Holy Trinity surpasses the solitary monotheism of the Old Testament.[3]

Since man does not come ready-made, if indeed he must create himself, he cannot do so in a haphazard way. Order and direction are needed. If he is spirit, this order must reach man *from within* as the fulfillment of his most profound aspirations. We must assure him of this by showing that he can attain his freedom only through self-liberation, and that, in order not to be subjected to his being—so as not to keep on being something—he has no alternative but to give it. And that is precisely the only way of becoming someone. It implies that man must

---

[3] This does not mean that there were no truly authentic saints in the Old Testament, because the Revelation it contains points to the definitive Revelation in the Word made flesh.

increasingly see God as partner in a relationship that realizes his full potential for knowing and loving. That is how we must present God to man, by constantly and repeatedly bathing him in the light of the Holy Trinity in whom he will find all his chances to be born freely to himself.

Shelley left an unfinished poem, written in 1822, which proves that an agnostic can desperately long for God, a God he does not name, but whom he seeks everywhere as the only presence that could come up to his expectations.

III

I loved — oh, no, I mean not one of ye,
Or any earthly one, though ye are dear
As human heart to human heart may be; —
I loved, I know not what — but this low sphere
And all that it contains, contains not thee,
Thou, whom, seen nowhere, I feel everywhere.
From Heaven and Earth, and all that in them are,
Veiled art thou, like a... star.

IV

By Heaven and Earth, from all whose shapes thou
flowest,
Neither to be contained, delayed, nor hidden;
Making divine the loftiest and the lowest,
When for a moment thou art not forbidden
To live within the life which thou bestowest;
And leaving noblest things vacant and chidden,
Cold as a corpse after the spirit's flight,
Blank as the sun after the birth of night.

In winds, and trees, and streams, and all things common,
In music and the sweet unconscious tone
Of animals, and voices which are human,
Meant to express some feelings of their own;
In the soft motions and rare smile of woman,
In flowers and leaves, and in the grass fresh-shewn,
Or dying in the autumn, I the most
Adore thee present or lament thee lost.[4]

These verses, from a great poet who was to die in an accident in 1822, the same year he composed them, echo in their own way St. Augustine's confession, that still rings so true: "Our hearts are restless until they rest in Thee."

People today are certainly capable of feeling such yearning for the divine and, starting from it, of discovering God as the Life of their life, and the Good—which, again, is God—as Someone to love. By freeing them from the yoke of the Law, this relationship of love will in fact allow them to obey it by surpassing it. That is why it is so important to constantly bring the people back—and ourselves along with them—to the inner sanctuary where the sacred is revealed as the infinite Presence that fills the space we become, as we disappear in Its light.

---

[4] *Op. cit.*, "The Zucca", pp. 703-704.

15

The Demands of a Morality
of Liberation

In our previous talk, I thought it fair and proper to admit that rejecting traditional morality (and religion) could be, for some and in the best of cases, a way for the spirit to protest obscurely against a discipline that supposedly issues from a particular community, at a given time, imposed from the outside in the name of a God who, like the community itself, is also outside ourselves. I tried to show that the requirements of the spirit—dignity, inviolability, interiority, freedom—imply in fact a much stricter morality, one that does include all the (non-cultural) dictates of the Decalogue, but surpasses them in its quest for the liberation that internalizes them.

Indeed, the spirit in us cannot avail itself of its autonomy without *conquering* it. Its absolute refusal of any intrusion, any constraint, any form of brainwashing indicates that the spirit rises above the world of things that can be used without their consent; as a result, it cannot be manipulated as things are, because it must be the *origin* of its choices. It can do this by allowing only those choices that confirm its vocation as *origin*, those which do not restrict it, lead to no partiality and will not make it a slave to any determinism.

If we condemn any attempt to violate the spirit as a sacrilege, wherever it may occur, it is because we realize that the loftiest human value is at stake here. We must absolutely assure everyone of the *power to be origin* and of the possibility to affirm it *effectively* in all commitments. That is what determines the existence of man. It is where the *sacred* first appears at the heart of life, and where I must become aware of it by venerating it in the recesses of my being.

Indeed, I could not respect this power to be origin (through which everyone is destined *to be the author of his own humanity* in each of his actions) in others without respecting it in myself, without keeping intact the virgin space within, since its presumed existence is the only foundation on which rests my personal inviolability that others (in principle) acknowledge in me.

But why (and for whom) should this virgin space be preserved, and how can the power to be origin be kept intact throughout the concrete decisions we face at every moment? Unless of course we meet within ourselves an infinite Presence, closer to our spirit than our own spirit, to Which it will surrender in the transparency of the total consent that fulfills it, a Presence the spirit discovers as the Life of its life. Our spirit will harness the Source of life into that space of complete receptivity it maintains within in order to welcome it, thereby becoming itself capable of communicating it, a source itself in the Source, inasmuch as the only tie that binds it to itself is the same tie that binds it to the Source.

Many of our contemporaries ackowledge and claim, in principle, the inviolability of the person *without seeing* that it is founded on a dignity that must be conquered. If every individual is to be assured of his power to be the origin of his very own *personal* life, it will entail on his part undergoing a radical transformation, creating the inner space that justifies respect and becoming, in the depths of his being, a universal good that the whole world can acknowledge as its own. In fact, people readily invoke the principle of inviolability to conceal a "private" life in which one does "as one pleases", supported by a kind of general complicity that simply ignores the preoccupation of becoming truly human. The need for inner liberation seems particularly alien to the "free" world, and yet, it is the necessary condition for the birth of the person whose rights it claims to defend. To say that in the West one can publicly scorn all moral values is a euphemism, since it firmly believes in none, having lost all reference to an absolute. One must try to save one's skin, one's position, one's comfort and one's pleasures, for as long as one can, and, if one has the means, let psychiatrists handle teenagers who call for free love, drugs and the right to bring the house down.

Fortunately, there are surviving elements of Christianity that cause sudden bursts of justice and generosity, and foster among many people of modest means a genuine honesty I never cease to admire. But by dint of suggesting to them, in every possible way, that they are fools for abiding by any discipline, society will succeed in making them weary of their own virtues.

In sketching this picture, I merely wish to express how urgent it is to "convert to our own selves", as Saint-Exupéry says, by living to the end our need for liberation about which we cannot cheat ourselves, for whenever we allow our instincts to control us, we compromise our dignity as creators and, eventually, we may forget it. And yet, the essential nobility of our life lies in this possibility of choosing ourselves, in the power to be our own origin actualized in an authentically personal self.

It is in this perspective of liberation that I would like to bring up briefly the problem of chastity, more than ever a timely topic and one that presupposes, it goes without saying, a stand with regard to sexuality.

François Jacob wrote that "what a bacterium seeks without respite is to produce two bacteria".[1] This means that living species, from the most elementary stage, escape destruction only by reproduction. The precision of this mechanism is astounding. Through countless perfectly coordinated reactions, programmed by a genetic code which we understand increasingly better, new individuals are born from those who preceded them. Except for some accidents, they are endowed with the same molecular structures, the same genetic heredity which they will be able to pass on, unchanged, for billions of years—our own fascinating history that comes down to us through the sexualization of our species. Beyond simple division (as in the case of bacteria), sex specializes the reproductive elements into egg and sperm, and they are entrusted, except in cases of hermaphrodism, to individuals of different sex—male and female—who will have to mate for

---

[1] François Jacob, *The Logic of Life: A History of heredity.* Translated by Betty E. Spillmann, New York, Pantheon Books, 1973, p. 4.

fertilization to take place in the mother's body. This necessity to join two complementary seeds (the two gametes) forms the basis for the carnal union from which we are born.

Genetic history, on a human scale, can be read on three different levels: physical, psychic and personal.

First, there is the union of the gametes, the fusion of the sperm and the egg that leads to a unique combination of genes for every individual (except in the case of identical twins). As far as the species is concerned, it is all there. The individual is but an ephemeral actualization of a structure which, it is true, cannot exist without him, but is organized is such a way as to outlive him, using him as a relay to renew its impulse. Could there be in this a suggestion of immortality, or the intervention of some form of anti-chance (which would be interesting to study)? Whatever we may hypothesize, that fact itself is clear. As soon as a living structure appears, it tends to last, perpetuating its type with such "invariance", in Jacques Monod's words, that any evolution would be impossible were the biological mechanisms so rigid as to exclude "accidents" that result in mutations (harmful or beneficial). In sexual reproduction, this tendency to last, in our species as in all the others, tries its luck in the chemical marriage of the sperm and the egg, an occurence as "innocent" as it is unconscious. No one would be interested in these elements (and their fusion)—except for scientists who observe them in the laboratory as they do any other phenomenon—if sexuality did not radically permeate our whole psyche. This makes it very difficult for us to perceive, objectively and dispassionately, these minute realities which, through a most complex hormonal chemistry, have an immeasurable emotional impact.

What strikes us first is the spontaneous dissociation, on the psychological level, between reproduction and the attraction of one sex for the other. Works of art about love, as well as all the songs written about it, always revolve around *two* partners, exhilarated by their meeting each other. Sexual union is constantly understood and suggested, if not explicitly manifested, as the ultimate goal of the love game. The child, however, has no place in this duo whose ecstasy does not seem to have anything to do with procreation. We can see here nature's cunning stratagem for the species. In order to bring the two bearers of complementary seeds in each other's presence, it casts a spell over their psyche, using a whole range of impulses that make their union appear as their *own good*, and a most pleasurable one which, if need be, they will fiercely defend against rivals, sometimes to the death.

To what extent do hormones (gonadotropins) or sexually charged fantasies, emanating from the unconscious or aroused by the erotic pressure brought to bear on individuals by the social environment, to what extent do they stimulate in our species this desire to possess? Three factors appear to intervene, to various degrees depending on individual predispositions and the prevailing social customs. Auguste Forel spoke of "engrams", or psychoorganic imprints that determine in each sex the knowledge of and attraction for the other. There must be clues for mutual recognition which mysteriously come into play at all ages (from early childhood) and can take all kinds of forms (even fetishism). The important thing to keep in mind in connection to our point is that the state of being in love, whatever the individual "charms" that trigger it, aims at physical union, while it ignores, even positively excludes, its natural outcome. This means that the determinisms of the species are so intimately intermingled with the traits of the two partners that they can only express their union by resorting to the language of the species. "That is the only way of holding on to them", said to me a virtuous wife who possibly needed to find some good excuses to "keep her husband". But you also lose them that way. The fierce hatred I witnessed between divided spouses, after happy beginnings, proves that the *anonymous* aspect in the "spell" cast by the species as a whole can leave them totally indifferent to each other when the "charms" have lost their power. Desire overvalues what it wants to possess and develops a distaste for what no longer stimulates it.

Love must be a path to the Infinite or it very quickly becomes a prison. Why bind one's life to someone whose limitations are all too obvious, unless two people make the commitment together to look beyond them and to try and find each day a new reason to respect each other? What chance will the spouses have of each *becoming origin* if their love is not centered on this very need, if they do not succeed in rising above the species by attaining, through each other, the autonomy and dignity of the person which, on the human scale, is the one universal good?

On the level of the person, where we seek *someone*, the sexual problem appears as one of *liberation* from the determinisms of the species to which eroticism *binds itself* in order to experience pleasure; it will do whatever it takes to get round them and avoid the consequences, the only natural link left with procreation, which can now be avoided by contraceptive means available to everyone. Partners can refine upon their pleasure in a vacuum, so to speak, like "lustful robots", as one outstanding educator once said, fully subjected to the impact of the species on the psychic level, while radically thwarting its plan on the physiological one. On the contrary, the quest for the person, through love, will begin with the partners acknowledging the natural link between sex and procreation, in other words, by the discovery of the *third person* —the child—potentially present in the complementary seeds borne by the man and the woman respectively. Then the physiological differences will organize themseves and be personalized in relation to a third party, and it is in connection with this third party that they will acquire creative significance. The spirit that will prevail then is one of total dedication; it will induce the spouses to conquer their personality, truly becoming their own origin, in order to give birth to a being conceived as a person and whom they will raise as a person, establishing with him the kind of person-to-person relationship which is often sadly missing between today's parents and children.

Every child would like to be born out of such a consecration: the respect surrounding his origin would show him the way to his own greatness and continue to foster his development by appealing to his interiority, which this very respect would constantly make real to him. Spouses aware of their own interiority, who always come together as persons are obviously the only ones who can create the atmosphere in which a child is imbued with the sense of his own dignity. For his educators cannot demand from him what they do not first demand of themselves, but if they fulfill this requirement for truth, their presence is enough to instill it as the most precious gift of their love. We speak, and rightly so, of the traumas suffered by children abandoned by their parents; nothing will ever heal the wounds inflicted on their unconscious by such a loss. But think of the ravages caused by parents who are unconcerned about discovering the human dimension in their own lives, and, as a result, are totally incapable of helping their children acknowledge and exercise their freedom as a liberating power. *Yet, it is in man's nature to transcend his nature,* to become his own origin by going from the given to the giving, from the possessive ego to the self-sacrificing self, from the prefabricated identity he takes from physical birth to the creative autonomy of a new birth.[2] Therefore, nothing is more harmful to love and to human procreation than to turn sex into an absolute that everyone must be able to enjoy unrestrainedly, as soon as possible, since pregnancy can be avoided with certainty. Indeed, we must *first* proceed to humanize ourselves organically, by overcoming the inner servitudes that make us psychological slaves to the species, in a dependence all the more absurd as we refuse to accept it on the physiological level. We are not meant to be subjected to what we call the body (which we are), but to create it like everything else. A body reduced to its erogenous zones is as far from a humanized body, vested with a soul, as the faceless individual slapped by the Nazi captain (who has not really seen him) is from Koriakoff suddenly

---

[2] A new birth that becomes supernatural in Christian baptism.

acknowledged as a person by the German colonel who makes amends for the insult he has just suffered.

Peace, justice, equality, education for all: what do all these terms mean if man is nothing but a pleasure-seeking animal into which we want to turn fourteen and fifteen-year-olds, solicited right outside their own high-schools by enticing propaganda that goes completely unchecked? What rights could possibly claim this pathetic creature, whom we insist on reducing to its sexual functions while systematically making them sterile?

One must choose: either man does not exist and what he does neither has meaning nor implies responsibility; or else, man exists with the power to create himself, and he achieves in an original self the supreme good of humanity and the universe.

The morality of liberation, which goes back to the Holy Trinity, introduces the same requirement in all spheres. It is always and everywhere a matter of turning oneself into a true human being, by actualizing the capacity for the infinite, which defines the spirit, and eliminating all that stands in the way of our full autonomy.

In his *Letters to a young poet,* Rilke noted about immature individuals who engage in precocious sexual relations that "they intermingle but they have nothing to exchange." Long before him, Kierkegaard had pointed out the condition for truly creative encounters in these magnificent words: "Absolute proximity lies in infinite distance." The distance of respect is what reveals the depth of love that each one must experience as the ultimate requirement of being, in that limitless space opened up by the other's trust. Indeed, *human* love concerns *persons*. What is more, it must shape them, with their individual subtle differences, in equal dignity. In the *human trinity*, the child is *ex-utroque* (from the one and the other) as is the Holy Spirit in Western theology. The child's father and mother are united in their indivisible relationship with him, which gives rise to the relationship he maintains with them. Woman "for whom everything is possible if she loves", as a woman-physician told me, appears as a mediator between the man and the child, "the fruit of her womb". Her desire is to be born of the man's heart (supposing that he has reached the same level of generosity as she has). In some way, she is his Son and his Word. And man finds fulfillment in giving himself to her; through his gift, life takes on a face for the woman, a face to which she can devote all her capacity to love. "He is alive" : I will never forget these words from a young woman whose fiance had been an officer on active duty throughout the Second World War. Before even greeting me, after years of absence, she uttered this cry of happiness : "He is alive !" Thus life keeps its meaning because it is always revealed through the same face.

The human trinity, undoubtedly the most beautiful image of divine Trinity, can only grow and blossom if founded on the same self-divesting that characterizes God's inner relationships. This may seem paradoxical in connection with the idea of possession one usually associates with love. But if love is directed at the person, if it wants to contribute to the birth and development of the self-as-origin in which the person asserts itself, it must keep virginally intact, in both partners, the capacity for the infinite. This is the condition for surpassing oneself more and more in a constant progress toward the boundless Presence that alone can fully satisfy the person. It implies constant self-effacement into that Presence so as not to intercept its radiant light. Everything that limits the person thus also limits love and augurs its end. The *human* body is a person. Impurity consists in making it an object (anonymous) or a cosmic fetish. It is a refusal to be, a refusal to be origin and, ultimately, a refusal to love.

To what extent do we find, at the center of this sexual problem, traces of the original test which led to the first transgression (Gen 3)? There seems to be a certain analogy of situation. Delighting *in* or being enraptured *by what* we are, without having had anything to do with it; remaining on the level of the species, losing ourselves in it and letting it carry us, instead of going beyond it and, as we ourselves rise, promoting it to the dignity of the person, and in the end, assuming the entire visible universe in a burst of creative freedom: these deficiencies that we find in the first refusal are fairly similar to those that underlie today's refusals to love.

Let me stress very strongly that they are *metaphysical deficiencies*. It goes without saying that organic reality, in itself, is perfectly innocent, and that it is perceived as such if we take it in its physical objectivity, without trying to make it more sophisticated than it is. But when the current of the species flows between the two psychic poles, male and female (at least in the imagination), then the species is bewitched, if we go along with it: it acquires a spellbinding power that includes every degree of irrationality that sensual turmoil can cause.

"Prehistoric" Venuses (Willendorf, Lespugne, etc.) show that humanity has always been sensitive to the mystery of fertility, to the kind of cosmic fascination that permeates the flesh when it is not transfigured (from within) by the spirit. The flesh is ambiguous, as are all our powers to be and to act. Destined to surpass ourselves to reach a personal Infinite, we can debase ourselves to the same extent and sink toward a faceless indefinite entity. But how wonderful when the ascending trend prevails, when a human being is revealed in the light of a gaze that contains the gift of his whole presence!

Dante must have felt the lustral effect of radiant beauty, transparent to his own contemplation, to have written the sonnets of *La Vita nuova* which seem to spring from his heart today.

> *Tanto gentile e tanto honesta pare*
> *la dona mia, quand'ella altrui saluta*
> *ch'ogne lingua deven tremando muta*
> *e li occhi no l'ardiscon di guardare.*[3]

Such sublime love turns towards the sacred mystery which will be unveiled in the marriage-sacrament.

We must certainly keep our eyes constantly fixed on these summits and arm ourselves with patience to climb them. We know the direction we should take; that does

---

[3] *My lady looks so gentle and so pure*
When yielding salutation by the way,
That the tongue trembles and has nought to say,
And the eyes, which fain would see, may not endure.
The Portable DANTE, edited by Paolo Milano, Penguin Books, New York, 1978, p. 594.

not excuse us from making this difficult ascent in which we rise through continuous self-transformation.

If it is true that we can commit ourselves to marriage for life only on the basis of an infinite Good—and the supreme exchange of love consists in the communication of this good—it is just as true that this Good, in the spouses' life as well as everybody else's, is not fully attained at one go. Many imperfections must be accepted, as steps towards a goal, to reach the balance of perfection; the only thing that matters is never to turn away from it. For instance, there is in marriage a world of tenderness which is the absolutely essential condition for a life together accepted in joy. Physical union may express it *spontaneously* regardless of any procreative intention. But, in that case, it is difficult to imagine intrusive contraceptive devices, incompatible with such an impulse. At any rate, in a morality of liberation, physical union can only be a step on the road of love-of-the-person, which transcends the species by becoming eternal in the sharing of the living God.

Chastity (which, on the contrary, is not broken by a procreative act aimed at the person of the child) is a privilege offered to spouses, as to anyone concerned with becoming a true human being by originating his own self.

Consecrated celibacy is a form of chastity particularly worthy of esteem and veneration, a testimony to authentic freedom actualized in self-liberation, which obviously implies the same detachment in all other areas of existence. If we assume this, we cannot think of a better guarantee than a life totally divested of self to give substance to a Gospel in which God reveals himself as pure giving in the eternal communion of love, the mystery of his own innermost being.

Nietzsche keenly perceived the two sides of the problem before us, as evidenced in Zarathustra's moving appeal: "May your love [man's and woman's] be pity for the veiled suffering gods, but most often it is an animal sensing another."[4]

This remarkable text acknowledges, in every human being, a mysteriously captive Infinite that love should strive to release.

Love seeks the person. Where indeed will the person be found if not in the translucent space where souls intermingle as they each live and breathe in the same God?

---

[4] He also wrote: "The most polished words I ever heard: 'In real love, it is the soul that envelops the body'."

16

The Meaning of a Miracle

The Gospel according to St. John, the spiritual Gospel *par excellence*, gives an account of Jesus' first miracle, the miracle at the wedding at Cana. The "secular" circumstances in which it is performed, the utmost discretion surrounding it, and the fact that the Mother of our Lord personally intervenes (Jn 2:1-11) are surprising. We can begin by tentatively defining it as the manifestation, through a phenomenon perceptible to the senses, of the *freedom of the spirit*. Our organic life roots us in the physical world, and we constantly experience our physiological and even psychological dependence on it. However, we rise above it by the spirit which unifies it in an overall view, and marvellously harnesses its energies, adapting them to our needs, depending on the control that knowledge gives us over their workings. More directly yet, we manage to discipline these energies within the limits of our own individuality through temperance, hygiene, moderation and chastity. But we have no immediate power over them outside our body. Indeed, it is not enough for us to *will* it for them to be transformed to our liking and to follow our own personal rhythm, as do the foods we digest. And yet, it seems that it should be so in the natural order of things. If the universe is our body in some way—or its matrix—the appearance *of the spirit* in us should affect it greatly, since it immediately puts it in tune with the need for interiority and freedom implied by the emergence of the spirit. All reality could then be personalized through us, as it were, spontaneously lending itself to the realization of creation's highest potentialities.

In fact, a *break* exists, between the physical world that carries us and our spirit which, in a sense, is its crowning achievement; it might be a consequence of original sin.

Miracles occasionally restore, in the realm of actuality, the *unity* that would have normally prevailed in the universe if the forces of nature were subordinated to the spirit's legitimate demands. A miracle heralds what will undoubtedly be the definitive order of the universe, when the physical world will itself be totally assumed by the spirit. It reminds us that we must not separate from the universe, as if it were irremediably outside ourselves, but rather that we must transmit to it, as much as possible, the sacrificial impulse in our heart, thus making the universe participate in the divine presence, which will be reflected on it insofar as that presence becomes the life of our life. Therefore, an authentic miracle does not conflict with the "laws" of nature which merely express (statistically) deterministic phenomena left to their own automatic processes. On the contrary, a miracle fulfills, intermittently, the most fundamental vocation of the universe which is to express God by letting "the light from his face" shine through, thereby suggesting a cosmic order in which we would move from being something to being someone.

The circumstances in which the miracle of Cana takes place are no less remarkable than the miracle itself. We refer to them as secular (in front of or outside a hallowed setting). But what does secular mean from Jesus' point of view? This nuptial feast, to which he is invited, represents a unique event in the lives of his hosts. If it becomes a source of embarrassment because they cannot honor the crowd of guests, larger than expected, who have rushed in to congratulate them, they will forever remember this day as a bad omen. On the contrary, if everyone is abundantly satisfied, they will always recall it, even unconsciously, as a happy prelude, a token of happiness. Indeed, the way man looks at life is one of the very elements that constitute it, and it is extremely important that he be able to view it with enough confidence to make it seem good. When St. John of the Cross writes: "One single thought of man is worth more than the whole world; consequently, God alone is worthy of it", he precedes Pascal on the heights of intelligence; but many will remain insensitive to this sublime statement because the world of thought is not where they seek to dwell. They have an *affective* understanding of what concerns them and, if we hope to convince them, we must touch them in the complexity of feelings rooted in their unconscious. In other words, their heart is what inspires their life choices, because they need to meet *someone* so as not to be hurt in the blind world of things.

This is precisely what lights up the whole scene at Cana, giving it the infinitely delicate shades that only Rembrandt's brush could have caught: a *presence* is about to come between the things that are running out and the hosts who would unexpectedly be deprived of them. The couple will not likely find out about the risk they ran until after the wedding, and they will be all the more amazed that the worse was averted as it was done with such power, hidden with such discretion. This is how, relatively speaking, liberation generally begins, when we begin to renounce ourselves and turn to God. A kind overture has implicitly revealed Him by opening up enough room for the spirit to breathe in. When it is acknowledged, the personality tends to actualize itself. One gratuitous act calls for another; we wish to become someone because we have met someone. The wedding feast at Cana concretely and eminently expresses the effectiveness of a simple gesture that awakens a sense of the sacred, while reaching down with absolute respect to the depths of man. The same thing happens to the Samaritan woman who discovers her soul in the infinite solicitude that unveils its value to her.

By contrast, a world deprived of its sacred dimension is one which an authentic presence no longer illuminates, I mean a presence that is truly a present, a gift that calls for a gift in return. Then we feel the full weight of all the internal and external necessities that condition our lives, when our humanity goes to sleep.

See the worker on the assembly line of a large factory, doing the same thing eight hours a day; he must fit, without any break, into a sequence of gestures in which his own becomes automatic; see the young woman who does piece work in a watch factory; she must put together minute works with a speed that determines her wages: how could they not feel they are robots, doomed to perform tasks that are meaningless to their heart and spirit, unless they bear within a face that mentally frees them from such slavery?

Generally speaking, the awakening of aspirations to an authentically personal life unquestionably depends on a certain quality of presence, and nothing, not even supernatural means, can ordinarily substitute for total absence of humanity.[1] Man is ready to rediscover the meaning of the sacred as soon as he meets someone who is really interested in what he is.

Fr. Georges tells a revealing story in *Le Maquis de Dieu* (God's Underground). During the Second World War, he was a military physician and a member of the Slovak resistance to Hitler's rule. Having joined the Russian army with his combat unit, he was invited by Stalin to come to Moscow, along with other officers from his group; they were billeted at the police station. Obviously, no one suspected that he was a priest. One evening, when he was waiting for everything to be quiet to celebrate Mass, a police woman knocked on his door to tell him that, since her husband was away, she thought she could spend the night with him. He made her sit down and was so attentive toward her, something she probably had never experienced, that she was induced to tell her story, beginning with her childhood and recalling her deceased parents whose memory was particularly dear to her. And then a question burst from her lips, one she had likely never had the opportunity to ask before: "Where are they, where are the dead?" Until dawn, Fr. Georges gave her

---

[1] Cf. the escape of St. John of the Cross from the prison in Toledo.

the answers she dared not hope for, and after fifteen days, during which time he kept on instructing her, she asked for and received baptism. She would surely never have thought of being baptized had he not received her with infinite respect, which had led her back, as a first step, to the silent regions where every soul keeps its secret.

In a yet more moving way, Oscar Wilde's *De profundis* confirms the prodigious effectiveness of a (unique) presence in the desert of universal absence. This great English writer, who died totally destitute in Paris in 1900 (the same year as Nietzsche), ruined his career, as you may recall, because of his affair with a young English lord. It created a scandal throughout the United Kingdom towards the end of the Victorian era. Oscar Wilde was forced to appear before a court of assizes and condemned to an infamous incarceration in the prison at Reading. There, in addition to his famous ballad, he wrote the *De profundis* that brings him so close to us. No one was less prepared for such a disgrace, which turned everyone against him, than this prince of dandies, spoiled and adulated in all the fashionable circles that had always competed for his company. His wife hastened to change her name, and succeeded so well in erasing all memory of her marriage to him that their two sons, small children at the time, learned that he was their father only in adulthood. His friends carefully avoided to show up in court, while his rivals gave free rein to their joy at seeing a fallen man. Once the sentence was passed, he was led back to prison, a terribly lonely man, through a hostile crowd of curious bystanders who stared at him with contempt. One man, however, waiting for him to pass, bowed down deeply before him. It was the only glimmer of humanity in the depths of despair into which Wilde almost sank during the first year of his emprisonment. Finally, having struggled in vain against what seemed a monstrous fate, this silent homage from the only friend who had remained loyal to him appeared as a promise of redemption. In spite of his fall, someone had believed in him, someone had seen that his worth was intact and that it justified the hope for a future of which it would be the foundation stone. From that moment on, he came to terms with his fate to the point of writing: "The greatest blessing in my life was the day society sent me to prison." It is in that dreadful jail, where he could see hanged men swinging at the end of their rope, that he was freed from his tremendous vanity and that he discovered the sacred as the ultimate meaning of what is specifically human. That is why the breakdown of his marriage took on a new significance in this admirable stroke of inspiration: "Love is a sacrament that one must receive on one's knees", as did his failure as a father which he accepted in this deeply moving confession: "The body of a child is like the body of the Lord: I am worthy neither of the one nor of the other."

One does not write such thoughts without living them. They truly spring *de profundis*, from the depths which we can only discover after having relinquished all things. Total relinquishment is the purest offering from us to the Presence in whom, without looking at ourselves, we see ourselves at last.

But, in order to come to that, there had to be, in Wilde's case, the infinitely discreet appeal to the best of him, in the form of a gesture of respect which showed him the possibilities the future held for him. And that, no doubt, corresponds to a universal need. Indeed, it is on the level of the *person* that we experience the "spiritual" as a reality, because the person is actualized in us in the process of self-liberation, and liberation implies *someone* to whom we give ourselves, in the depths of our being.

That is how, it would seem, the original core of spiritual life is formed. Unless we perceive a presence within ourselves, how can we emerge from the narcissism that makes us cling frantically to what we are, and whereby we gauge reality solely with the subjective passions in which we are trapped? This is precisely why the first concern of one's apostolate should be to lead others to the Presence within them: we can, as our own self disappears in It, let It shine for them through our human presence.

An English priest, Fr. Tyrrell, showed in his book, *The Unreality of Words*, that words that do not bear life are tragically ineffective; since they do not flow from life, they cannot lead to it. This warning seems more timely than ever.

I often wonder about the appeal that so many concerts and other high-quality shows have for thousands of listeners or spectators. What they look for, and often find, is a source of wonder that, for one moment, will set them free from themselves in that silent encounter with the Presence. Any great artist will make It perceptible to the audience when, as Ansermet used to say about Dinu Lipatti, his performance becomes "the communication of a person through the gift of self".

How fruitful the priestly ministry would be if it always aimed at bringing about, in everyone, this encounter with "the Spring of life eternal," while constantly remaining united to it!

Jesus' most bitter enemies were religion specialists, locked in a world of concepts with no roots in the deeper regions where the communion of men is achieved in an exchange with God. It is not without a touch of humor that He proposes the heretic Samaritan as a model for them: he may not have been so learned, but he immediately recognized his neighbor in the wounded man lying by the roadside.

To genuinely know God is necessarily to know him as Love personified, and only giving of oneself can reveal him as the Gift that he is.

A priest is doubtless called upon to give so much more than himself in the mystery of the sacraments of which he is the minister, but what better way for him to spark the wish to receive them than to manifest the transformation they bring about in himself?

At Cana, the Mother of the Lord surely knew that her Son's presence was infinitely more important than all the miracles. Still, this Presence had to be recognized and welcomed. Thanks to the intervention that she suggests and obtains from her son, It first comes joyfully into the hearts of the newly-weds as the most beautiful of their wedding gifts.

There is a whole program of pastoral action in that, and it can be admirably summed up in this phrase, modeled on the liturgy: letting the "gentleness of Jesus' joyous face shine forth".

17

Meditation on the Sacraments

A world with no one in it is an uninhabitable place. The very last word of Camus' *Le Malentendu* (The misunderstanding) conveys this with implacable cruelty in the face of a murder the authors of which have committed suicide. Absence, faceless indifference raise a wall before the woman who must face alone her husband's murder. On the other hand, even in the most desperate of circumstances—Oscar Wilde is living proof of it—a human presence is enough to dispel the unbelievable anguish of a cry that goes unheeded. It counterbalances the feeling of the absurd, which can drive wild with grief those who have been totally abandoned, by enabling them to glimpse, behind a universe that seems alien to them, a Face that can give it a meaning.

In the parable of the good Samaritan, Jesus very clearly invites us to become this presence which will make us a true neighbor for others. But it is not merely an exhortation to exclude all forms of indifference from our relationship with others. Jesus makes such a requirement an integral part of the *sacramental structure* that establishes our relationship with our neighbor, as if the salvation of others were inseparably linked to ours. We can even say, I believe, that the sacraments are instituted on purpose for us to be that presence for others in our quest for God, because this quest implies, along with the self-liberation that attests its authenticity, universal communication with others. If the search for God were strictly an individual concern, there would be no need for common signs to prompt it and express it. But such a "private" religion cannot exist if the presence of God in others is as precious and as necessary for the coming of his kingdom as it is within myself.

That is why we can state from the outset that we always receive the sacraments with others and for others as much as for ourselves. This is what I try to explain to those who do not attend Mass because they find it boring. The Mass will interest you if you take part in it for the sake of others, and if you understand that they need your presence: because you bear witness to it, the Lord's presence will be confirmed in their eyes.

This *ordinatio ad alterum*, our relation to others at the heart of the sacraments, seems to me of paramount importance. It immediately universalizes our relationship to God and prevents us from bringing it down to the emotional level. A feeling of elation does not necessarily entail true self-denial, no more than the thanklessness of prayer without solace suggests, in itself, any disloyalty.

We can find such greatness in the *baptism* of a child if we view it as an event that affects the whole world. Once the child is integrated into the Mystical Body of Christ and has become the temple of the Holy Spirit, it is enough for him to exist in his new dignity as a baptised Christian to be the bearer of the divine presence and offer it to those around him. He no longer is just a voracious consumer whose only worth lies in his future. He is a shrine, like the one before which Emmanuel Mounier knelt for years, his young daughter whose mind had been destroyed by a fatal vaccine at the age of six months. In that little being, seemingly closed to communication, this great man discovered, thanks to his faith, a host to offer up for all abnormal children; at her bedside, he spent long hours of fruitful meditation that put him in touch with all the miseries of the world.

Confirmation is for each one of us what Pentecost was for the Apostles. It activates the ferment of liberation planted in the soul of every catechumen at the time of his baptismal initiation. It calls Christians to bear witness personally to their faith in such a way that others may always recognize their own good in it. A Chinese boy, at the time of the cultural revolution, had understood this perfectly. The Red Guards had closed down the local church and were preventing anyone from going in; so totally committed was he to the Lord that, when they said: "Go away, there is no Church any more", he simply replied: "What Church are you talking about? I am the Church."

The sacrament of *penance* is no less open to others. "The soul that rises lifts the world with it" (Elizabeth Leseur) and enriches the communion of saints with all the light it becomes, as long as it keeps on rising. But, by the same token, the soul that falls brings down the world by depriving it of the common good it might have been for all through self-denial; it thus reinforces the communion of darkness in which evil spreads. In other words, I am guilty toward others insofar as I am guilty toward God. This is what I acknowledge when I confess my sins to a priest who represents both God and man, and who can grant me the forgiveness of God and man by absolving me in the name of Christ, the Word made flesh, indivisibly God and man. I believe it was Fr. MacNabb who emphasized this twofold aspect of confession and sacramental absolution, something Pascal had understood when he wrote: "How unjust and unreasonable is the heart of man, which feels it disagreeable to be obliged to do in regard to one man what in some measure it were right to do to all men! For is it right that we should deceive men?" The sincerity with which we "undeceive" the priest by confessing our sins appeared to him, and rightly so, as a kind of atonement to those we "deceive" by showing them a face that does not correspond to what we are.

The *anointing of the sick*, while it implores for a cure, aims first at invigorating the life of grace, debilitated by the after-effects of sin, thereby reviving the flame of charity that kindles the whole of creation. This sacrament induces the sick person to live through his illness with the spiritual dimension of an organism consecrated by divine presence. Through the *anointing*, his ordeal comes within the communion of the whole Church whose intervention makes it fit into the overall plan of the kingdom of God. The sacrament prepares him either to take his place again within the community with renewed fervor, or to turn his death into an act of life by offering it for the growth of others, as Fr. Kolbe did with absolute freedom at Auschwitz.

This sacrament of the ill provides a basis for the special mysticism that inspires the nursing religious orders. It allows them to have a better grasp of their admirable vocation which consists precisely in making illness a source of life, up to and including the time of death. These sick human beings, greatly undermined on the physical level and in the realm of action, can in fact achieve endless progress in the order of being, where only love sets the levels. Hence the supreme concern of the Church for those it describes, in truly evangelical terms, as the suffering members of Christ.

Matrimony which, by its very nature, is a unique opening onto another, becomes that even more when it is assumed as a sacrament, whereby it rises above the species by aiming to humanity-as-person of which Christ, as the second Adam, is the leader and the head. Called upon to become persons through mutual giving, the spouses will discover in Him the way to self-divesting as the only path to liberation; this in turn will lead them to live the human trinity mentioned above, in which family relations are stripped of all attachment to oneself. Inasmuch as they can fulfill this infinitely demanding love, the *sine qua non* condition for lasting happiness, they can universalize their union and extend fatherhood and motherhood to the entire world. Whoever has shed his own self to the point of being completely open to receive inside him the personality of another is capable of experiencing each person's worth as his own. It is through this intimate universality that marriage as a sacrament symbolizes and accomplishes, in its own sphere, the mystical marriage of Christ with the Church.

The sacrament of *Holy Orders*, inasmuch as it confers the power of ministering the sacraments, includes most explicitly this relation to others found in each sacrament. We can even say that it does so exclusively since, as a rule, the consecrated minister cannot give himself the sacraments. He is a deacon, priest or bishop for others, but not for himself. He has been handed over to them, so to speak, as the hostage of God, and they have the right to demand God of him.

But it is the sacrament of the *Eucharist*, the "sacrament of sacraments", from which we all derive, as it were, and around which we order our lives, that expresses and realizes to the fullest the reference to our neighbor implied in all sacred rites. I try to make it concrete to children by telling them this parable.

A French engineer was invited to South America around 1895 to build a great dam on the Amazon river. Since he had ten children and wanted to ensure the best possible future for them, he let himself be tempted by this offer that would free him of all financial worries. Circumstances forced him to be away from his family for some twelve years, during which time he had the misfortune of losing his wife. After her death, his children split up into two hostile camps. When the father returned to France, now almost a stranger to them, he was unable to reconcile them and, overwhelmed with grief, he in turn died. His children, naturally, all threw themselves on his will which would give them access to his wealth. The will was locked away in a chest that could only be opened by spelling a code word on a key with movable letters. The will specified that the children had to look for the word *together*. They thought of all the names used in the family and tried them each in turn, but to no avail. The lock did not budge. They reread the will and noticed that the word "together" was underlined. They spelled it on the key and fit it in the lock; the chest opened. Then they understood their father's intent and, touched by this call from beyond the grave, they made their peace with one another.

Together is also the key word of the Eucharist. If we put John's testimony together with that of the synoptic gospels, we can underline, at the Lord's last supper, the washing of the feet (Jn 13:1-15), the proclamation of the new commandment (Jn 13:34-35) and the institution of the Eucharist (Mk 14:22-24 and par.). It is only natural to connect these three events in which love is illustrated successively with an action, a precept and a sacrament. Ecumenism, part of Jesus's personal structure, is expressed in a kind of irresistible *crescendo* as the requirement we must meet so that he may dwell in us and we in him. For the whole question lies there: Jesus must be able to live in us, as the source of a new life that will spring with the consent of our whole being. Our relationship to him is not that of the disciples to the master who offers teachings they must put to good use solely with their intelligence. His word is geared to his presence, to the gift of his person that must become the principle of inner liberation, as St. Paul reminds the Galatians: "It is no longer I who live, but Christ who lives in me" (Gal 2:20).

We know from experience that a person's innermost being can only be received by another's innermost being and according to that person's capacity for welcoming the other. Total self-divesting will be needed before we can "don the mantle of Christ" (Gal 3:27), so as not to bring him down to our level and turn him into an idol, which would prevent him from being "formed" in us (Gal 4:19). It is precisely to avert this danger that Jesus invites us to a meal, where we come *together* and accept responsibility for one another. Together, indeed, does not simply mean to gather in one place, but actually to take charge of one another. This concerns all of humanity, as it is destined to be most deeply united in the "mystical body" of the Lord.

I believe we can say that the presence of the mystical body is essentially implied in the advent of the eucharistic presence. The words of the consecration, which result in the mysterious Parousia of the Lord under the sacred species, were entrusted to the Church whose name is *Agape*, Love (Ignatius of Antioch), because Love is its breath in the Holy Spirit. These are not magic words to be uttered anywhere at any time. When the Church uses them, they constitute both the call from the mystical body to its Leader (to its Head) and the Lord's answer in his actual presence.

One can hardly imagine a eucharistic liturgy that would not be lived somewhere in the world in authentic love of the soul; at the very least, it would assume its communal dimension in everyone's name and for everyone's sake. Otherwise, Christ would be called by no one and for no one and, in fact, there would no longer be any Church. Nor can we accept as valid a consecration deliberately performed outside the Church and against it, as supposed in the movie *Le Défroqué* (The Defrocked priest). The main character, played by Pierre Fresnay, is an apostate priest who, in a bar, wants to consecrate a champagne-bucket for fun, even if he has no intention of doing what the Church does. St. Ignatius of Antioch had already declared invalid such a sacrilege when he wrote to the Smyrneans: "Shall be held as valid only the Eucharist presided over by the bishop or by one delegated by him" (VIII, 1). We must also reject the idea of a "private" eucharist reduced to meeting individual "religious" needs. The Eucharist is always a public act and a universal gift. It always concerns *the whole Church*. It implies its presence, it exists through it and for it. If every time the Eucharist is celebrated "our redemption is being carried out", it is because it embraces everything that the sacrifice of the Cross (actualized by it) meant to recreate.

In his great book, *The Christian Faith Yesterday and Today*, Ratzinger admirably brings out this link between the Eucharist and the Church by reminding us that the term *"communio sanctorum"* first meant the communion or sharing of the same "sacred gifts", and that "it refers to the eucharistic community which unites the Churches scattered throughout the world in *only one* Church by virtue of the body of Christ", the "true link of [this] unity." By a natural extension of this first meaning, the community of persons, "united and sanctified" by the *sancta* (sacred things), came to be itself designated as the communion of saints.

These considerations are enough to establish that the Eucharist requires universality and that, in order to approach its mystery, we have to become the Church. We must indisputably be present to the whole Church community and, indeed, the Eucharist has possibly been instituted to this very end. Christ as the Word *Incarnate* is conceivably already present in every soul in a state of grace, since his humanity is indissolubly linked to his function as mediator of all graces. Thus, in a certain sense, he is already there; we, on the other hand, are not (not always enough) and must actualize our presence in order to rejoin his; he offers it to us under the appearance of a meal so that, by partaking of the same divine nourishment, we may become one body. St. Paul says it explicitly in this verse of the *First Epistle to the Corinthians*: "Because there is one bread, we who are many are one body, for we partake of the one bread" (10:17).

Just as the Incarnation makes Christ's humanity inseparably present (by his "assumption unto God"[1]—who was already there) to the Word in whom it subsists, similarly we could say that the Eucharist makes us present, as a community, to the already-present Jesus by requiring and bringing about the self-divesting that roots us in the Eucharist's universality. This is what Pope St. Gregory suggests when he writes: "When we celebrate the sacred mysteries, we must sacrifice ourselves in contrition of the heart because, as we celebrate the mysteries of the *passion* of our Lord, we must imitate what we celebrate. Our contrition will then truly become our host (an expiatory victim) in the presence of God, when we ourselves will have become hosts."[2] Before him, St. Leo the Great had said as much in other words when he stated that the Cross was foreshadowed by the prophets as the altar "where, through the Host of salvation, the offering of human nature is celebrated".[3]

No doubt, the offering of the whole universe can justifiably be included in this offering of human nature. This leads us to question ourselves about the *cosmic* significance of the Eucharist, in reference to the cosmic primacy of Christ, so powerfully expressed by St. Paul in the *Epistle to the Colossians* (1:15-20). If what we have

---

[1] Cf. *Creed* of St. Athanasius.

[2] Fr. de la Taille, *Mysterium fidei*, Dial. 4, 59 ap., p. 8.

[3] *ibid.*

to do is transform the given in us into giving, and also transfigure "matter" within ourselves with a view to the spirit, how can the physical world share in this transfiguration? The great biblical *Benedicite*, in the wake of the psalmists, and all the traditional liturgies with their varied symbolism, St. Francis' *Canticle to the Sun* and the *Spiritual Canticle* by St. John of the Cross, all magnificently praise the whole of creation. Science in its quest for truth and art in its hymn to beauty, each in its own fashion, orchestrate these sacred lauds with inexhaustible inventiveness. But these "elevations" promote humanity without directly modifying the universe; however, they may contribute in various ways to create a climate in which miracles can more easily appear, in the physical world, as manifestations of the freedom of the Holy Spirit whose presence is revealed in us by our own liberation.

Here a question comes up: what does a miracle in general, and the eucharistic miracle in particular, mean to the universe? A scientist like Einstein felt he was in communion with "the highest wisdom and the most radiant beauty" manifested in creation. He experienced a kind of inner contact with this "incomprehensible universe," in a "profound emotional conviction of the presence of a powerful and superior reason revealed" in it. Someone who has witnessed a miracle, as Carrel did in Lourdes, no doubt lives with the perception of a personal intervention from divine power, a much clearer experience of the harmony that could exist between the inside and the outside, between cosmic energies and what Bergson called "spiritual energy". This harmony could lead to a unification that would transform the universe, as it would be entirely and definitively assumed by the Spirit, when humanity itself had been sufficiently liberated.

The eucharistic miracle is above all the conversion of substances—the bread into the Body and the wine into the Blood of Christ—and it works on the deeper level *of being*, but only on the elements of bread and wine, Christ himself undergoing no transformation. Perhaps such a miracle plants in the universe a particularly active ferment for this final transfiguration alluded to in the Bible as "a new heaven and a new earth" (2 Pet 3:13), just as it arouses in us the desire to restore our inner virginity, by internalizing all our powers to be and to act in a kind of anticipation of the resurrection positively promised to all those who eat of the "bread of Life" (Jn 6:50-58). A progressive evolution of the whole of creation, driven by the powerful attraction of the Eucharist, would bring about, at least in one aspect it seems, the Lord's cosmic primacy we have referred to in Paul's message to the Colossians.

Once we have accepted the miracle, or rather miracles, which result in the real presence (in a substantive mode) of our Lord in the sacrament of the Eucharist, it might be useful to add some corollaries that derive precisely from the mode of this presence. St. Thomas maintains that it is not of itself a *local* presence,[4] although the species (of bread and wine) under which it is communicated are in a specific place. Therefore, it is not multiplied by the multiplication of the species, nor divided by their

---

[4] St. Thomas, *Summa*, III, 76, art. 5.

division, nor affected by their distance. Fr. de la Taille makes it clear that we must reject the notion of distance "between the body of Christ, as it is specifically found in heaven, and the body of Christ present in the sacrament", as well as the distance "between the body of Christ that exists in a (consecrated) particle in Rome and another one in Paris". Since the consecration produces no change in the body (or the blood of Christ), "he must be found in the Eucharist such as he exists in heaven"[5] without undergoing any transfer (from heaven to earth). The change takes place entirely in the bread, which is always transmuted into the one and only body of Christ who forever remains unchanged.[6] An image comes to mind, that of millions of mirrors turned towards the sun: they all reflect the same light equally without the sun being affected in any way. It is only an image, since each mirror does not actually become "the Sun"—every host, on the other hand, does become the body of Christ—but it gives a good idea of how in Him nothing is changed.[7]

Finally, allow me to mention briefly a few notions that do not call into question in any way the real presence of the whole person of Christ in the Eucharist, but which may be of some importance for its presentation.

Claude Tresmontant forcefully reminds us in two works, *Comment se pose aujourd'hui le problème de l'existence de Dieu* (The problem of the existence of God today) and *Le problème de l'âme* (The problem of the

---

[5] F. de la Taille, *op. cit.*, pp. 642-43.

[6] *Ibid.*, pp. 620-21.

[7] *Ibid.*, Scotus' and Tolet's hypothesis, p. 638.

soul), that every living being is a *subsisting structure* that lasts as long as there is life, "even though each of the integrated material elements is renewed". This structure "is not an element, a material thing", although "it integrates" and organizes, as an architect would from inside his work, "a material multiplicity" in perpetual motion to turn the structure into a living body. It is as if the torrent of cosmic energies had been contained and channelled into these *islands of inner life* that living beings are, where they work to execute a "creative program" which, while surpassing them, gives them form. The appearance of life represents the emergence of autonomy; it will grow in stages and lead to consciousness and freedom. A kind of immateriality thus rises from matter which becomes subject to the "specific morphological plan" (Bounoure) according to which every living being builds, maintains and reproduces itself. The ascent of organisms from the simplest to the most complex implies a growth in immateriality, in interiority, in unity and in autonomy, and also that the cosmic energies are increasingly better adapted to the "logic of life" (F. Jacob). It has gone from a bacterium to man, whose mind can hold the whole universe and who can turn his very own death into an act of life.

And so, starting with man, the "inside" can counterbalance the "outside" to the point of prevailing over it (even to the point of immortality), while autonomy is affirmed in self-liberation, in that offering which is born of the encounter with subsisting interiority (pure *intus*), the living God of Augustine.

In the progressive internalization of the universe, the Incarnation shines forth as the supreme communication (eminently supernatural) of divine interiority to humanity, and through it, to creation. The Eucharist can be placed in the same perspective. In a miraculous shortcut, it promotes the non-living structure of the bread and the wine (structure here = substance) to the body and blood of the risen Christ, the supreme living structure. Thus, in its own way, it summarizes and prefigures in a transcendent achievement the slow ascent of the universe toward the spirit. That is, at least, how I perceive the cosmic significance of the Eucharist when I raise the consecrated host and silently recite the remarkable verses of Monday's Lauds:

Verusque sol illabere
Micans nitore perpeti
Jubarque Sancti Spiritus
Infunde nostris cordibus.[8]

---

[8] *And you, the true Sun, imbue us with your light,*
You who are resplendent with an eternal fire,
And pour into our hearts
The (morning) splendor of your Holy Spirit.

18

Jesus *Is* the Church

One more or one less crucified man did not count for much in the Roman justice system. In the year 4 B.C., Quintilius Varus, the legate of Syria, had inflicted the torture of the cross on two thousand Jewish rebels; history did not record their names. Thus, humanly speaking, there was every likelihood that we would never have heard of Jesus' death and that he would have been forever obliterated from memory, especially in view of the fact that he had not written anything that might have kept his name alive. His death meant a failure which his disciples could not remember without seeing in it the collapse of all their hopes. Only the Lord's resurrection revived their faith, which had been buried along with his body, by giving the tragedy on Calvary the divine dimension that opened it onto the future, even though its precise meaning still escaped them.

Two things appear certain. The first is that the resurrection was a *confidential* event, as it were: it was revealed only to close friends, distraught by the catastrophe that called into doubt all their reasons to live. Enemies only heard about it at the very most; they were not confronted, to their embarrassment, to tangible evidence that the Lord had himself previously deemed inappropriate in the parable of poor Lazarus (Lk 16:19-31). The second thing that stands out from the texts at our disposal is that those who actually saw the risen Christ were unable to draw any conclusion regarding the mission they were to carry out. From the account in the Acts, it seems that they were simply waiting for their Master, who had overcome death, to realize the objectives for which they had followed him and which they themselves sum up in their last conversation with him when they ask: "Lord, is this the time when you will restore the kingdom of Israel?" (Acts 1:6). The fact that they bring up their old dreams again at such a moment shows that, on their own, they were incapable of taking the initiative that, a few days later, would lay the foundations of the first Christian community.

That is why we can say that, without the miracle of Pentecost, the miracle of Easter would have remained incomprehensible to them, as is suggested by an impression of unsolved mystery that emanates from the accounts of Jesus' appearing on different occasions.

We are all the more startled to see, in these same disciples, the total absence of hesitation about what they have to do as soon as they receive the "power" of the Holy Spirit. We sense that the Master they had lived with for so long was suddenly and definitively *internalized* to become the innermost principle of their life and action. It is no longer a question of a kingdom for Israel, but of total acceptance of Jesus' Person through baptism, conferred in his name for the remission of sins (Acts 2:38). The Church thus inaugurates its career by facing, from her first successes on, the opposition from the nation's religious leaders. The twelve Apostles, Peter in particular, do not seem aware of the rift that is widening between the community for which they are responsible and the Synagogue whose customs they scrupulously observed. In fact, they are so far from thinking that a break can occur with the Synagogue that, at first, they present Jesus as the one whom "God exalted... at his right hand as Leader and Savior that he might give repentance to *Israel* and forgiveness of sins" (Acts 5:31). This belief is so firm that it will take divine intervention for Peter to bring himself to enter the house of an uncircumcized man and baptize him and his household (Acts 10).

Saul, the fanatic and brilliant enemy, is the first to see how radically incompatible the two ways, the Jewish and the Christian, are. He understands this with the passionate clearsightedness of love that refuses to share and that is ready to use any means to wipe out the evil which, in his eyes, the new Church represents, and this in spite of the moderation shown by his master Gamaliel (Acts 5:34-39 and 22-31). For him as well, the debate will suddenly be internalized in the stunning reversal of his whole being, which will be forever given over to love of Christ in a tireless apostolate among the uncircumcized. On their behalf, he will claim equality with the converts from Judaism by inveighing against those who want to impose circumcision as a condition for salvation. Henceforth, largely due to the impact of his ministry in the pagan world, the break with the Synagogue will become inevitable, in the name of the very principle that makes it necessary, expressed in this quote that sums up the main theme of the Epistles to the Galatians and the Romans: "The Mosaic order served its purpose as preparatory stage and is now over".

This negative conclusion, powerfully motivated, is obviously rooted in the experience of grace that overwhelmed him on the road to Damascus, throwing him at the very heart of the new order where *all* of humanity, infused with new life by Christ's grace, is destined to abolish frontiers and become united in the mystery of the *Church*.

And so, it is *as the Church* that Saul, later known as Paul, meets the Lord for the first time and is blinded by his light (Acts 9:3-8): *I am Jesus whom you are persecuting*. This reply from the Power that takes hold of him as it frees him of himself reveals to Paul, in a flash, that the community he is bent on destroying is the sacrament of the Presence rising inside him. Those he is about to put in chains and whom he is ready to kill, as he took part in the stoning of Stephen, these men and women live of a Person who dwells in them, and now in him. Jesus, who appears to him, identifies with them as the head with the members that it permeates with its impulses. For the *revelation that he is*, as the Word Incarnate, cannot be separated from him. Reduced to discursive reasoning *about* him, revelation would be trapped within the limits of language—it can never express divine reality adequately—made worse by human beings who, under its patronage, might well only express what they themselves would have understood of revelation. And even if such reasoning came *from* the Lord, it would not be enough, for he often had to adapt his teaching to his audience and speak in parables (Mk 4:10 and par.); furthermore, he referred his own disciples to the Holy Spirit to guide them to the whole truth (Jn 16:12). Therefore, he must forever remain the guardian of the definitive revelation contained in his person, and constantly bring back the words *about him* to the infinite Word that *he is*.

In fact, the first speeches attributed to Peter by Luke in the *Acts of the Apostles* are evidence of a rudimentary Christology which cannot but surprise a reader of the canonical gospels, and particularly of the gospel of St. John. The gospels themselves and the other writings from the New Testament have not cleared up all the ambiguities concerning the essence of the Christian message. Indeed, it took centuries to arrive at the *homoousios*[1] of Nicaea (325), *the théotókos*[2] of Ephesus (431), the asunchútôs[3] of Chalcedon (451), all admirable expressions that have considerably enriched our understanding of the faith.

Whatever the future developments, when Christ appears to Paul and says : "I am Jesus whom you are persecuting", thereby making him one of his Apostles, he is identifying with the early apostolic message which has already begun to organize as a community with an embryonic hierarchy, but still remains purely oral and is effectively imprinted in each new member through baptism "for the remission of his sins" (Acts 2 :38). Thus, the words that convey the teachings on Christ (like sacramental rites) lead to his person and are always surpassed in him. Eventually, they will take the form of the inspired Scriptures that will incorporate part of the oral Tradition. This Tradition will continue to complete and interpret the Scriptures, and it will support the definitions by the

---

[1] Consubstantial.

[2] Mother of God (Mary).

[3] Without intermingling or without confusion (of the two natures of Jesus).

Church which, throughout the centuries, will attempt to explain the "one and only sacred trust of the Word of God", which indivisibly comprises both Tradition and the Holy Scriptures.[4]

To find Jesus, who did not himself write anything, we only have the testimonies of those who saw him and who, with the exception of Paul, lived with him (Acts 1 :21-22). The accounts take many forms and they evolved, during the apostolic period, in the light of a personal experience imbued with Christ's presence, which, not surprisingly, must have influenced the presentation of the "strictly historical facts". The Apostles and their collaborators are not academics, in love with history and anxious to tell it while avoiding to appear affected by the facts they are relating. On the contrary, they feel totally involved in the life of the Lord; it has become their own, and they tell it only to spark it in the hearts of others. They naturally stress those aspects that personally touch them or which are most likely to arouse interest in their listeners or readers. They all agree on Jesus' unique transcendence and, apparently without the slightest difficulty, they all bridge the gap between Judaic unitarian monotheism and trinitarian monotheism, implied in this transcendence. If we do not accept transcendence, because we have no other sources, we are necessarily reduced to conjectures based on fragments we take from them, more or less arbitrarily isolated. If we do accept transcendence, we find a particularly enlightening manifestation of it in the words that

---

4 *Vatican II*, 4, p. 47, Éditions du Centurion.

we are focusing on: "I am Jesus whom you are persecuting."

These words mean that Jesus, who has overcome death, remains present *in person* in and through the Church community and, for this reason, "the Revelation that he is" is completely transferred to the Church, while remaining open, in the same immutable *direction*, to an inexhaustibly new understanding. We have said over and over that, in the final analysis, Revelation always brings us back to the infinite self-divesting that shines at the heart of the Trinity as the foundation of God's freedom and the principle and meaning of our own liberation. It is precisely this reference to God's innermost being that maintains the immutable direction I have just alluded to, and that ultimately guarantees the truth. For where can truth be found if not in this pure act of taking hold of being, in the light of absolute relinquishment?

But, of course, the mystery of the Church is the first to benefit from this *identification* with the divine Source which directly affects it, and all we can say about it is summed up in these words: "I am Jesus." It follows that the whole Church is a *sacrament*. If indeed the Church is Jesus, everything that is not Jesus can only be a sign that represents and communicates him. This immediately confers on the Church the status of self-divesting, which is the seal of divine Charity, by making the Church's mission coincide with the self-effacement of all its members, who can effectively bear witness to Jesus only by merging with him. However, it is important to note that this self-effacement implies a twofold aspect: the first, specifically *sacramental*, concerns the apostolic function;

the second, *personal*, concerns the sanctification to which every Christian is called.

When St. Paul writes to the Corinthians, who are breaking up into factions, some claiming to take their inspiration from him or Apollos, others from Kephas or Christ, he asks: "Has Christ been divided? Was Paul crucified for you? Or were you baptized in the name of Paul?" (1 Cor 1:12-13). He concludes: "What then is Apollos? What is Paul? Servants through whom you came to believe, according to the role the Lord assigned to each" (1 Cor 3:5). By these words, he affirms the sacramental self-effacement whereby the Apostles and their successors completely disappear in Christ, in everything that relates to their Church ministry, regardless of their personal worthiness or unworthiness. This ensures the *authority* of the hierarchy, which derives entirely from Jesus and which Paul claims most firmly, in particular in his *Epistle to the Galatians*: "Even if *we ourselves* or an angel from heaven should proclaim a gospel different from the one we have preached, let it be accursed" (Gal 1:8); in the first part of his statement, he acknowledges that this authority would lose all its rights should it turn against the mission of the Church. At the same time, the self-effacement of God's servants guarantees the *freedom* of the faithful who, through the hierarchy, always deal only with Jesus.

It is certainly most desirable that the hierarchy also express this sacramental self-effacement in personal renunciation, another name for godliness, but the effectiveness of apostolic ministry does not depend on the minister's godliness. If we are not baptized in the name of Paul, neither is it Paul's virtue, when he baptizes, that confers on baptism its sanctifying power, but only the holiness of Christ whose "servant" Paul is. The same can be said about the doctrine. We are bound to the revelation transmitted by the Apostles and their successors, but not to their personal interpretation of it.

This seems very important to me. If the Church *is* Jesus, it is in order *to give* Jesus in person. It is on this condition that the definitive revelation, which the Word *is*, becomes really accessible to everyone, either as a source of knowledge or as a sanctifying principle. Otherwise, we would be left with nothing but commentators to pass on his word and jurists to apply his morality in a confusion of ideas mingled with uncontrollable prophetism. Some would give us their "version" of the Gospels, others the products of their unconscious. The proliferation of charismatic movements in Corinth gives us an idea of the kind of anarchy, in thought and behavior, we would come to if Christ had not endowed his Church with an instrument to ensure that his word, as well as the sacred rites that convey his person and his grace, be reliably handed down. And we can see that, in Corinth, apostolic authority has the last word in deciding the use of charismas. This authority has a sacramental character, as does everything that relates to the Church. Those who hold it disappear in Christ, and they can legitimately exercise it only in His radiant presence, wholly found in the Eucharist.

Sign and bond of unity in charity, the Eucharist is also the burning bush of faith: *mysterium fidei* (mystery of faith). In it, Christ sanctifies us in person and becomes the master within us through whom the word proclaiming him bears fruit in his light.

This means that apostolic teaching is directed towards that spiritual understanding in which words come to life in the fiery presence that consumes their limitations, so that they can become *someone* and always bring us back to the interpersonal dialogue in which our innermost being merges into the Lord's. As "a preparation is made to receive or to consecrate the Eucharist through the sanctification of all the sacraments"[5], so are we led to our encounter with Jesus through the preaching of the Gospel (in its own way, also a sacrament, a eucharist of truth). He will remain with us until the end of time as the "one bread" that unites us in one body (1 Cor 10:17).

If I insist on the giving of Christ in person as being the essential mission of the Church, it is first of all because the words spoken to Saul undoubtedly induce me to do so: "I am Jesus whom you are persecuting." But it is also because I think the mission thus understood is the foundation of the Church hierarchy, among the Apostles and their successors. No one will ever match the Word Incarnate in wisdom and holiness; thus, no one, on his own, is capable of communicating the plenitude of Christ. Inevitably, each individual will bring his own limitations to it, unless he be nothing but *pure sacrament* through which Christ in person can operate to the full extent of his power "which knows no limits". That is what the Lord is aiming at when he chooses his twelve Apostles (and, through them, those who will succeed them). He makes them permanent sacraments of his presence, so that we will know where to find him, unerringly, in the doctrine as in

---

[5] St. Thomas, *Summa*, 73, 3.

the Eucharist and in the entire sacramental organization of which his presence is the source. And, through this very supernatural self-divesting, the Apostles receive the power to give Jesus in person.

This is exactly what the Christian people have always expected from their priests who represent concretely the apostolic hierarchy: that they give them Jesus in person. And, clearly, this expectation implies that the priest must act in conformity with what he is. Yet, for all that, the godliness expected of him is not to be confused with Christ's incomparable holiness. There will be necessarily a gap between the virtue of the minister-sacrament and the virtue of the Lord, as St. Ignatius of Antioch acknowledges so movingly: at the dawn of the second century, this most steadfast witness of the "monarchic" episcopate wrote that it was through martyrdom that he would at last become "a true disciple of Jesus Christ" (Rom. IV, 2).

Therefore, one must not equate the example of a respectable life that every priest is obliged to give, as is every Christian, with ministerial power, which has as its mission to actualize sacramentally Jesus' real presence: in his Word as well in the sacred rites, "infused with life by the Eucharist."[6] St. Augustine makes the difference quite clear: "Should Peter baptize, it is He [Christ] who baptizes, should Paul baptize, it is He who baptizes, should *Judas* baptize, it is He who baptizes"[7], however worthy or unworthy the baptizer may be.

---

[6] Fr. de la Taille, *op. cit.*, p. 575.

[7] St. Augustine, *Tract. I in Joan ante medium.*

Understood as the radical self-effacement of all the ministers in the person of Jesus, whom they are called upon to communicate, the Church hierarchy is a matter of faith, as much for the minister as for the faithful who turn to him in this capacity. How would I know that I am a priest if I did not believe that the sacrament of Holy Orders is permanently effective? How could a penitent feel he has been absolved from his sins through me, in the sacrament of penance, if he did not share the same faith, if he did not see infinitely more than the man in the priest? Thus I cannot pride myself on my priesthood, since it is not mine, and the faithful are in no way subordinated to me since they turn to me only insofar as I am not myself. The freedom of the soul remains intact in these relationships if they are established, as they must be, in the person of the Lord.

It is all too evident that there have been abuses on the part of the hierarchy, inasmuch as it has used, in a spirit of possession, a power that was founded on complete dispossession. Judas betrayed his Master and Peter disowned him. That did not prevent Jesus from entrusting Peter with the responsibility of feeding his sheep (Jn 21:15-17) and strengthening his brothers (Lk 22:32). It is no less certain that there were abuses on the part of the faithful. On the one hand, the powerful naturally tried to bend to their own interests the ambiguous power the Church held inside a religion the State recognized as its own. The weak, on the other hand, were possibly too often induced to pass off the responsibility for their own salvation onto the priests by relying on a more or less magic power they attributed to the sacred rites. These abuses, the worse of which St. Catherine of Siena recorded in her *Dialogue*, did not hide from her the true face of the Church (I am Jesus) and she continued to revere the pope, in his pastoral role, as *"il dolce Cristo in terra"* (the meek Christ on earth). This is precisely because she placed the Church on a sacramental level that faith alone can reach, where it appears "without stain or wrinkle... but holy and immaculate", as St. Paul presents it in his *Epistle to the Ephesians* (5:27).

In the light of this faith, it is impossible to accept that the "people of God" be divided in two classes, the clergy dominating the laity. By stamping the seal of total self-divesting on the minister, ministerial power aims at liberating and not subjecting. Besides, this power is conferred for the benefit of others. In his personal life, the priest is just one of the faithful. In other words, he is a priest only for others, as a sacramental medium of the presence destined to become for *each one* the Life of his life.

Sacramental sociology, peculiar to the Church, entails that the Good, which is the life of the whole community, be totally communicated to *each one* of its members. This life, eminently personal since it is Christ in person, can be received only by persons to whom it is offered in its indivisible unity, and not as an object of which each one could get a piece. From this viewpoint, each member bears the indivisible life within himself, each one is its center, each one is totally and equally responsible for it. The sacraments essentially imply that this life flows from the Head (Christ) to the members who make up his "mystical" body. They are not concrete things that can be set down before us; veiled by signs perceptible to the senses which appeal to our faith, the Lord himself gives us his heart. The hierarchy, custodian of the sacraments in charge of perpetuating them, exists only for this purpose: to bring the living Christ to the hearts of men. The "privileges" it has been granted, particularly doctrinal infallibility (as we have defined it) and the intrinsic efficaciousness (*ex opere operato*) of its specifically sacramental power, are not bestowed upon it for its own benefit, but, on the contrary, they explicitly signify the very self-effacement inherent to its mission. Through these powers, the clergy says: the word we proclaim is not our own and we accept it as you do in faith, under guarantee from the Holy Spirit; we are not the source of the grace that flows through our hands, and it bears fruit in us, as it does in you, in keeping with our love. Thus, ministerial priesthood is not opposed to the universal priesthood of "God's people", nor does it restrict it in any way, since it seeks to inspire it by uniting the whole Church community in the "body" of Christ, through the permanent communication of the Lord's presence that constitutes it.

One is always free in the Church one has freely joined. Moreover, one is free through the Church if, by freedom, we mean self-liberation. We find its supreme example in trinitarian self-divesting, in which the mission of the Word Incarnate is precisely to make us participate.

We are at the heart of the mystery of the Church, and it can only be apprehended through the eyes of faith, the light cast by the flame of love.

To what extent are today's protests inspired by this vision? To what extent do they aim to achieve total relinquishment which alone makes us akin to God?

The hierarchy's response, in the exercise of its indispensable ministry, can only be to live fully the self-effacement in Christ that is imprinted in the very ordination which hands down the apostolic legacy. Indeed, if the Church is to succeed in interesting the minds and touching the hearts of humankind, it must always appear as a Person and never as an institution. This is how the Lord wants it to be, the Lord who, to give himself to all, conceils himself under the veil of the sacrament that the Church is, as he reveals to Paul in those overwhelming words: "I am Jesus whom you are persecuting."

19

"Human Rights"
and the Transformation of Hearts

In the Academy of Florence, you can see some unfinished works by Michelangelo, figures beginning to emerge from the marble that holds them captive in a yet formless mass. These rough-hewn shapes can bee seen as an image of humanity trying to find itself, unable to break free from the constraints that subject it to its needs and instincts. When it is not weighed down by destitution, it lcts itself be won over by ideologies that stem from subjective passions and that are sure to trap it in its own limitations, all the more so as they claim to be the voice of science and progress, of justice and liberty. Once again, we find Pascal's "circle" in the collective experience of humanity ("You would not seek me if you had not found me"). It can be generalized as follows: in order to search in the right direction, we must at least have sensed the goal we are pursuing. But the ideas on which we claim to base our behavior (science, progress, justice, liberty) remain so ambiguous that they easily lend themselves to whatever interpretations coincide with the instinctive choices of groups or individuals.

This is borne out in the area of justice, particularly on the quesion of the right to property, which we shall now consider.

The fundamental ambiguity lies in the concept of right. Indeed, we may ask: "What is right (*rectum*) by contrast to what is crooked (*pravum*)?" In other words, what is the *criterion* for righteousness in human relationships and, especially, in relationships that involve property? It was a poor woman who made me think of this when she said: "There is nothing I would like more than to pray and meditate, but how can I, with five children to feed and nothing cooking in my pots?" The obsession created by the urgency of material needs stands in the way of spiritual growth. Her life was tragic and she was asking for some basic security so that she might make room for generosity inside herself. She was perfectly aware of the essential values on which human dignity is founded and only wished to devote her whole being to them. But she was racked by her children's hunger, and that hindered her thinking. She was simply asking to have sufficient means so as not to feel harassed by her worries that alienated her from herself. If, indeed, as a rule, man here below cannot escape the organic necessities that bind him to the physical world, he can put a distance between them and himself, and thus loosen their hold on him. He manages to forget them when he is sure of being able to satisfy them. Then he can apply his energies to tasks that are specifically human, the first being to make himself a *universal good*, which is precisely what *rights* acknowledge and guarantee in each one.

If we proclaim and defend "human rights", it is because we attribute to every human being, as a human being, a value that concerns everyone else and that everyone is interested in protecting as his own good. What can this good be which is created in one's innermost self and touches others in their innermost selves? The path we have followed so far dictates the answer: it is self-liberation through self-divesting which transforms our possessive ego into a sacrificial self, totally open to others, and carries our whole being away in a love relationship with the Presence that is closer to us than our own innermost being.

"Human rights" imply such a transformation deep in our hearts. They are not meant to protect narcissism whereby everyone clings to self-interest, but that generosity through which each person becomes a good for others. Kant admirably expressed this intent when he said: "Whatever you do, treat humanity in yourself and in all other people as an end but never as a means."[1]

Obviously, "human rights" cannot be based on our biology reduced to its animal manifestations. If that were the case, bugs and scorpions could just as well claim their rights and domestic animals could rebel against their own domestication by forming unions to oppose their breeders. Our rights stem only from our *capacity for the infinite* which frees us from all external and internal constraints and summons us to transcend our limitations, so that it can be offered up to divine Poverty in its pristine potentiality.

---

[1] Immanuel Kant, *The Metaphysical Foundation of Morals* in *An Immanuel Kant Reader*, edited and translated by Raymond B. Blackney, Harper & Brothers, 1960, p. 187.

In order to become this common good that enriches all humanity, it is certainly not necessary to acknowledge God explicitly as the infinitely personal Other to whom our sacrificial self relates; however, it is essential to shed the self completely and to keep our inner space inviolate in anticipation of that Someone who alone can fill it, alluded to with such respect by Shelley and Keats in the verses quoted above. And it is this secret creation, whereby each one of us becomes human, that "human rights" mean to protect. For humanity comes into being inasmuch as each one becomes truly human.

Human rights do not affect humanity as a zoological species, labeled *homo sapiens* in the order of primates, that includes all the individuals that inhabit our planet, but the *humanity-as-person* that must emerge from it through voluntary surpassing of oneself. In the latter, unity does not arise from common anatomical and physiological traits inherited from the same carnal origin, but from an inter-communion of persons, each one being open to all the others. A balance is achieved here between the two poles of a specifically human sociology, *together* and *alone*, of which the Church community is a good example. The current that propagates unity flows through each one's *solitude*; the richer the solitude, the stronger the current. All the people listening together to a concert are immersed in a silence that transports them in a common experience; that shared silence results from the most secret encounter of each one in the audience with the music, and is all the more intensely felt by all as it is more deeply experienced by each. Similarly, the interpersonal tie that constitutes true humanity is established in the depths of one's being, and it binds men together all the more strongly as it is more deeply rooted in that invisible generosity whereby each person is a common good.

This is the end that "human rights" and Kant, in the maxim we just mentioned, have in mind; it is not given to us ready-made; we must become that end.

In this perspective, the right to property, like all rights, can only aim at protecting this inner creation whereby we become our own *origin* through self-divesting. Therefore, its ultimate foundation is also "poverty of the spirit" which conditions the giving of oneself. The only thing that it can claim is thus the opportunity for each one to accomplish this act of giving, without any obstacle, by ensuring a sufficient degree of security for the spirit never to be prevented from acknowledging and affirming the primacy of such giving.

Once this minimum is guaranteed, which, clearly, must be in keeping with individual duties—a nuclear physicist needs equipment and space different from those of a cobbler (equal to the former in dignity)—an individual cannot appropriate more possessions as long as *everyone else* does not enjoy the same basic security. On the one hand, "human rights" are as valid for others as for himself and, on the other hand, he cannot be truly human unless he takes responsibility for the humanization of others, which is implied in the common good he becomes.

The fact that favorable circumstances may allow him to acquire wealth, that the laws of his country guarantee him the peaceful enjoyment of his possessions without breaking the law, does not extinguish his debt of humanity towards others. It is written in the right to property, and this right is rooted in generosity and cannot exist unless it is open to others. Whoever does not acknowledge this debt of humanity destroys the very foundation for the right to property on which he relies to keep his possessions.

Quite remarkably, St. Thomas Aquinas introduced a doctrine very close to the one just presented, in Question 66 of the *Secunda Secundae*.[2] While accepting the legitimacy of personally appropriating external goods, which by natural law belong to everyone, he distinguishes, within this personal ownership, two distinct rights: the right to manage and distribute to ensure the *better* management and circulation of goods, a right unconditionally acknowledged to belong to the legitimate owner; and the right to use which obliges the owner "not to look upon external things as his own but as common to all, so that he will promptly share with others to meet their needs, since by *natural law*, we owe the overabundance of goods to the poor for their sustenance". He goes yet further and teaches that, in cases of dire need, a man with no other recourse can *licitly* take from someone else's possessions whatever he needs to relieve his poverty. By virtue of necessity, what he takes to sustain his life "becomes his own" because "when one is in need, everything is common." This *"efficitur suum "*[3] (becomes his own) clearly indicates that the primitive order (common property) spontaneously reappears because it underlies personal appropriation which exists (by virtue of a human contract[4]) only

---

2 St. Thomas, *Summa*

3 *Ibid.*, art. 7 ad secundum.

4 *Ibid.*, art 2 ad primum.

to better ensure its fulfillment. The Decalogue's "Thou shalt not steal" has never been interpreted in a more human way; it corroborates, with indisputable authority, what we have said about the right to private ownership.

Since *work* is the normal means of acquiring earthly goods, it must be considered in the same light as property itself, that is, work like property must be directed to the liberation of man. In other words, its aim must be *to make men* before making things. It cannot be treated as a piece of merchandise purchased at the lowest price. Work involves people who generally do not have other resources to achieve the security without which they cannot become themselves. Therefore, wages must be set on the basis of human needs, which the worker must be able to satisfy with dignity, and not of profit, which equates man with machines that are only rated in terms of output. The error of economic liberalism, known as free enterprise, is precisely to have thought it could simply give labor a numerical value and factor it into production costs, in an impersonal system of faceless employees.

This in turn led to another error, *non-participation.* A tool does not need to know the forces behind a company's actions; it merely fits into it like a link in a chain. For whom does the factory work? With what country? For what cause? Where does the capital come from? What are the profits? How are they shared? All this had nothing to do with the worker. The owner's business was not his concern. He was attached to it like a foreign body, the only link between the two being a salary the worker could not discuss. The surveys reported by Marx in *The Capital* give a distressing picture of the poverty-striken working class of his time in England: children could be forced to work in mines sixteen hours a day; entire families were crammed in one filthy room, where promiscuity led to the most dreadful consequences. The existence of two classes living their separate lives side by side—a situation that prevailed in all industrialized countries—inevitably gave rise to a class mentality that Marxism was to stir up by turning class struggle into a new religion. Marxism was to attain the power that we know, not only in the empires it founded, but also in the vast network of propaganda that it spun like a web over the planet.

If the right to ownership had been well understood, we could have avoided this worldwide experiment that has divided humankind in two camps and cut Europe in two. By its very essence, it excludes any attempt at monopolizing property by unconditionally legitimizing only the appropriation of those goods necessary to promote the giving of oneself.

Since the problem is still not solved in the "free world" today, it remains appropriate to speak of participation in the form of co-ownership and joint management. If, indeed, work is to make men before making things, all workers must share in taking responsibility for it. If it is not a product of fraud and injustice, capital that becomes available is abiding by the rule "of use" to which it is held by "natural law". Thus it cannot claim the lion's share. The human goals of the company will allocate for it a return compatible with the requirements the company has to fulfill. Similarly, all positions should be remunerated according to the same principle. People should accede to them by a vote open to all the people working together on an equal footing. New opportunities for promotion should constantly be provided, and the required training given by and paid for by the company. Indeed, as long as work will not be understood and organized as an instrument of liberation, we will not be able to speak of a "free world." Nothing is more urgent than to humanize work; it is imperative, first, for the sake of justice, and then because, if it is not done, Marxism will overtake the whole planet.

Marxism does not offer a human solution, not because of the collective ownership of the means of production and of the goods produced (that is the rule in monasteries), but because of its atheistic materialism. This ideology sets up the community as an absolute (represented by a dictatorship) while it radically ignores the autonomy of the person and the primacy of the inner creation which is the sole true common good. In the Soviet Union, we have tragic evidence of this in the psychiatric assaults waged against opponents of the regime; they constitute a particularly atrocious way of robbing human beings of their humanity and a flagrant contradiction of the very program for human promotion of which the proletarian revolution was supposed to be an exemplary realization.

The "free world," as I have already pointed out, has lost, to a very large extent, any sense of the absolute. It has nothing substantial to set against Marxism which, especially nowadays, applies itself to win over its intelligentsia or to reduce it to helplessness when it does not prove to be a sufficiently obliging ally.[5]

Can the Church do anything in the face of a huge communist bloc in league against it, and in the face of the

---

5 Jules Monnerot, *op. cit.*, last chapter.

"free world" where it is questioned from all sides, even from the ranks of its own faithful, and where disillusioned youth are fired with a desire for revolution?

I have just used the expression: robbing human beings of their humanity. it does not apply only to the inevitable consequences of atheistic communism, but also to the silence, typical in the West, on that inner creation in every man where the dignity of the spirit is affirmed. Meanwhile, eroticism is all-pervasive and skepticism in every quarter is sowing doubt with respect to any kind of belief or obligation. I am not implying that Marxists, on the whole, are deliberately planning to crush in man what makes him human, or that the best brains of the "free world" are consciously trying to prevent man from attaining his true self. That would be false and unfair. I rather think that neither of these two groups have ever reached ultimate humanity within themselves and are thus unable to direct their fellow men toward a reality unknown to them.

This, I believe, can be the meeting point where the Church can connect with today's world, by drawing its inspiration from Pascal's words: "We must begin by showing that religion [...] is venerable, because *it has a perfect knowledge of man*; lovable because it promises the true good."[6] Paradoxically, it is incumbent upon it to awaken or restore *faith in man*, that "infinite abyss that can only be filled by an infinite... object"[7], by insisting on

---

6 Pascal, *op. cit.*, No 187, p. 67.

7 *Ibid.*, No 425, p. 138.

that inner creation which constitutes, for each human being, the only authentic way of actualizing his humanity.

Indeed, what is the point of a call to justice if the supreme injustice is first committed, that of robbing men of their humanity? Only subjective passions will make it ring out. Some will arm themselves to keep their privileges of ownership or domination and others will arm themselves to snatch them away. The result will be a justice *against*, a justice of class, race or fanaticism. It will only shift the oppression, amidst hatred and bloodshed, and provide dictators with a choice springboard to pull themselves up to a position of power and the best argument to hold on to it.

If we do not acknowledge the same identical worth in everyone, which is the only basis for equal justice, people will never agree on what justice means, and violence will decide. Nor will there ever be equality if it is not founded on that inner creation by which every man becomes a universal good.

The Church believes and teaches that Christ died for each one of us, that God wants to make each one a shrine of his presence; the Church can contemplate in the Holy Trinity the supreme model of a personalism founded on total self-divesting that gives us the key to our own liberation: for these reasons, the Church can reveal man to himself as profoundly as it can reveal God to him. If it persistently applies itself to showing him his true greatness by carefully avoiding any collusion with partisan ideologies, it will be heard by what is most human in man and thus contribute to set all the debates on an *internal* basis common to all men, beyond all the false absolutes that involve them in insurmountable conflicts.

The encyclical *Populorum progressio* of Pope Paul VI points out "the turning toward the spirit of poverty" as one of the conditions for "full humanism." Nothing sheds more light on the problem of the right to property in our attempts to reach down to its roots. As all "human rights," it must be based on self-divesting, the only road to authentic freedom. That is why it is, in essence, open to others and concerns them as much as myself, since it revolves around the same Good within each one. The sharing to which *Populorum progressio* calls, in all areas where property rights can be exercised, is a requirement, and its fulfillment brings into question its validity. I cannot claim this right for myself without wanting it to apply for the benefit of others. The peaceful revolution (for the benefit of all) that it requires stems from its being exercised with a view to that space of generosity deep inside that it means to protect in each one. I betray it when I cling to my possessions in the face of the guiltless indigence of others, and I undermine its very foundation by wanting it to work only for my own benefit. "Human rights," of which it is but one aspect, can only command respect from everyone if everyone feels equally concerned.

That does not exclude reasonable differences in distribution according to the importance of one's position which may require more resources to cope with greater responsibilities, once the basic necessities have been guaranteed to all. Nor does it imply that anybody can grab other people's belongings (except in cases of dire need) without taking into account the right to manage goods which St. Thomas clearly distinguishes, and rightly so, from the right to use them. But it presupposes, above all, another vision of man in which he conquers his humanity by liberating himself and by changing from a possessive ego to a sacrificial self.

To have or to be: we must choose between these two terms that Gabriel Marcel made familiar to us and which are so often opposed in *Populorum progressio.*

Such a choice involves the whole person in all spheres of action. We cannot clamor for disarmament out of respect for life and, at the same time, promote free abortion, which concerns the same life. And we can truly respect this life only by acknowledging the inner creation in which each one becomes the origin of his own humanity.

"How beauteous mankind is," wrote Shakespeare in one of his sonnets. There is no greater truth, provided humanity is and is not prevented from being by refusing, if only to one man, the security that will allow him to become generosity.

20

An Inviolable Capacity
for the Infinite

Any man can say "I exist," but he must immediately add "I have no hand in the matter". A coronary, a cerebral hemorrhage or a rupture of the aorta can make him die in a split second. He lives, but he knows neither how nor why, nor if he will still be alive the next minute. He says "I", "me", and he perceives and presents himself to others as the subject, as the autonomous center of past or present experiences. He cannot communicate how these experiences affect him, for they take place in a domain exclusively his own, from which he cannot come out and which others cannot penetrate. He not only exists, he experiences *himself*. But there again, most of the time, this is not of his own making. He experiences himself through a prefabricated ego—the "I-me"—that he is subjected to and of which he has only a narcissistic awareness, thus becoming an accomplice of his subjective passions, the roots of which escape him. The instinctive attachment he feels for himself induces him to try and increase his standing in his own eyes and in those of others. He praises himself and expects to be praised for what he is (even if he has no hand in it), and he resents those who do not admire him as much as he does. However, he may suddenly lose sight of himself: he may experience the wonder of an encounter that reveals to him his need for the infinite, as it fulfills it, or, in the highly emotional state caused by misfortune, he may feel a sense of tremendous emptiness. He then discovers another self inside himself which comes into being in a mysterious effacement into a Value, or Presence, on which his whole being hangs. He finds himself in Another and for Him. Through the giving of himself, he transcends himself and ceases to be subjected to his ego. He no longer defends his innermost being as a threatened possession, but as the shrine of a Good which is everyone's Good.

The self-sacrificing self is opposed to the possessive ego as freedom is to enslavement, as the highest affirmation of man to his most dangerous negation. The latter generally claims the privileges of the former and an autonomy that it cannot found on anything; this leaves the self at the mercy of impulses from an anarchic unconscious.

Which "I" (individual and collective) are we dealing with in ourselves and in others? One can easily grasp the importance of this question: it relates to a difference in *perception* which necessarily leads to different visions, for we see according to what we are. Hence, those dead-end dialogues between people for whom the "obvious facts" are never the same. Flaubert went to the root of the problem in the little sentence we quoted above ("Why wish to be something when we can be someone?"), in which the difference between the instinctual ego and the personal self is quite obvious, as Rimbaud possibly sensed when he wrote: "I is Another."

These considerations essentially affect the presentation of the Christian message which calls us into question deep inside ourselves, since we can only hope to assimilate it by being born again, as Jesus himself teaches Nicodemus (Jn 3:3).

If the *Gospel* is meant to penetrate the depths of our being to bring forth a new man, it is important not to set against it personal autonomy, as misunderstood as it is passionately defended, thereby hurting, with a narrow exegesis, a legitimate feeling of inviolability, since this inviolability must be the source of infinite autonomy. Nietzsche's words: "If there were gods, how could I bear not being god?" show how far the rejection of god can go when it is conceived as a limitation to someone who longs to live life fervently.

Thus, in keeping with the truth, it is a matter of *showing* that nothing is dearer to God than our freedom, and that it finds its meaning and fullness only in Him. Moreover, to become free and to meet God are one and the same thing, for our authentic self can only emerge in this relationship with Him. It makes us move from without to within, from darkness to light, from death to life.

Two magnificent and particularly timely texts, each in its own way, remind us of this.

The first is by St. John of the Cross in the commentary on stanza 28 of the *Spiritual Canticle*: "... God is pleased with naught save love;...if anything pleases Him, it is that the soul *may be exalted*; and since there is no way wherein He can exalt it so much as *by making it equal with Himself*, for that reason alone He is pleased when the soul loves Him. For the property of Love is to make the lover equal with the object of his love. Wherefore, since its love is now perfect, the soul is called Bride of the Son of God, which signifies equality with Him; in the which equality of friendship all things of both are common to both."[1]

The second is by St. Catherine of Siena and is taken from the *Dialogues*; it is presented as words that God spoke to her: "I do not want to violate the rights of your freedom. But as soon as you wish it, I myself transform you into me and make you one with me."

Concern for our own greatness, to the point of equality on the level of love, with respect for our freedom, those are the key words for presenting the Gospel in a way that will reach the spirit, that *inviolable capacity for the infinite* which cannot accept to be limited in any way, and will not rest as long as we remain locked in our prefabricated ego, clutching its possessions.

That is where the human journey begins and acquires its true dimension. It is important to show how Christianity lights the way and gets us involved by living the adventure ourselves with the enthusiasm kindled in us by our ever-renewed discovery.

The revolution which is to change the world starts with ourselves. Indeed, we cannot liberate anything unless we liberate ourselves, since we will necessarily bring to any action, seemingly motivated by the best of intentions, the inner constraints that still rule us. The point is not to either keep or systematically throw out everything

---

[1] *Op. cit.*, pp. 323-324.

there is, but rather to redirect the means at our disposal, or those we will invent, to this *end*, which is man, by first seeking to guarantee each one the *creative solitude* he needs to be the origin of his own self. Nothing is more exciting than this inner creation whereby each one is called to become a universal good, in an equality based on the same requirement for every human being to give totally of himself.

The Church can cast a supreme light on this process by drawing from trinitarian revelation the revelation of man for whom it is meant and who must find his fulfillment in it. Because of our craving for greatness, as I have said time and again, and our need to show ourselves off to best advantage, we risk losing ourselves in inordinate pride and perpetually frustrated rivalries. A repressed and stunted humility—perhaps little more than helpless pride —would be unable to counterbalance them if we did not find in intradivine relationships the absolute self-divesting that offers us the incomparable model for our own liberation. Every moment of our lives, we discover evidence of how impossible it is to achieve a truly original self without realizing, within ourselves, the total relinquishment whereby we go from the given that enslaves us to the giving that makes it radiant.

Such a solution to the problem that we are is so new and so unexpected that it is not surprising to see enormous mistakes being made, in all areas of thought and action, by most of those who have not received this enlightenment. That is why, rather than denouncing these errors and reprimanding those responsible for them, we should first explain this truth, showing how fruitful it is for understanding man and helping him attain his true greatness.

Besides, believers themselves will be the first to benefit from a teaching centered on divine Trinity, whose liberating effect in their personal lives and all human relationships they rarely understand.

But, naturally, the best way to substantiate that message is to bear witness to it in our own lives. To be effective, it must touch man's innermost being, like a nuptial invitation summoning him to joy.

We ourselves are men and we must appear deeply committed to this divine adventure; it is up to us to make others feel how wondrous it is. If Christ were not our delight, how could we convince others that he can become theirs?

True, neither the state of the world today nor that of the Church are cause for rejoicing. But if we believe in the power of the leaven that Jesus is in humanity, we cannot doubt that he offers our times a chance for salvation. Finally, those who openly come out against Christianity rarely object to the mystical essence of our faith, in its nuptial aspect where our freedom reaches its peak. It is usually unknown to them, and we have good reasons to hope that they would not be insensitive to it if they saw it affirmed in our lives without any compromise. In any case, the fact that some have never seen the radiance of the "pearl of the kingdom" does not diminish its worth for those who have been fortunate enough to discover it. The joy of the latter cannot be wiped away by the failure to recognize it on the part of the former; perhaps someday they will open to its light.

Nothing is more moving than to read this call to joy from Our Lord, one of the last things he said on the eve of his Passion, as related by St. John: "I have said these things to you so that my joy may be in you, and that your joy may be complete" (Jn 15:11). That clearly means that the Cross leads to joy as it frees us from the evil that dries up its source. St. Paul experiences this in the midst of his tribulations when he writes to the Philippians: "Rejoice in the Lord always; again I will say, rejoice" (4:4). St. Augustine, in turn, discovers the same joy after his long stumbling journey towards the truth: "And so, this is happiness: to rejoice in Thee, for Thee, on account of Thee"[2], and Pascal remembers it in the famous parchment on which he has recorded the memory of that fiery night of November 23, 1654: "Joy, joy, joy, tears of joy."

The crowning testimony, and there are many, comes from St. Francis of Assisi in his jubilant *Canticle to the Sun*. He asked to hear it sung as he greeted "our sister" death. How can we give a sense of this translucent scene in which the "Poor Little Brother", lying on a bed of ashes and bearing the stigmata of the divine wounds on his body, listens to a song of praise of God's creatures. Never did love of the world burn with a purer flame in the heart of man; never was there a greater love for God than on that evening, when the eulogist of Poverty happily waited for the thin screen of mortal flesh, which still prevented him from seeing the Lord, to break and reveal the Face so deeply etched in his heart. He was leaving nothing because he had given everything. Transfigured, the whole of creation exulted in his gaze, and he embraced it like the

---

[2] St. Augustine, *Confessions*, X, xxvi, 32.

monstrance of God, up to the last breath, at the moment when he entered that heaven he carried within himself.

Our mission is none other than to introduce every man to this great secret of love that illuminates St. Francis' death with its unique brightness, effacing ourselves in Jesus, who eternally utters it in the Word that he is. This is how we will know joy; this is how we will recognize our experience of God, closely akin to St. Augustine's, and be able to express it in these words, still vibrant with the longing that made them burst out: "When I shall with my whole self cleave to Thee [...] my life shall wholly live, as wholly full of Thee."[3]

---

[3] *Ibid.*, X, xxviii, 39.

Appendices[1]

THE PRESENCE-SACRAMENT

As a child, I had the privilege of meeting a woman who died in her eighties some twenty-five years ago. She had never known her parents; they had died shortly after she was born. She had been brought up in an orphanage where she had never been shown the slightest affection. She reached the age when she had to go to work, her heart still craving for love. She thought she had found it in a co-worker and she married him. She soon found out that he was a drunkard who subjected her to the unrestrained brutality of his fits of anger. All her dreams of happiness crumbled under the blows that hurt her soul more than her body. And then, she met God, as a hidden presence inside her that gave her the courage to live. Her husband understood that this inner refuge, in some way, removed her from his power. He determined to take revenge and, being unable to take her faith away from her, he forbade her to pass it on to the child she gave birth to in that miserable home. He took on the task of raising the child himself according to his own principles, jealously thwarting the

---

[1] These appendices summarize a talk on the general theme discussed briefly here. Another talk was incorporated into a section where it could fit.

mother's influence, and he turned him into an unstable individual who, because of a lack of self-discipline, led a totally dissolute life. His mother kept him in her prayers; it was the only way she could reach him since he would see her only when he needed money to pay his debts and buy new clothes.

At thirty-five, he was burned out. So ill with incurable tuberculosis that no sanatorium would take him, he came back to his mother. "He messed up his life", she told me, "I would not want him to mess up his death." And her prayer became more earnest than ever to obtain for him that flash of grace that would open his heart to God. But she let nothing show of her wish that he make of his death an act of life. She felt that any intrusion into his private feelings could only induce him to a rejection, possibly definitive, and that, Like the Lord at the washing of the feet, she had to kneel before the shrine that he could still become.

"I never had any religion, but now I want my mother's." In the middle of a conversation with a friend to whom he was confiding the many disappointments of his life, it is with these words that, all of a sudden, he revealed the fruit of a thought he had been secretly entertaining.

I attended his first communion a few weeks before the feast of All Saints, day on which he died, as his mother had wished. But before dying, he had made a point of telling his mother: "If you had spoken to me about it, I would never have done it. It is because you never said anything that I discovered everything through you."

I never understood so clearly the power of a human presence, through which God shines forth, than in this conversion of a son for whom his mother's face was the only gospel.

THE WORDS OF A CHILD

A group of children, who had made their first communion in the chapel of the Benedictine sisters on the rue Monsieur in Paris, were talking about this event, not suspecting that an adult could hear them. Each one was trying to impress the others by repeating a quote from a book likely to create the biggest stir. Only one little girl contented herself with saying what she had really felt: "Well! As for me, He makes me disappear in Him!"

There is a word "that carries life," that expresses what is important. The whole mystery of poverty of the spirit, the full experience of true freedom, in one word, the whole truth about love ("I is Another") is contained in these few words straight from the heart of a child.

I AND WE

Francis Jeanson, in *La Foi d'un incroyant* (The faith of a nonbeliever), opposes the *I* who can do nothing to the *we* who can do everything in order to eliminate God and replace him with the community of men as a valid and perfectly adequate substitute. If I am not mistaken, this is the most naive expression of the "absolute" that sustains Marxism. We must nevertheless distinguish between the *we* which represents the merging of all the individual instinctual subjectivities, resulting in the "we-against" of a race, a nation, a social class or a party, and the "we-for" that emerges like a communion of love from the coming together of all the personal solitudes, when each one, overcoming his limitations, opens up to the Infinite that awaits him in the depths of his soul. There, at the very center of being, is created the only universal absolute that can embrace *all* men and lead them to become truly human.

Achevé d'imprimer
en août 1996
sur les presses de
Imprimerie H.L.N.

Imprimé au Canada – Printed in Canada